RIPE

RIPE

Arthur Allen

THE SEARCH FOR
THE PERFECT
TOMATO

COUNTERPOINT • BERKELEY

Library of Congress Cataloging-in-Publication Data

Allen, Arthur, 1959–
  Ripe : the search for the perfect tomato / by Arthur Allen.
    p. cm.
  ISBN 978-1-58243-426-1
  1. Tomatoes. 2. Tomatoes—History. I. Title.

SB349.A285 2010
635'.642—dc22

2009038162

Jacket by Silverander Communications
Interior by Amber Pirker
Interior illustrations by Sean Bellows

Printed in the United States of America

COUNTERPOINT
2117 Fourth Street
Suite D
Berkeley, CA 94710

www.counterpointpress.com

Distributed by Publishers Group West

10 9 8 7 6 5 4 3 2 1

To Margaret, Ike, and Lucy

Who are sweet and surprising

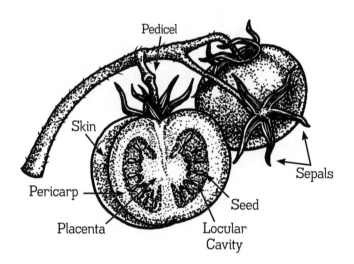

Pedicel

Skin

Sepals

Pericarp

Placenta

Seed

Locular
Cavity

CONTENTS

RIPE

La Ribera, Mexico

 ONE SUNNY APRIL DAY, I SAT IN THE FRONT SEAT OF A pickup truck driving north on Highway 1 from San José del Cabo, at the southernmost tip of Mexico's Baja Peninsula. After an hour or two, we turned up a broad dirt road that took us deep into a desert landscape pulsating with the activities of spring. Brightly colored birds darted through thorny shrubs and cacti. Pink flowers like ruffled piñata paper sprung from the armored shoulders of prickly pears. Fiery orange blossoms burst from the tips of gangly ocotillo plants. Here and there a palo verde thrust up mild green limbs feathered with tiny white blossoms. For as long as anyone could remember, this arid land hadn't been used for anything besides subsistence farming and cattle grazing. Every few years, hurricanes howled

across the Mexican mainland and the Sea of Cortez and flooded the area. It seemed like a crazy place to look for tomatoes. Yet the desert soil held a secret fertility.

After a long, jolting stretch, the road climbed and entered a wide canyon between two bluffs near the coastal village of La Ribera. Here, several months earlier, bulldozers had crashed through the dry arroyo, ripping out the mesquite and barrel cactus and piling up the sand and debris to form dikes. The *campesinos* working the land here were *ejidatarios*—villagers whose land was collectivized by the Mexican revolution. In September, they had laid out a few tons of steer manure and fish meal, driven sticks into the ground to stake the growing plants, and then transplanted young cherry tomatoes. And now the first crop was up.

A California farmer named Sandra Belin had brought me to this oasis to give me a sense of the trials and joys of helping organize poor people to successfully grow vegetables for the remote taste buds of the American middle class. Sandra and her husband, Larry Jacobs, owned Del Cabo Farms, a company that exported tomatoes and other organic produce from Baja farms and that employed, directly or indirectly, about five thousand families. Kanti Rawal, a University of Illinois–trained geneticist and plant breeder, was also along that day. A young Mexican agronomist named Fabiola Rodriguez, who was learning the finer points of tomato breeding from Kanti, was driving the pickup.

Kanti—I have never heard anyone call him by his last name—was a sprightly sixty-eight-year-old with a beak nose and honey-colored eyes, dark brown skin, and a shock of white hair reminiscent of Danny Kaye's. Before he'd become Del Cabo's breeder, Kanti had worked in nearly every aspect of the tomato business. In the 1970s, he'd helped the U.S. Department of Agriculture organize its tomato genetics database and then went to work developing canning tomatoes for Del Monte. In the 1990s, the biotech company Calgene hired him to help design the first genetically engineered vegetable, the Flavr Savr tomato.

Kanti had patents on yellow canning tomatoes, and his vegetables had appeared on the cover of the Burpee Seeds catalog. But he was old enough to be thinking less about money and more about his life's purpose, which drew him to Larry and Sandra. In exchange for a small wage and expenses, Kanti was developing new cultivars, or varieties with a simple but difficult goal. He wanted to produce delicious tomatoes that were hardy enough to be transported over many miles and through much rough handling from a poor farmer's field in Mexico to the supermarket emporia of America. If he succeeded, it could mean the difference between these farmers staying with their families on the farm and being forced into the wrenching life of emigration—a life that had uprooted so many millions of their compatriots.

Here, in short, Kanti could make a difference. "Larry and Sandy are open and frank and honest and generous. They're like Peace Corps volunteers who never grew up," he said. It wasn't that hard to sell his seeds for decent money. "But what do I do with that five million dollars? My legacy will disappear like everybody else in this business. Even if Fabiola and the others don't stay in this company, they're getting a feel for breeding and how it works, the whole tomato trail from here to Chicago or Philadelphia or L.A. And they'll be proud their products are making somebody smile."

From a distance, the farm near La Ribera looked like any other anonymous human postage stamp in the desert, a vague green acre backed against forbidding sandstone. The field was surrounded by wild growth—banana plants and sunflowers, hummingbirds and butterflies, datura and castor beans growing along the edges. As we got closer, threading our way through the barbed-wire enclosures that kept cattle out of the pockets of cultivation, we could see that something unusual was going on. Kanti was the first to notice. The tomatoes were Golden Honeybunch, a cultivar he had been tinkering with for fifteen years, and they were growing in magnificent clusters. In twelve rows, each as long as a football field, tens of thousands of spherical golden berries were hanging in thick masses off pale green vines that roped luxuriantly around the training twine.

Kanti made a beeline for his tomatoes. He started walking down a row, eating as he went, and soon he was shouting his questions and frustration at anyone who'd listen, in the mixture of Spanish and English that he spoke with a Gujarati brogue. "I'm at a loss as to why no one is harvesting these," he said. "This is like gold, man!"

Taste is as personal as love, as ephemeral as the fish that got away. First impressions are as important in taste as they are in love. A bad sensation tends to close the mind; a good one opens pathways of pleasure, comfort, and acceptance. Over time, the intensity of taste fades. Today's thrill can be bland or sour in the morning, or even in half an hour, and bittersweet is just a sentimental recollection from inside a bitter present. Tomato flavor is complex, fleeting, impossible to describe.

For all that, I'll be damned if those weren't the best tomatoes I'd ever tasted.

At the time, I wrote in my notebook that they communicated cantaloupe and fresh pulpy mango, with only a piquant tang at the back of the mouth to remind you they were tomatoes. They crunched when you bit into them, releasing bursts of extravagant flavor, an encyclopedia of delight. If you closed your eyes, you might think you weren't tasting tomatoes at all, but some tropical fruit. And they were so sweet that

Kanti broke into a corny 1960s ditty. "Sugar, Sugar," he sang, dancing around like a child, "Honey, Honey."

We ate them continuously over the next three days—riding up and down the peninsula checking out the farms, sitting around with Larry and his computer at the dinner table on the porch of their house in San José del Cabo. Like Jehovah's Witnesses of flavor, we brought bags of the tomatoes everywhere we went, proselytized for them, imposed them upon friends. If we could have bottled that flavor, we'd have made a mint. There was a hitch, though. These tomatoes were at the height of ripeness, but the people for whom they were grown lived at least 1,200 miles away. The buyers talking on their phones in warehouses in places like Nogales, Arizona, San Francisco, and Chicago didn't know about them. Whole Foods and Trader Joe's didn't know about them, and neither did the Zuni Café or Alice Waters. As for the discerning shoppers, those willing to pay a premium for these exotic tomatoes, they were doing what upper-middle-class people do—typing on their Macs with family photographs push-pinned to cubicle walls in Manhattan and Minneapolis; listening to NPR in their bathrobes in Bethesda, Maryland; driving on Interstate 70 through Golden, Colorado; or stopping for coffee at a Starbucks in Santa Monica. They were all far, far away. Would the flavor of these tomatoes survive the journey?

From Wild Edible to Political Vegetable

ONCE UPON A TIME, THE TOMATO WAS THE PERFECT FRUIT for political expression of a certain kind. In 1959, the Venezuelans shelled Richard Nixon with rotten tomatoes during a visit to Caracas. Filipino mobs threw tomatoes at the Beatles when they snubbed Imelda Marcos in 1962. And every time Henry Wallace campaigned in the South during his 1948 presidential run, farmers turned out with bushelfuls to express their scorn for Yankee ideas of racial justice. In 1958, a jealous stripper showered Anita Ekberg with tomatoes during an appearance with Bob Hope in Miami. That was poetic justice of a kind; in those days, "What a tomato!" was a slangy expression of appreciation for a woman with opulent curves.

Times have changed. Tomatoes have gotten harder. People

hardly ever throw them at politicians anymore. They throw politics at tomatoes instead. Once upon a time, we just ate tomatoes, or used them to share our feelings about politicians and lousy musicians. But in the decades since the baby boomers started raising their voices, first to struggle against injustice, then to rage against the sorry state of the earth, then to contradict their fate as mortal beings, and then against the lack of "authenticity"—an aesthetic problem posing as a social one—tomatoes have been handy metaphors for controversy. Perhaps it's because in fighting over tomatoes, we're fighting over a piece of our experience, a sensation whose meaning is all the more powerful for being indefinable.

In the 1970s, the student radical Tom Hayden stood up at meetings of the University of California Board of Regents to decry the inhumanity of the mechanical harvester developed at the UC Davis campus. By saving labor, the harvester took menial jobs away from unskilled migrant workers, forcing them onto food stamps. A decade later, the protest centered on the rubbery tomato, picked green, gassed with ripening agents, and sold cheaply at the great democratic food emporia called supermarkets. The educated middle classes despised these little red cannonballs. Calgene had tried to improve things with the Flavr Savr, designed to stay juicy for weeks after picking. But in that battle, the American appetite for high tech lost out to nostalgia for no tech. Jeremy Rifkin, the neo-Luddite conscience of the boomer generation, led radical students in tomato-smashing parties to drive off the fearful Frankenfood. Most recently, immigrant farmworkers have again become the focus of a campaign for rights. If anything, these workers are worse off than they were in the 1960s; after making the long trek from their villages in Chiapas and Huehuetenango, they gain little or nothing for the backbreaking work of picking slicer tomatoes for McDonald's and other fast-food chains. Well-heeled foodies have made pilgrimages to the Everglades to demand better wages for these poorest of the poor, who pick the off-season tomatoes that the foodies would never eat. In Italy, too, postmodern tomato warfare rages. Is it possible to admit that a Chinese tomato sauce is as good for veal parmigiana as an Italian one?

The quest for the perfect tomato carries a lot of aesthetic, political, and social weight. I have always wanted to tell a story about agribusiness through a single crop, examining its travels from a seedsman's laboratory or greenhouse to our tables. There's history, anthropology, politics, and science involved, but more than anything else, there are interesting people. During my search, I've met a lot of farmers and breeders and canners who have tried both to make tomatoes that tasted good and to make maybe a little money in the bargain. The tomato industry, it turns out, is a pretty small business, in which most everyone knows everyone else. And despite the lines that have been drawn between the players, most everyone is struggling with the same curveballs that nature throws at them.

This book is a voyage of discovery that will take you from Mexico to California to Florida and from China to Italy to my backyard. We'll explore where tomatoes came from, how they became important to our cuisines, the techniques that scientists and gardeners have used to improve them, and finally, why they tend to taste so bad in the wintertime. At the end of our journey, you may feel no less indignant and standoffish about your Safeway tomatoes, but at least you'll have some compassion for the poor guy who produced them. Books like *Fast Food Nation* and *The Omnivore's Dilemma* have delivered strong arguments about what's wrong with our agricultural systems and foodways, and while I concur with some of their points, I feel it's important to separate aesthetic judgments from issues of justice, health, and the environment. There's not much evidence that organic food is healthier for those who eat it. Big farms may upset our sense of the agrarian idyll, but they also produce food cheaply—and reflect the generations-old migration of people from their farms. Pesticides and petroleum-based fertilizers may be harmful in large doses, but so are some of the powders and sprays used by organic farmers. Cheap food stimulates obesity, it is true—does that mean expensive food is preferable? Most importantly, it's silly to think we can return to some prelapsarian time in food production. In the words of historian James E. McWilliams, "writers who believe that achieving truly responsible food production requires rediscovering some long-lost harmonious environmental relationship are agricultural idealists who do not know their history."

Politics, politics. "Politics has penetrated the heart of things," the Cuban poet Cintio Vitier wrote in a different context.

> Into the atoms, the very electrons
> The skies are free for now
> Butterflies too
> Nature, except where the bombs are falling
> is still an Ivory Tower.
> But don't worry, not for long
> They've planted devices in the center of the flower.

Can't we all get along? Can't we just talk tomatoes? I'm going to try.

The taste of a fresh tomato, like the juice of a perfect peach or the smell of roasting peanuts in the bleachers, is one of the sweetest memories of summer. A tomato bursting with flavor is exquisitely unique. It contains sugars and salts and those ineffable, oily flavors that we call *umami*, in a nod to the Japanese who lent us the word and the distinction. There's something about biting into a tomato picked warm off the vine or sliced and doused in vinaigrette—It's a blitz-taste that stimulate memories in a way that the stolid, reliable flavors of an apple, an orange, a cucumber, or even the best plums can't.

That first bite is a somehow discomfiting experience, from the perspective of what food scientists call "mouth feel." The tomato lacks the crunch of an apple, the yielding smoothness of a peach, the snap of a carrot, or the simple squelch of a grape. The tomato is a peculiar conglomeration of diaphanous-slick skin, wet, rubbery, granular flesh, goo-embedded seeds, and emptiness. The tomato is an awkward fruit, unique in shape and flavor, yet transformable in a thousand ways. As a plant, the tomato symbolizes home and bounty and the irrepressibility of nature. Its seeds, swept across vast distances by Hurricane Katrina's floodwaters, sprouted hopefully in wrecked New Orleans gardens a few weeks after the storm passed. I've found tomatoes growing in suburban median strips, alongside chicory on dirt country roads, in dung heaps at a horse stable in Washington, D.C., from a few inches of silt on a log-jam in an urban stream. It is a most opportunistic plant. It is often what you'd call a weed.

The tomato is also the epitome of the genetically parsed, overdetermined product, a crop-food that has been manipulated for centuries or even millennia to meet human needs and tastes, a constantly evolving product of human sophistication. Today's tomato—whether the strangely crunchy specimens on your fast-food burger, sliced from a tomato picked green in southern Florida, the yellowish purple heirloom sold at the farmer's market, or the paste on the slice at the corner pizza shop—is the product of countless human hands. Whether it is sprayed with pesticides, fertilized with sheep manure, or pollinated by specially bred bees, the tomato has not been a "natural" product for a long time. It is a very human tomato. Yet at its core, it maintains a certain purity and humbleness. It's an easily grown plant from Home Gardening 101, the ultimate backyard food.

Mexico is the birthplace of the tomato, or to be more precise, the probable birthplace of tomato *cultivation*. Plant geneticists and linguists have traced the original cultivars, or cultivated varieties, to the semitropical mountains where the states of Veracruz and Puebla come together, near where the Olmecs left their enormous, Asian-looking stone heads. Linguistic evidence indicates that the Maya, who lived in the swathe of land stretching from southeastern Mexico halfway down the Central American isthmus, also grew tomatoes during antiquity. When Spanish soldiers arrived in 1521, they found a wide variety of tomatoes for sale in the markets of Tenochtitlan and Tlatelolco, centers of Aztec power. As the Aztec nation's last Nahuatl-speaking scribes died off in the mid-sixteenth century, Bernardino de Sahagún had them record their memories of the wildly diverse precolonial tomato market, which I'll describe more in the next chapter.

The Veracruz-Puebla border is a land of heavy rains, profuse vegetation, and dark soils that produce coffee and oranges, bananas and cacao. But it is the coastal plains of western South America—the arid lands of Peru, Chile, and Ecuador—that spawned the wild tomato and its relatives. At least seventeen tomato-like species are currently recognized by taxonomists. These species, which belong to the *Lycopersicon* and *Solanum* genera, often grow in rugged, dry terrain where rainfall is a rare event and ocean mists may provide the only precipitation.

The conquistadors and their priests brought the tomato back to Spain, but unlike corn, potatoes, and chocolate, it languished for centuries as an oddity in the gardens of Europe. It was not until the vegetable had been domesticated by canning that it fully conquered European cultures. Compared with other products of the Columbian exchange, the tomato was a late bloomer in the Old World. The bland potato quickly swept through Europe, adding caloric heft to the Spanish omelette and the French *pot-au-feu* and enabling the rapid population growth of formerly rye-eating northern European lands; the sweet potato and hot peppers transformed Chinese and other cuisines; and corn quickly became Italian polenta and British gruel. But colonial-era tomatoes may have been bitter, judging from early European accounts and from the genetic history of the plant. They resembled poisonous plants like Deadly Nightshade, which is a member of the Solanaceae family, to which tomatoes also belong. For these and perhaps other reasons—could it have been the tomato's peculiar smell and texture, its perfectly strange taste, neither sweet nor sour exactly, that alienated the Renaissance palate?—professional cooks shunned the tomato for centuries. Botanists and doctors, who were the gatekeepers of the European table, spoke of it as a dangerous and unhealthy fruit.

Tomatoes love sun, abhor mold, and thus grow best in Mediterranean climates, where the growing season is hot and dry. But the tomato only gradually entered the southern Italian diet, mostly in the nineteenth century. When Goethe visited Naples in 1787, noodles were still eaten with cheese only. The first published recipe for spaghetti and tomato sauce appeared in a Neapolitan cookbook in 1837. Even in the 1880s, a battle raged in the agricultural community of Parma between the *pomodoristi* and the industrialists who would have preferred that Po Valley farmers grow mainly sugar beets. Familiar tomato-centric dishes like veal parmigiana and spaghetti bolognese were late-nineteenth-century inventions, better known among expatriate Italian populations than in Italy. Yet today there is scarcely a culture in the world where tomatoes are not regularly eaten.

The tomato took hold slowly in North America as well. Though it came to New Orleans in the eighteenth century with Spanish—and Mexican—cuisines, the tomatoes seen in Jefferson's Monticello garden in 1809 were mainly ornamental. The standard story about the introduction of the tomato to the United States is that a farmer named Robert Gibbon Johnson ate a tomato on the steps of the Salem, New Jersey, courthouse in 1820 to prove that it wasn't harmful; Salem began hosting a tomato festival in 1987 to commemorate the event. The Johnson story has been debunked, however, apparently made up by a Salem booster in the early twentieth century. The Salem festival, too, has disappeared—local farms no longer produce enough tomatoes to make it worthwhile. Like most foods, tomatoes undoubtedly found their place in U.S. cuisine gradually, and for much of the nineteenth century, there seem to have been as many people who feared them as who ate them. One person who helped their popularity was John Cook Bennett, a quack doctor and pretender for the leadership of the Mormon Church who proclaimed the tomato as a new cure-all in the 1830s. In the wake of his tomato propagandizing, patent medicine vendors developed tomato pills—made from the boiled paste of the fruit—which they peddled as curatives for heartburn, measles, indigestion, and whatever else ailed you. It was an early American nutritional self-improvement craze.

During the Civil War, canning technology made the tomato into a durable food; the camps of the Union Army were littered with rusty tomato cans. But it was under the careful tutelage of plant scientists at the Heinz and Campbell Soup companies that the tomato became the first Taylorized vegetable. Well before Ford created the assembly line, the pioneers of the mass food industry bred uniform tomatoes and delivered their seeds for planting to the farmers in Maryland, New Jersey, Pennsylvania, and Ohio, who grew them under contract. Heinz's and Campbell's exacting standards created the mold for industrial attitudes toward food in America, an ideal of consistent production that became iconic with the McDonald's hamburger (and Andy Warhol's painting of the Campbell's Soup cans). Outside the Campbell factory, "a line of trucks and farm wagons, sometimes nine miles long, began forming before daybreak along Second Street in Camden," a contemporary wrote in the early 1900s. "The streets literally ran red" with tomatoes. By 1928, ten million cans of soup rolled off the Campbell's Soup No. 2 factory every day, and John Dorrance, the MIT-trained chemist who owned the company, was the third richest person in the United States. Pittsburgh-based Heinz, possibly the world's first company to have a quality control department, was producing 400 million—nearly half—of the world's bottles of ketchup. Ketchup and tomato soup were essential components of the transformation of American foodways from homemade to store-bought. Yet before long, they had become so familiar that generations regarded them as traditional comfort foods.

But before the tomato could occupy a truly stable position on the American table, a peculiar semantic question had to be settled, namely, was it a fruit or a vegetable? Food importers John, George, and Frank Nix sued Edward Hedden, collector of the port of New York, for duties he had levied on a shipment of tomatoes from the West Indies in 1886. Hedden imposed a 10 percent levy on vegetables, while fruit entered free. Tomatoes were fruit, the Nixes argued, so they should have been tax-free. The high court disagreed. "Botanically speaking," it acknowledged, "tomatoes are the fruit of a vine, just as are cucumbers, squashes, beans, and peas. But in the common language of the people, whether sellers or consumer of provisions, all these are vegetables, which are grown in kitchen gardens and which, whether eaten cooked or raw are, like potatoes, carrots, parsnips, turnips, beets, cauliflower, cabbage, celery, and lettuce, usually served at dinner in, with or after the soup, fish, or meats which constitute the principal part of the repast and not, like fruits generally, as dessert."

That solved that. But some debates about the status of the tomato are more heated than ever. Over the past five years or so, the revolt against the supermarket tomato has given birth to a nostalgic craze for old varieties. Everyone has his or her pet tomato. In New Orleans, they'll tell you you've never had one until you've tasted the Creole, which they use in gumbo. Up north in the Garden State it's the big, juicy Rutgers and other "Joisey tomatoes." And there are people who'll tell you that the best tomatoes they ever ate were in Greece . . . or Italy . . . or Thailand . . . or Afghanistan. A lot of American cooks swear by Italy's San Marzano—elongated and angular, a bright red Venus de Milo–shaped tomato for making sauces and stews. But in southern Italy, some food snobs scorn this type. The San Marzano is dead, proclaim the aesthetes of the *mezzogiorno*, as they traipse up Mount Vesuvius through trash left by Mafia hauling companies to pick the dour, unirrigated *piennolo* tomatoes from that hard soil.

Increasingly, American tomato lovers swear by the ultimate tomato throwback—the heirloom tomato. An heirloom is a variety that has been around for fifty years or more, handed down by farmers from generation to generation. The assumption is that anything worth saving that long must be really good. Sometimes, heirloom cultivars aren't particularly flavorful, but they are almost always distinctive— these are weird tomatoes, ugly tomatoes, tomatoes with irregular shapes and odd colors and peculiar folds and cracks and zippers.

Heirlooms have made inroads even in the supermarket in the last few years, but most all of the tomatoes to be found in your local Kroger or Giant—as well as most of the seeds you buy at the gardening store— are hybrids. Hybrid seed results from crossing two pure strains in a way that heightens certain traits from each. Breeders try to create hybrids that have particular characteristics not found in any one "pure" cultivar— traits that are important to commercial growers, like hardiness, resistance to microorganisms, consistent size, and increased yield. But some hybrid breeders focus on flavor as well. Those who bemoan industrial agriculture and the lost flavors of yesterday tend to carry grudges against hybrids. Nowadays, if you want to sell a tomato to a cultural critic, it had better be an heirloom. Its individuality and diversity—apparent diversity, that is, since few gene variations are involved in the varied morphology of the heirloom—produce a feeling of happy proximity to the vastness of nature's manifestations. Heirlooms are a frowzy, indifferently groomed answer to the Futurist pyramids of red rubber ball tomatoes. They're Wild Things, juicy and rebellious, a thumb in the eye of mass-marketing. They're nice if you can afford them.

But heirlooms are for fun, not for feeding the world. All those crop failures and famines in history? The starving children in China and India you heard about as a kid as you poked at the liver and onions on your plate? These disasters came about because the farmers had no seeds but their heirlooms, which stopped producing because of crop diseases or poor soils. The problem with heirlooms is the same problem that the heirloom people of the Americas faced when they came into contact with Europeans: A lack of genetic diversity made them vulnerable to disease. Molds, blights, rusts, and insects are always on the attack, withering foliage and spotting fruit. The fact that heirlooms have passed from generation to generation shows they have some worth. But you'd be a fool to plant the same heirlooms year after year on a large commercial farm. Sooner rather than later, bugs would ruin your crop.

The heirloom tomato is perfectly capable of fulfilling its evolutionary destiny of self-reproduction. For that goal, it's a good thing to have a soft-skinned, cracked tomato fruit that quickly rots and tumbles off the vine, providing nourishment to the seeds inside it and the creatures who feed upon the seeds and sometimes carry them to new destinations.

We humans have other designs for the tomato. Since the days of hunter-gatherers, we have always influenced the plants we use as food, and the tomato is no exception. Early humans selectively chose which plants to gather and which to leave behind, and this affected where plants grew. Later, as agriculture developed—relatively recently, since humans have been around for over a million years, whereas the earliest evidence of agriculture, in the Middle East, dates from only ten thousand years ago—human impact on plants increased. Over the millennia, as humans saved the seed from plants that thrived in their fields one year and planted it the next, they molded and shaped wild plants, domesticated them, and transformed them into "crops." They kept the plants that thrived, and those that didn't either died or were discarded. The act of selecting plants with desirable characteristics is what plant breeders do. Early farmers were plant breeders without knowing it. The techniques they used—selecting and keeping seed from plants that performed well—didn't change much for thousands of years. In fact, they didn't change at all until the middle of the nineteenth century, when Gregor Mendel, a monk living in the Austro-Hungarian Empire, began conducting experiments to investigate differences he observed in peas growing in the monastery's garden, creating what became the first systematic study of genetic variation. Humankind might have gotten off to a slow start with genetics and plant breeding, but since Mendel, we've been making up for lost time. Our understanding of genetics has advanced rapidly, and the tools and methods of plant breeding have developed apace.

We humans have come to be cruel taskmasters of the tomato. We want it to leave its vine and go places. The average tomato consumed in America, according to a study conducted by Adel Kader at UC Davis in the 1980s, moves 1,028 times from when it is picked on a Sinaloa ranch to when it turns up in a Los Angeles supermarket. When tomatoes are in a truck, they bump against hard surfaces and each other. That can cause external and internal bruising, which sets off inside the fruit various ripening processes that soon turn even the best-tasting cultivars into sour mush. The skins of heirlooms are too thin, often too prone to cracking, to be able to truck long distances. For some purists, the answer is to not eat tomatoes unless they are grown nearby. But many people would like to eat a tomato out of season and would rather eat one grown halfway across the world than not eat one at all. There may be questions about the environmental impact of this goal, but there are also wholesome reasons to eat tomatoes year-round.

And so, many people in the business have sought another way to create tomatoes that people want to eat. In doing so, however, they don't want to throw out decades of research and plant breeding that have created a vegetable you can sell any time of the year and that at least resembles a tomato and provides the same nourishment. They don't want to throw out the industrial tomato with the bathwater. They want to transform it—to go back into this highly civilized tomato and somehow reinsert the lost secrets of the backyard tomato. This goal may ultimately be unachievable, but it's not outlandish, and as research and field tests progress through the decades, some real progress is being made. Like all scientists, the breeders of today can only see as far as they do because they're standing on the shoulders of giants.

CHAPTER ONE

The Architect
of the Tomato

O, Mr. Burbank, won't you try and do some things for me?
A wizard clever as you are can do them easily.

—Peter Dreyer, *A Gardener Touched with Genius*

 A BREEDER USES SCIENCE TO SYSTEMATICALLY IMPOSE HIS or her will on an organism, yet the unpredictable and unexplained, for which there is no resort other than intuition and resignation, are an undeniable part of the professional experience. Because evolution is an accidental, nonrational process, there's no purely scientific basis for breeding. A breeder's line is a free-flowing, adulterated stream that can end in a cul-de-sac (like the fossilized creatures of the Burgess Shale) or produce some happy exception to the disorder that rules genetic chance.

But science has given tomato breeders a set of markers on the road to designing new tomatoes, which is why any tomato breeder you meet will say that Charles M. Rick—who wasn't a tomato breeder at all—has contributed the most to the field. Many of these breeders even have photographs of Rick on their walls or desks. The undisputed father of tomato genetics, Rick gave the field a set of important intellectual discoveries and a habit of generosity that was contagious and spread throughout the world of tomato science and even further into the field of genetics and plant breeding. Kanti Rawal, the tomato breeder who guided many of my explorations, would often pause in the middle of an explanation and say, "None of this would have been possible without the work of one man, Charley Rick." He was not alone in that assessment.

Rick's friends like to describe him as a mixture of Charles Darwin and Indiana Jones. Physically, he looked like any other back-garden doodler from the Midwest—a tall, thin, serious-looking gentleman who had lots of facial hair and nerdy specs and who always, back to his high school days, wore a floppy fishing hat. Rick was neither an armchair evolutionist nor a whip-handling treasure hunter. Everything he did was simply in the name of science. But he had so much fun doing it that he inspired several generations of botanists.

Rick trained at Harvard and taught at the University of California, Davis, for nearly six decades. From 1948 to 1992, he took thirteen trips to South America to bring back wild relatives of the tomato, and the DNA from these plants added immensely to scientific understanding of plant genetics and to the commercial value of the tomato crop. Practically all the disease resistance that has been bred into modern tomatoes was drawn from related wild species, many of which Rick gathered on his botanical prospecting trips. He gave the seed away to anyone who wanted it. If it weren't for Rick's collection, and the network of unfettered research communication that he fostered through the Tomato Genetics Resource Center at UC Davis, we might not have cheap, year-round tomatoes, pizzas, or spaghetti sauces. Perhaps we wouldn't have cardboard supermarket tomatoes, either, but that's another story.

Rick was a well-known fixture in Davis, riding his rattletrap single-speed bike over the flat Central Valley roads that linked his lab, his greenhouses, and experimental fields. If it were a hot summer day, he'd be shirtless. Rick had dragged his family along on a yearlong adventure to Peru in 1956, driving a beat-up Volkswagen van through the desert and the Andes in search of wild tomatoes. When the van broke down, which it did frequently, and his wife and children were forced to hitch a ride into a town big enough to have a garage, Rick would stay back in the van, typing up his notes while the family hunted for parts—to the bemusement of the busloads of Peruvian peasants riding past. Once, he stayed in the van for two days by himself. Back in Davis, he grew millions of plants in his greenhouses and fields, testing thousands of hybrids and mutants. He created a geneticist's paradise, and dozens of superb graduate students and fellows passed through his program. To truly get the measure of the man's good-natured dedication to his science, though, you had to hear the turtle shit story.

Rick's visits to South America twice included tours of the Galá-pagos Islands, where he collected samples of a tomato relative called *Lycopersicon cheesmanii*. Normally, when he returned to Davis with his collections of wild tomatoes, Rick would plant the seeds and grow them in his greenhouses. But the *L. cheesmanii* seeds wouldn't germinate, no matter what he did. He exposed the seeds to solvents and even scraped them with sandpaper, but that didn't work. Many seeds in nature have to pass through an animal's digestive system to sprout. So Rick fed the seeds to mockingbirds, which were common in the Galápagos. "But it didn't do any good," recalled Rick's son, John Rick. The mocking-birds happily consumed the seeds—and digested them. Rick next tried feeding the seeds to iguanas, also common in the Galápagos. No luck. Eventually, a process of elimination (no pun intended) brought him to the legendary Galápagos giant tortoise, *Geochelone nigra*. There weren't any on the UC Davis campus, but Rick had a friend at San Francisco State University, an expert on finch evolution named Robert I. Bowman, who had brought two tortoises back from Santa Cruz Island and kept them in his backyard in Berkeley.

Rick sent Bowman the seeds to feed the tortoise, and in return, Bowman sent him mounds of turtle shit every couple of days, carefully sealed to fool the U.S. Postal Service, since it was and remains illegal to mail feces of any kind. "He would be sorting this stuff in the lab, to the great wide-eyed amusement of his grad students. But they still couldn't find anything," John Rick recalled. Rick consulted with an animal scientist, who suggested he try a marker dye. So Bowman started feeding the tortoises *L. cheesmanii* seeds at the same time that he fed them salads marked with carmine red dye. "By then, my father was starting to run out of the seeds, so it was getting serious." After about a month—tortoises have a *very* slow metabolism—the red started showing up.

"I remember coming into the lab one evening around nine o'clock or so," said Ghurdev Khush, one of Rick's illustrious students. "Charley was washing the feces off the seeds and the place really stank. He was a bit embarrassed." But he was undaunted. After passing through the tortoise, the seeds germinated, and this was no irrelevant trick. By crossing *L. cheesmanii* with garden-variety tomatoes, Rick was able to recover a trait that would prove vital to the mechanical harvest of tomatoes—the *j-2*, or jointless pedicel gene. The gene is involved in the formation of an abscission zone, an area of dead cells that forms between two plant parts—say, the stem and a fruit—and ultimately causes the furthest extension to fall off. Tomato plants with the jointless mutation form the abscission zone between the fruit and the stalk it's attached to, but not on any other section of the stalk; this means that the fruit comes off the vine without taking a piece of stem with it. As a result, the harvested tomatoes aren't attached to pieces of stem that jab and spoil other tomatoes while in transit to the cannery or packinghouse. This was an invaluable trait to the tomato business. For them, Rick had almost literally woven dross into gold.

Rick was unusual in that he was both a gentleman naturalist and a specialized lab rat. He was a lumper and a splitter, a fox and a hedgehog, an encyclopedic generalist and a laser-eyed reductionist. There aren't a lot of scientists like that anymore—maybe there never were. The hands-on genetics he performed at UC Davis is mostly done at private companies now, or by academic scientists using sophisticated molecular techniques whose mastery requires a career-long commitment. It's certainly nothing that a single individual would attempt.

Rick was born in Reading, Pennsylvania, in 1915. His father was an engineer who, during World War I, moved the family to Tennessee, where he managed electrical plants. After the war, young Rick returned to Pennsylvania with his family and worked in an orchard managed by his father. A studious lover of the outdoors—even in photographs from those early years, he's wearing the fisherman's cap—he enjoyed a circle of friends that revolved around his Boy Scout troop. Rick met his wife, Martha Overholts, at Penn State, where they were both undergraduates and her father was a distinguished mycologist. One summer, Rick and some friends drove an old Model A out to Lompoc, California, where he worked for Burpee Seeds and got a heady taste of the Left Coast. After earning his doctorate at Harvard, Rick was eager to head west. In 1941, the opportunity arose, when the University of California's new Davis campus invited him to join its Division of Truck Crops.

UC Davis, at the time, was a farm school in a cow town of a few thousand people. There were only four paved streets. The university had been established as an experimental farm during World War I and hadn't offered four-year degrees until 1933. As late as 1960, it was simply part of the agricultural school of the University of California, which was at Berkeley. When Davis students wanted to take other subjects— including cytogenetics—they rode the train to Berkeley. None of that was of the least concern to Charley Rick. He bought two lots on Parkside Drive, several blocks from the campus. He built a house on one lot and grew fruits and vegetables on the other. Cutting his ties with the East, he set to work bringing genetic advances to the expanding universe of California agriculture.

Rick at first continued studies begun at Harvard on X-ray-induced mutation of genes in plants like spiderwort, and sex determination in asparagus. Not long after his arrival, though, he took a stroll through the fields with plant physiologist John MacGillivray, a canning tomato expert who suggested it might be interesting for Rick to study the causes of infertility in "bull" tomato plants. About one in one thousand seedlings of any variety produced large, bushy plants that did not bear fruit. Farmers wanted to know if something could be done to get rid of such plants. But the inquiry led Rick far afield.

From a scientific perspective, the tomato is a welcoming species with which to work. Its genome has 710 million base pairs on twelve chromosomes with minimal internal duplication, which makes it relatively easy to match attributes of the tomato with specific regions of DNA. Thanks to such features, the tomato is probably the vegetable crop that has been most improved by hybridization with materials from its wild relatives. This work hadn't advanced far when Rick entered the field.

Some of the "bull" tomato plants were Down syndrome children of the tomato field, carrying an extra copy of one of the twelve tomato chromosomes in their cell nuclei. Certain others, like the male sterile mutants, Rick quickly noticed, might be suitable to use as parents in hybridization experiments, since they didn't produce pollen of their own (traditional hybridization, still in use today, involves removing pollen from the male parent, hand-stripping the anthers from the female parent, and rubbing pollen from the male on the female's stigma). But that was just the beginning of the uses to which Rick put these mutants. By conducting cytogenetic studies in which he correlated the chromosomal abnormalities of the trisomic bull plants (a trisomic has three copies of a chromosome in its nucleus, instead of the standard two) with their unique characteristics, Rick began to map tomato genes on the different chromosomes. Rick and his students did this by crossing thousands of plants and using a combination of microscopic examination and traditional Mendelian genetics to dope out the genes' location. A recessive trait has a one-in-four chance of appearing in the progeny of a typical, diploid plant carrying the trait. In a plant with an extra copy of the chromosome where the gene is located, the ratio is one in eight. Rick and his colleagues could determine the chromosome on which the trait was located by looking at differences in the ratios.

In 1948, Rick won a Guggenheim Fellowship that enabled him to spend a year in Peru, the first of several trips to South America that would energize the other major arm of his tomato research. On this and five subsequent trips, Rick collected thousands of wild *Lycopersicon esculentum* plants and specimens from many of the seventeen related species of the *Lycopersicon* and *Solanum* genera. This wild germplasm, catalogued at UC Davis, would make the tomato one of the best-understood plants and contribute enormously to the genetic diversity of the tens of thousands of domesticated tomato cultivars that exist in the world.

The trips were also an awesome source of material for Rick. As

Khush and Steven Tanksley, two of his most illustrious students, noted in a memorial essay, "Charley could recall details of almost everything he had read or experienced. A nature walk with Charley would open up your sense and awareness to everything around you, making you wonder how you could have ever missed those things that he so readily saw." John Rick, now a distinguished archaeologist at Stanford University, concurred: "I don't think I ever saw him consult a botanical text." He carried what he needed in his head, including the Linnaean system of botanic classification, which he'd committed to memory.

He was also a charming storyteller with an idiosyncratic take on the world: "the Mark Twain of plant genetics," Khush and Tanksley called him. In a November 23, 1948, letter he wrote from Lima, Rick complained genially about his "many hours of bouncing around in rattling busses and standing in long queues waiting for the privilege of riding the uncomfortable things." Later he described a long, alcohol-soaked visit with a local landowner.

> It is fruitless for me to try to recall how many times the glasses were raised or how many different kinds of things were offered. I offered a prayer of thanks that it was a dark night and that there were lots of large plants in the garden and that no one was too sharp to be watching what the other fellow was doing . . . How could I forget the most famous wine of all: "*quita calzón*" it is named ["get naked"], and I shall leave for you the translation and connotation of the name. The old fellow was very friendly and jovial, even though he had partaken rather sparingly as I noticed . . . I was astounded at how easy it was to speak and understand *castellano* in this state of affairs . . . the farewells were so belabored that one might think the parties were never to see one another again . . . The worst aspect of this indulging was that none of us had eaten since noon. The less said of the return trip down the mountain road the better.

In the days when there were smoking and nonsmoking sections in the airplane, Rick always made a beeline for the smoking section. "He didn't smoke," his son said, "but he'd say, 'The people in the smoking section are much more interesting.'" He was an extrovert and a joker, in any setting. Colleagues recalled a meeting in the early 1990s, when the USDA was trying to figure out how to work with transgenic plants and their theoretical perils. The talk had gone on for the better part of the day when Rick grew tired and raised his hand. "Dr. Rick?" the organizer called. "Yes"—Rick sat up and cleared his throat—"Well I don't think these plants are going to be dangerous because before they reach the public they will jump out of their petri dishes and kill the scientists who work with them. Then we won't have to worry about this anymore."

The garden lot next to Rick's house in Davis produced excellent cherry tomatoes, which few people were in the custom of eating in the early 1960s. Rick and his wife served them at annual dinners for the grad students and fellows. From the age of ten, John Rick was given his own business, raising sweet corn in the garden and selling it. Through his connections at Burpee, Charley Rick had obtained an extremely sweet experimental cultivar that became wildly popular in the neighborhood. "My parents forced me to sell below supermarket prices, but I still made a lot of money. I was sought after. People would leave notes on the door saying, 'I need urgently two dozen ears for Saturday.' I remember that I sold it for fifty cents a dozen. And my guess is we probably harvested maybe a couple hundred dozen. That was a lot of money in those days."

Though he was not a tomato breeder, Charles Rick performed hundreds of crosses of wild and domesticated species. The purpose of these crosses was to bring to light genes in the wild species that, once hybridized into commercial tomatoes, could prove useful in a variety of ways.

"His role in the breeding program was huge," said Don May, an agricultural extension agent in Fresno County since the early 1960s. "He was the foundation. He was the architect. He was also a fantastic person. Gentle, kind. Best guy to sit down and talk to in the world. But he wasn't a field person. Once Charley figured out the gene, he lost interest."

Rick's work, along with that of others such as tomato breeder C. Gordon "Jack" Hanna, engineer Coby Lorenzen, and various Davis extension agents, would transform the California tomato industry. Between 1945 and 1980, most of the canning tomato business moved to California, where yields tripled to about twenty tons per acre. A state that produced about two million tons of tomatoes in 1965 was producing eleven million tons by the end of the century. But Rick's influence extended well beyond California. "He was kind of a holistic scientist—breeders tend to be. He integrated his interests in a coordinated scientific effort," said John "Jay" Scott, a University of Florida professor who has bred tomatoes for farmers in that state for three decades. "Five minutes after meeting him he'd seem like your best friend," Scott recalled. "He was a nice, personable human being, and very funny. I think the best scientists are like that— they don't perceive other people and their work as threats."

From an academic perspective, it was Rick's remarkable energy and openness that were his biggest contribution. The Davis collection of tomato germplasm was an open book. Rick would send out seeds, free, to anyone who requested them. He published a monthly newsletter in which scientists from around the world shared their latest publications and discoveries with one another. The free distribution of information would become a model to other botanists such as Ghurdev Khush, who later headed the International Rice Research Institute, based in the Philippines. Collaboration in the rice breeding field helped speed the development of innovative new varieties for the Green Revolution. "There are many jealousies in the academic system, but Rick wasn't closed-minded. He shared materials with anyone who wanted them. And his attitude infected the whole field. When I got to the Philippines I never refused a request for material. Using that system, we turned rice into a model organism."

Many of the world's leading tomato scientists passed through Rick's lab as grad students or fellows at one time or another. His circle of friends extended around the world and even behind the Iron Curtain to East Germany, home of Hans Stubbe, director of the Institute of Plant Genetics and Crop Plant Research at Gatersleben.

Stubbe was an unusual German—a brilliant scientist who managed to pick his way through the ideological minefields of the mid-twentieth century to accomplish work of lasting importance without having to flee into exile. Recent research has shown that he collaborated with both the Third Reich and the East German Communists to maintain his funding and scientific stature, but these compromises were not grave enough to severely damage his reputation, unlike those of so many others in his cohort.

The Nazis fired Stubbe in 1936 from his position as chief of the Institute of Plant Breeding Research at the Kaiser-Wilhelm Institute, the nation's leading scientific center, but he maneuvered his way into a comparable position at another Kaiser-Wilhelm station. From there he joined in the wartime German policy of "autarky"—self-reliance, based in large part on the looting of southern and eastern European lands that were being starved by the German SS at the same time. Stubbe led botanical expeditions into the mountainous hinterlands of the Balkans and Russia following in the tracks of the Wehrmacht. In German historian Susanne Heim's words, he "used the Nazi expansionist policies as a means to scientific advance."

No doubt some scientific good came out of these expeditions, which were modeled on the remarkable globe-trotting research of Nikolai Vavilov, the Russian geneticist whose contributions to agriculture included the conceptualization of how crops came into being. In 1927, Vavilov had published his influential theory of "centers of origin," the idea that in certain geographical regions, huge varieties of cultivated species proliferate and provide a wealth of genetic material. Vavilov was especially interested in wild relatives of plants with desirable qualities. Though he apparently never published anything about tomatoes, the principles of Vavilov's work were of fundamental importance to Rick and his colleagues.

Vavilov was eventually a victim of Lysenkoism, the repressive campaign against agriculturalists who hewed to generally accepted Mendelian genetics rather than the Lamarckian "heritability of acquired characteristics" theory, which was championed in Russia by breeder T. D. Lysenko. Stalin adopted Lysenkoism because it fit in with the Leninist view of humanity as an easily transformable organism (and also because of Lysenko's peasant roots and his toadying to power). In 1940, as Stalin had Vavilov sent to Siberia, where the scientist perished three years later, the Germans were hot on the trail of Vavilov's ideas. Nazi scientists like Erwin Baur had followed his lead in scouring the world for germplasm that would strengthen German self-sufficiency and dominance. Stubbe and his colleagues seized Vavilov's valuable grain and fruit archives in the Ukraine and Byelorussia. Perhaps Stubbe, a secret skeptic of Nazism, thought he was safeguarding Vavilov's work in a time of war.

After the war, Stubbe remained in East Germany, where he became one of a handful of Soviet bloc scientists willing to stand up to Lysenko, whose notion that organisms could change the genetic makeup they passed along to offspring had a disastrous impact on Soviet agriculture and science. The idea that plants, through striving, could change their DNA was even more wrongheaded than the overestimation of what prodigious feats of labor the heroic Stakhanovite worker could achieve through proper class consciousness.

Stubbe, for his part, employed chemicals and radiation to produce changes in the DNA of plants ranging from snapdragons to wheat to tomatoes. Using X-rays, ethyl methane sulfonate, and other substances that provoke DNA mutations, Stubbe and his colleagues created about three hundred *L. esculentum* mutants and another two hundred in *L. pimpinellifolium*, the tomato's dainty cousin (its fruit is roughly a third the size of the cherry tomato). To explore the evolutionary linkage between the two forms, Stubbe experimentally expanded the size of the *L. pimpinellifolium* fruit by exposing successive generations to radiation. He was able to create plants producing fruit that were the size of *L. esculentum* varieties. Then he reversed the procedure; radiation and selection of the offspring of these *L. esculentum*–like plants produced *L. pimpinellifolium*–sized fruit.

Rick frequently drew attention to Stubbe's work. He invited him to tomato genetics conferences in the United States, but the East German authorities never permitted Stubbe to attend. Fortunately, Stubbe would send samples of his mutants to UC Davis, where they were used by Rick and others working to unravel the tomato genetic blueprint. The samples are still preserved there today.

Decades later, Steven Tanksley took Stubbe's work forward with a remarkable discovery about how DNA mutations affected size in the tomato. Tanksley, a Rick protégé who went on to become a distinguished professor of plant breeding at Cornell, showed that the DNA mutation affecting size was in an area of chromosome 2 that regulates the expression of a gene called ORFX, which affects the protein that stops cell growth. The mutation in ORFX—a gene that is expressed early in flower development—is structurally similar to the alteration of a gene that causes cancer in humans. In a tomato, it results in a fruit that has proliferating cell division—"the plant version of a tumor," as Tanksley described it. In the wild plant, large fruit are evolutionary losers, because birds—the vectors for wild tomato seed dispersal—can't pick up a large tomato. Humans, of course, have other feelings about cell proliferation in fruit. "We don't call them tumors; we call them luscious tomatoes," said Tanksley. "But it's all the same biology—a mutation that creates cancer in humans, but in plants it created agriculture."

Using his mutation experiments, Stubbe was able to link damage to specific chromosomal areas in the tomato to specific traits in the plant and its fruit. With this information, he laid out a map of markers and genetic variants for investigations into the size, shape, and fruiting habits of the tomato. Rick eventually built his own tomato genetics map upon a blueprint that Stubbe had laid down.

In the 1970s, when young people began questioning the way things were done in America, including on its university campuses, some of the criticism centered on academic scientists and how, for example, they had contributed to the transformation of agriculture in California and the world. To an extent, these were Luddite concerns that accompany any industrial transformation. But they were also specific to modern agribusiness and to feelings about how and what the baby boomer generation ate and fed its children. Was it good to have created tomatoes that were most valuable for their yield and not their flavor? To have created tomatoes that could be harvested by a machine, rather than the hands of poor farmworkers? To have transformed an agricultural system that employed four thousand small farmers to one in which a few hundred farmed vast acreages, their crops harvested and processed by a few conglomerates using pesticides and artificial fertilizers? As a radical critique of agriculture developed, activists in some poor countries moved to prevent outsiders from bioprospecting for their native plants and seeds. In the United States, critics charged that the incorporation of wild DNA into plants like the tomato had created crops that were unhealthy or inferior to their earlier ancestors. Developing nations' governments had other ideas about the value of this germ-plasm. In 1995, the Peruvian government stopped allowing scientists like Rick into the country, charging that they were taking the nation's patrimony and selling it for a profit.

To questions about the political orientation of agriculture, Rick had pragmatic responses. "On pesticides, Dad would say, 'You're going to have pesticides whether you like it or not; otherwise you're going to starve.' He felt we'd gone much too far on this to go backwards. He was very convincing on that point. He had a very perverse sense of resisting trends," said John Rick. "He thought organic was the funniest thing he'd ever heard of. He'd say, 'Everything's organic.' He definitely had a sense of environmental dangers coming from pesticides and so on. He was very well read in terms of what had gone wrong with pesticides. But when someone would come at him with a hyper-liberal line about genetic engineered stuff, or 'Pesticides are all bad,' or 'Why can't I get a good tomato in winter?' he'd say, 'You've got to understand how the system works. How much money are you willing to pay for a pound of tomatoes?' and people would give some low figure and he'd say, 'Well, you're going to be eating cardboard, so just live with it! You're barking up the wrong tree. If you think you deserve to eat tomatoes at a time when they aren't grown locally you're either going to have to pay for it, or eat awful stuff. You're not thinking through your argument.'"

One of the great botanical questions that motivated Rick during his career was the origin of the cultivated tomato. That the tomato first appeared in South America is not in dispute. The valleys of the western Andes have provided as many food crops to the world as any region, except perhaps the Middle East. Potatoes, peppers, yams, and peanuts all originated in the Andes. The last ice age never reached as far south as this great mountain chain, and its deep, fertile valleys maintained a wealth of plants, including many types of wild tomatoes. Yet the bulk of evidence indicates that while the Andeans of antiquity may have eaten wild tomatoes, they never cultivated them.

Studies by Rick and others showed that the only related species that commonly crosses with *Lycopersicon esculentum* in the wild is the so-called currant tomato, *Lycopersicon pimpinellifolium*. Nineteenth-century botanists found vast quantities of both species in the nearly rainless coastal deserts of Chile and Peru. During the hot Southern Hemisphere summers (that is, the northern winter), when the two species produce fruit, they provided a cool, sweet refreshment to the desert traveler. While the currant tomato's berries were smaller than those of the cherry tomato (*L. esculentum* var. *cerasiforme*), Stubbe's work suggested a gradation of forms between the currant and cherry. Luther Burbank, the plant-breeding wizard of Santa Rosa, California, may have been the first to knowingly cross them, creating a cultivar that his marketing reps called the Burbank's Preserving when they listed it in the 1916 Burpee's catalog.

Rick's many travels to South America included a yearlong 1956 jaunt with his family. "We soon arrived at a mutually acceptable understanding," the elder Rick wrote of this sojourn. "The sooner Daddy started working on the wild populations, the sooner the others could visit nearby beaches or archaeological sites!" The trip left a profound impression on John Rick. He was six at the time; his sister Susan, now a retired biology teacher at Santa Rosa Junior College in California, was ten. The spotting of tomatoes at high speed—although their Volkswagen bus never went that fast on those roads—became a game for the children, the botanist child's version of "I Spy." "We'd say, 'There's a tomato!' Usually he'd say, 'We're not stopping for that one.' And we'd say, 'Why, Daddy?' He'd explain that he already had something similar."

John Rick's first word in Spanish was *ruina*—not surprising, perhaps, given that tomatoes of interest to his father could often be found near the ruins of prehistoric settlements. Perhaps the "disturbed" ground these populations left behind provided prime soil for the propagation of diverse tomato populations. The overlap of ruins and interesting tomatoes points to the early, unconscious work of crop domestication that was done by our early ancestors. In the decade before Rick began scavenging the Andes for tomato relatives, a geneticist named Edgar Anderson, who worked at the Missouri Botanic Garden, had published a fascinating theory about how this development of new species and varieties of plants proceeded. His hypothesis of "hybrid swarms" held that at the edge of a plant's natural distribution zone, or within the zone but in disturbed areas that had unusual soil makeup (like what you'd find in a prehistoric human garbage dump, for example), natural hybridization would occur among different varieties, producing a profusion of new plant types. Vavilov's central observation was that most varieties of a given crop tended to concentrate in proximity to their related wild relatives. Anderson hypothesized that when humans and other animals inadvertently transported seeds to new environments, they catalyzed diversification.

Rick never published any observations about this phenomenon, but breeder Kanti Rawal believes that he must have had a nose for "hybrid swarms," because he managed to collect so much diverse tomato germplasm in his wanderings. "One of my yellow pears comes from Dr. Rick's collection," he told me. "He picked it up somewhere mid-altitude in the Andes. It was a village with a couple of houses, and he found them growing there. Best he'd ever eaten, he said. I got the seed, grew them up, and something happened. I had one thousand genotypes in thirty seeds—some were red, some orange, some yellow. For me, this is evidence that the place Rick picked these tomatoes was a border area for different subspecies. A lot of cross-fertilization was going on."

In any case, the proximity of ruins and tomatoes set the younger Rick upon his career path. One of his earliest memories is of a ruin in the remote Culebras Valley, two hundred miles north of Lima. While his father collected tomatoes in the valley, John and his mother could see, on the adjacent slope, adobe walls poking up through the sand. "We trudged up there, and my mother spotted some textile coming to the surface. We knelt down, cleared the sand off the textile, unfolded it, and we were looking straight into the face of a mummy. She had a necklace on her chest with ears of corn still in place, and a *manta* around her shoulder with a bone pin securing it. It was a very, very clear memory to me. I call it the decisive moment in my own career, going into archaeology."

Twenty years later, as a graduate student at the University of Michigan, John Rick was driving up the coast, and "almost like a homing pigeon, I drove straight to that site, although the Culebras Valley was the least indicated place for any of the work I was doing. I looked around, took some pictures, but had no idea where I was. But when I got back home, my father pulled out some old slides and said, 'That was Culebras.' It was as close to a mystical experience as I've ever had."

It was almost as if Charley Rick had raised his son to untangle one of the great remaining mysteries of the tomato, which was who, exactly, had first cultivated it. The Inca and other ancient Peruvian peoples often depicted their favorite foods on pottery that archaeologists continue to unearth from mountain, jungle, and desert sites. Yet there is some doubt whether any of their pottery contains an image of the tomato. There are some ribbed, round crops depicted on ancient Peruvian pots, but these fruit were probably squash rather than tomatoes. And there is no word for tomato in the aboriginal tongues of the region. Rick spent hours in the UC Davis special collections looking through old prints for the definitive answer. When his son had become an established archaeologist (in 2008, he was chairman of the Stanford Department of Archaeology), "he sort of commissioned me to report any evidence of tomatoes that I found in the literature or otherwise," said John Rick. "I can't say I contributed to an answer with any good level of confidence. But my father felt pretty confident that the tomato was never domesticated in Peru—that if it was used, it was a casual use." The first tomato cultivator remains an enigma. What was undeniable was the incredible diversity of edible tomatoes, wild and cultivated, in Mexico.

When the Spanish conquistador Hernán Cortés and his ironclad warriors arrived in the Mexican capital, Tenochtitlan, in 1521, they encountered a civilization that in many ways had advanced far beyond their own. The Aztecs and their subjects lacked horses, guns, steel, and, most importantly, resistance to common infectious diseases. But their art and architecture were, in their own ways, as impressive as those of Europe, and their agricultural practices were extremely productive. More to the point, their diet was a hell of a lot better than that of most Spaniards.

At Tlatelolco, sister city of the Aztec capital, pyramids of corn, chocolate, chilis, and squash reached skyward. Market men and women sold thick brown, orange, red, and yellow bowls of prepared foods—salsas, moles, pipians. The lords of Mexico ate well. Their meals often included tamales and turkey pies, roasted rabbit and fish, fried winged ants, maguey grubs, boiled lobster, fresh avocados and greens. Everything was wrapped in piping-hot tortillas made of corn softened with lime, and smothered in sauces. As accompaniment, they feasted on a profusion of fruits washed down with honey-sweetened cocoa (chocolate was also consumed, with nuts and chilis, in the fiery moles).

The fabulous table set by the Aztec nobles emerges most poignantly in the Florentine Codex, also known as the *General History of the Things of New Spain.* Three decades after the conquest, as he tended to Indians falling prey to smallpox, measles, and other germs that were as foreign to the Mexicans as their food was to the Spaniards, the priest Bernardino de Sahagún hired seventy industrious scribes and wise men to collect information about the ways of the dying civilization, "that there be some memory thereof, that the evil and imponderable might be better refuted and, if there were something good, that it might be recorded even as many things of other gentiles are recorded and remembered," as the royal court put it.

In the part of the codex referring to the Aztec table, tomatoes had pride of place; there were frequent references to the *pipian*, a continuing staple of Mexican cuisine, made of ground squash seeds, chilis, and the small, green, papery-veiled tomatillo, a close relative of the tomato. The sauce was ladled out on venison, hare, fish, rat, frog, and turkey—even, on special occasions, over the tender flesh of the inner thigh of a slave sacrificed to appease Huitzlipochilli, the Aztecs' bloodthirsty god of war. A mixture of tomatoes, chopped lilies, and peppers was also appropriate for serving on slave flesh. In his chronicle of the conquest,

Bernal Díaz del Castillo, justifying the massacre at Cholula, claimed that the city's warriors "wished to kill us and eat our flesh, and had already prepared the pot with salt and peppers and tomatoes."

"The tomato seller (Tomanamacac)," reported Sahagún's informants, "sells large tomatoes (xitomatl), small tomatoes (miltomatl), leaf tomatoes (Izoatomatl), thin tomatoes (xaltotomatl), large serpent tomatoes (coaxitomatl), nipple-shaped tomatoes (chichioalxitomatl), serpent tomatoes (Coatomatl). He also sells coyote tomatoes (coiotomatl), sand tomatoes (tomapitaoac), sweet tomatoes, those which are yellow, very yellow, quite yellow, red, very red, quite ruddy, ruddy, bright red, reddish, rosy dawn colored. The bad tomato seller sells spoiled tomatoes (tomapalaxtli), bruised tomatoes (tomapitzictli) . . . Also he sells the green, the hard ones, those which scratch one's throat . . . the harsh ones, those which burn the throat."

The apparent diversity of the Aztec tomato market is tantalizing. We may never know what some of these tomatoes were, but the distinct names suggest varied shapes and flavors. Many of these fruit were not tomatoes per se, but related members of the Solanaceae, including the husk tomato, *Physalis philadelphica*. Known in the United States as the tomatillo, the husk tomato is called *tomatl* in the Nahuatl language of the Aztecs, *p'ak* by the Maya. A native plant, the tomatillo was the ur-tomato of Mexican cuisine. This probably explains why its South American tomato cousins, which arrived later, tended to have names in various indigenous languages that compounded the original—*miltomatl, coiotomatl, Mehen p'ak*, and so forth. Perhaps birds had brought *Lycopersicon's* wispy seeds north to Central America across the Darien Gap, or Mayan sea voyagers brought them back to the Yucatán Peninsula. Research in recent decades has turned up quite a bit of evidence of trade among pre-Columbian Americans.

Most early European depictions of the New World tomatoes show them as wrinkled, yellow or red fruit with hollow areas inside their ribbed sections—similar, perhaps, to modern heirloom cultivars like the Zapotec Pink and the Genovese Costoluto, which Thomas Jefferson grew at Monticello. The first account of the tomato, written in 1544 by the Italian physician Matthiolus, described it as being "eaten in the same manner as the eggplant—fried with salt and pepper." Matthiolus's account may have come from the botanist Dioscorides, or from a Turk named Busbecq, but Matthiolus was frequently misquoted in later accounts as saying the tomato was "eaten in Italy with oil, salt and pepper." There are numerous accounts of the tomato in herbals and travel literature from the late sixteenth and seventeenth centuries, but they shed little light on where tomatoes came from, and not for lack of wild speculation on the subject. It was claimed that the tomato came from Peru, North Africa, Syria, and Ethiopia. Its scientific name, *Lycopersicon*, was another red herring. The seventeenth-century Italian botanist Anguillara Semplice christened the tomato with this name because he became convinced that it was the same plant Galen had called *Lycopersicon*, or Wolf Peach. When Galen was puttering around in the second century, of course, no one in Europe knew from Mexico or tomatoes.

The early accounts were deeply suspicious, abounding in descriptions of the fruit's supposedly unwholesome qualities. The editors of the 1600 British book *The Countrie Farm* said that while "pleasant to the sight" the tomato "provoketh loathing and vomiting" when smelled or eaten. Italians eat them, wrote the Dutchman Matthias de l'Obel in 1581, "but the strong stinking smell gives one sufficient notice how unhealthful and evil they are." The earliest European statuary depicting a tomato is apparently the 1601 bronze door of the cathedral at Pisa, which also features peppers. Like most accounts from this period, l'Obel's describes the tomato in medicinal terms, along the lines of the modified Galenic thinking of the time, which held that health was all about balancing the humors. Different substances contributed to this apparently delicate equilibrium in ways that seem particular and arbitrary to the modern way of thinking. Tomato, for instance, was a "very cold" substance that "not only drives away the power of superfluous dampness, but it tempers also the heat as it has been put to the test by our modern doctors . . . It is also very good against wild fire (erysipelas) because it is very cold, diminishing the heat when it is applied."

In the literature of tomato history, many authors attribute the tomato's slow conquest of Europe to the reluctance of Europeans to trust a fruit that was closely related, in taxonomical terms, to datura, nightshade, and other deadly plants. I wonder, though, whether taxonomic knowledge was widely enough diffused to make people fear tomatoes for their familial connections. It seems to me that its being unusual, strong-flavored, and distinctive may have been enough to create mistrust in the tomato. Its leaves stank, and it was not like anything else that Europeans ate, and therefore suspect. You say tomato, I say no thanks.

The Spaniards, having seen the Nahua people eat tomatoes and undoubtedly having partaken themselves, were apparently willing to give these fruits a go. But the traces of early Spanish tomato cookery are scant. There apparently weren't any Spanish cookbooks published between 1611 and 1745, so it's difficult to track where and how quickly the tomato penetrated the cuisines of the Iberian Peninsula. From Spain the tomato may have spread first to Africa and the Middle East; early reports describe the tomato as a borrowing from outcast European Jews or Arabs around the same time that Spanish nobles of the House of Bourbon brought them to their subject peoples in Sicily, Naples, and Parma.

It was Italy that provided the first European name for the tomato, although the etymology is somewhat confused. By the eighteenth century, the French called it the *pomme d'amour*, an apparent bastardization of the Italian *pomodoro*. The Italian word, in turn, may have referred to some yellow—i.e., golden, or *d'oro*—tomatoes that appeared in Europe early in the tomato's adaptation. Or, the Italian might have been a musical tergiversation of the French *pomme d'amour*. (Which came first—the love or the gold?) Whatever the case, the French name created a lingering mystique that suggested the tomato had aphrodisiacal qualities. Tomatoes are no more aphrodisiac than any other food that, simply by providing nutrients, helps put lead in your pencil. The historian Rudolf Crewes offered a radically different theory about the origins of the name. He speculated that *pomodoro* was no more than a botched version of the word Italians earlier had used to describe the eggplant. The eggplant came to Europe from the Arabs and is a member of the Solanaceae family, like the potato and tomato. "The apple of the moors," or *pomo del moro*, may have been shortened and twisted to *pomodoro*, or golden apple. This was the seventeenth century. Spell-check wasn't available, and poetic licenses flowed like wine.

In 1948, a Berkeley colleague of Rick named James A. Jenkins published the most definitive paper on the origins of the cultivated tomato. Up to Jenkins's time, most authors believed the tomato had been cultivated in Peru, since its wild relatives all lived there. Indeed, it is impossible to rule out isolated Peruvian cultivation of the tomato in antiquity, but even if that's the case, it was Mexicans who immersed themselves in the tomato and its uses and who shared it with the world. Genetic analysis shows that wild Mexican "cherry" forms of *Lycopersicon esculentum* bear the closest resemblance to the tomato blueprint that now circulates around the world.

Jenkins, who traveled all around Mexico in his investigation, tackled the question initially from the linguistic angle. A Paduan scholar had called them *tumatl* as early as 1572. (Sahagún's account of the tomato seller was published later.) There was no record of a separate word for tomatoes in any of the pre-Columbian Peruvian tongues. By the 1940s, when Jenkins did his survey, wild cherry tomatoes were growing in subtropical areas from Hawaii to Africa to China. In subtropical Mexico, Jenkins found them in streambeds and disturbed ground bordering fields and roads. "It does not behave like a well-established native plant, but one that has been introduced and has spread in association with man," he wrote. Yet Mexicans had obviously been eating tomatoes in these regions for centuries, and the range of the fruit's size and shape, while nothing like the extravagant diversity of Andean *Lycopersicon* species, was extensive. "In the poorest markets and in the remotest villages there are usually tomatoes for sale during the season, and nearly every housewife, no matter how poor, buys at least one or two." Sometimes the wild cherries, considered especially tasty, were sold side by side with the larger cultivated tomatoes. "It is highly improbable that a people who have retained their ancient food habits as tenaciously as have the Mexicans could possibly have incorporated the tomato so extensively into their diet in the comparatively short period since the Spanish conquest," Jenkins wrote.

Jenkins found that Nahua speakers continued to refer to tomatoes with a variety of names such as *xaltomatl, jaltomatl, miltomate, tomate silvestre, cuatomate,* and *cuatomatillo.* In Veracruz one variety was known as *chitalino, chitalillo, chitalito, sitalillo* (star tomato), *tomate de venado, ojo de venado, chiltomate* (red tomato), or *tomatillo* (not to be confused with *Physalis,* the *tomatl*). In Oaxaca, the Zapotec called them *Chinana, pethoxi, bethoxi, bituixe.* In northern Mexico, the

Tarascans called the cherry tomatoes *tinguaraque*. The Summer Institute of Language, whose mission was to translate the Bible into every
language in the world, assisted Jenkins by collecting names for tomatoes from natives living in isolated jungles, deserts, and mountains.

Other names referred to tomato sizes and shapes. You had your
perón (plum), your *calabacito* or *guajito* (pear), the *durazno* (peach),
the irregular *costillón* (ribbed), the *gajo* (segmented), and the *riñón*
(kidney-shaped). For Jenkins, the concentration of varieties in the
Veracruz and Puebla escarpment and lowlands, which included types
that did not grow elsewhere, "indicates that much if not the bulk of the
evolution from the small, two-loculed tomato took place in Mexico."

Yet even in a largely rural, premodern Mexico, it was hard to be
sure that what you were seeing was authentically prehistoric. In Puebla
state, for example, Jenkins found a cultivar very similar to the Italian
San Marzano. The San Marzano–type tomato may have resulted from
a very early mutation of the cherry. A San Marzano chopped in half
reveals that while the fleshy part of the fruit (the pericarp) is elongated,
the gummy, seed-bearing area (the placenta) is no bigger than that of a
cherry tomato. This would suggest that a simple mutation was behind
the creation of the San Marzano type, and would argue in favor of its
having evolved in Mexico before coming to Italy. On the other hand,
Jenkins wrote, "since there is an Italian colony in the state of Puebla it is
difficult to know whether [the San Marzano or its predecessors] originated from the Mexican variety, or vice versa."

In a 1943 letter to Jenkins, Edgar Anderson described encountering
currant tomatoes growing wild in the scrub desert surroundings of Tuxcacuesco, Jalisco. The locals called them *jaltomates*, and "they snuggled
up against rough stone walls at the edges of gardens and the outbuildings
of haciendas; they clambered about and sometimes grew all over the big

mescal plants which were grown for tequila . . . Picked by the handful and eaten sun warm they taste almost like a sweetish tomato catsup." But "the only man in Tuxcacuesco who was growing tomatoes for the market told us that he got his seeds from California. He was so impressed by the big American tomatoes that he saved the seed from a ripe tomato in a restaurant and all his crop have descended from that."

The collectors frequently heard stories like this. The Mexicans wanted to be modern, with modern tomatoes. And once the 1960s came along, Americans started to crave the wild, unimproved flavors of these aboriginal tomatoes. It often seemed that the further people got from the agricultural grind, the more they wanted its oldest, pre-civilized products.

There's no record of how tomatoes were brought from Mexico to Spain, but it's fair to assume that whoever brought over the plants didn't have a background in the fundamentals of plant breeding. If this were the case, the royal collector would have sought out as many diverse tomato plant types as were grown in Mexico, to generate the kind of diversity that would produce hearty, high-yielding tomatoes. But tomatoes were nothing more than a court curiosity. We know from early European tomato iconography that the tomatoes distributed in apothecaries' herb gardens in the sixteenth century were a medium-sized, ribbed sort, though there is also discussion in the early herbal books of smooth fruit. Whatever the case, not many tomatoes formed the founder generation of the tomato cultivars that soon spread around Europe and from there back to the Americas and throughout Africa and the Middle East. A little more diversity entered the global gene pool when the Spaniards brought Mexican tomatoes to the Philippines in the sixteenth century—from there they traveled to India, Thailand, and the

rest of Asia. Early accounts of tomatoes in the American colonies suggest that some tomatoes had arrived from the Old World, and some
directly from Mexico or the Caribbean.

The cultivated tomato, as we know it today, rests on narrow genetic
shoulders. Before expanding into the multitude of shapes, colors, and
sizes that we know from the seventy-five thousand varieties available
in international collections, it had to pass through the bottleneck of
sixteenth-century Spanish selection.* In the course of its cultivation,
L. esculentum increasingly became a self-pollinating plant; that is, each
flower on the plant pollinated itself, rather than relying on pollen that
drifted over from a neighboring flower or plant for pollination and
fruiting. By contrast, some tomato-like species are *self-incompatible*—
meaning that the flower will only create fruit if it is pollinated from
another plant. These plants have a kind of built-in incest taboo—a fruit
that results from self-pollination fails to develop seeds and therefore
doesn't propagate. The result, as Tanksley and other geneticists have discovered, is that there is more genetic variation within a single collection
of some of the self-incompatible species, such as *Lycopersicon peruvi-
anum*, than there is in the entire collection of cultivated *L. esculentum*
tomatoes around the world. "The total variation in this single species,"
Rick wrote of *L. peruvianum*, "is indeed staggering. In truth, we cannot
comprehend the extent of this genetic resource and have only scratched
the surface in analyzing, let alone utilizing its genetic resources." Out of
all the known tomato and tomato-related gene sequences in the world,
cultivated tomatoes contain only 5 percent.

When Rick came to Davis, few scientists or breeders had attempted
to bring wild genes into commercial tomatoes. Yet there was an intense

---

* The actual number of varieties is probably lower; there are no doubt duplications
within collections.

need for it. Almost all of the commercially grown tomatoes were subject to a variety of rots, blights, and wilts caused by a seemingly endless number of bacteria, viruses, fungi, and parasites, not to mention the predations of the insect world. Entire crops were routinely wiped out when a new pathogen swept through an area. Tomato breeding to withstand these and other challenges was a piecemeal art.

The Trophy, the main cultivar used to make canned tomatoes for Union troops during the Civil War, was still a staple of gardens and commercial operations well into the 1930s. But by then it was accompanied by cultivars developed by Alexander W. Livingston, a Reynoldsburg, Ohio, seedsman who was the first important tomato breeder in the United States. Livingston introduced his first creation, the Paragon, in 1870. Prior to Livingston, tomato breeders seeking to improve their stock would select attractive individual fruit and grow out the seeds. Livingston's innovation was to select entire plants that showed attractive qualities. By growing out hundreds of seeds from promising plants, he created the Paragon, which he called "the first perfectly and uniformly smooth tomato ever introduced to the American public." Livingston developed more than a score of new cultivars. Yet there were limits to how much he could achieve by simply selecting attractive mutations in the field. Many of the "open-pollinated" cultivars (nonhybrids) he created remained susceptible to numerous microbes.

It wasn't until breeders began using hybridization techniques, rather than simple selection, that they were able to take advantage of all the germplasm in the tomato and its relatives. In 1917, Frederick J. Pritchard of the U.S. Department of Agriculture (USDA) crossed a cultivar called Marvel with one of Livingston's tomatoes, the Globe, creating the Marglobe, which was coveted by growers for several decades because it was tolerant of fusarium wilt.

In the 1920s, inspired by the success of the Marglobe, agriculture extension agents in Ohio and Indiana began screening tomatoes for resistances. In the 1930s, well after Vavilov and the Germans had gotten the idea, USDA scientists toured Latin America in search of wild species. They found some wild tomatoes that were of interest to commercial breeders, but failed to properly maintain the seeds. Tomato seeds are only viable for about ten years; they must be grown out regularly, or they lose their viability. And the early bioprospectors didn't understand the proper germination techniques or growth requirements of many of the wild species. They also failed to recognize the diversity of germplasm that might be contained in a single collection of plants.

While cultivated tomatoes are largely self-pollinating plants, this isn't generally the case with their wild relatives. In many tomato-growing areas of Peru, numerous species of bees can pollinate the tomato flower. In fact, bees are the only insect that can fertilize the tomato—they do it by thrumming the pollen out with their rapidly beating wings. In wild *L. esculentum*, the stigma—the female part of the sexual apparatus—extends outside the flower, so that it can be pollinated by a visiting bee. But as the species was cultivated further and further from its home, especially in areas that lacked good bee populations, this out-breeding became a disadvantage. Evolution favored plants with a shorter stigma, which could be pollinated from the flower's own anther (the "male" sexual organ). Out-breeders, lacking bees to spread or bring pollen, would not set as much fruit. This evolutionary process is visible in a geographic and genetic study of the tomato's past. Some of the old Mexican cultivars—closer to the wild tomatoes of Peru—have stigmas that are partly enclosed in the flower. In modern cultivars, the stigma is entirely enclosed within the flower, where pollen from the anthers falls on it. Thus the modern tomato is entirely inbred.

The shape of the flower makes it relatively easy for tomato breeders to create hybrids. To create a hybrid tomato plant, the breeder strips the anther off the flower chosen as the "female," then rubs pollen on it from another plant. If the cross is successful, the seeds in the fruit it forms will have genetic material from both parents. The result of the recombination of the chromosomes of the two parents is a jumble of DNA, resulting in offspring that may have the traits sought by the breeder, along with many other, undesirable ones. To get a single trait into an established line of tomatoes is a long, difficult, painstaking process. It often requires multiple crossings and backcrossings. And it isn't always successful. Sometimes, unwanted traits can't be separated from the desired ones—perhaps the DNA that codes for the two sets of traits is located too close on a given chromosome to segregate out during the juggling of gene sequences that occurs during the creation of sex cells. A good breeding program requires a large, well-organized collection of plants with well-documented traits. Livingston didn't have anything like that. And his collection lacked the genetic diversity available to later breeders.

As the tomato business expanded, this became a serious deficit. When ripening tomatoes get wet, various blights can set it—as was seen in June 2009, when tomato farms throughout the eastern United States were struck by *Phytophthora*, a mold also known as potato blight or late blight. Frosts generally prevent some of the other bad organisms, like the fungi fusarium and verticillium, from spreading beyond small areas. But in California and Florida, these organisms remain in the soil year-round. So as early as the 1920s, extension agents at UC Davis and other campuses were trying to breed tomatoes that were resistant to these two wilting agents. And it was here that Rick's travels in South American began to pay off.

By crossing domesticated breeds with wild varieties like *L. peruvi-anum* and *L. chilense*, Rick uncovered from the wild tomatoes certain genes that either weren't expressed or were masked by other charac-teristics in the plant. In other words, there were hidden resources in the wild tomatoes, invisible to the naked eye. In 1952, Rick crossed an established breed called Pearson with *L. chilense* and got plants with a coppery orange color in the corolla and anthers of the flower. He called it the "old gold" or "crimson" gene because it also gave the fruit of the *L. esculentum-chilense* hybrid a rich red color—though the pure *L. chilense*'s berries were hard and purplish green. The "crimson" gene is now frequently bred into fresh-market tomato cultivars, especially as inter-est has grown in lycopene, which causes the red color and may have some protective effect against certain cancers.

In 1951, Rick and his colleagues established the Tomato Genetics Cooperative (TGC), a clearinghouse of information. As they grew more systematic in their categorization of genes, these scientists decided to define a genetic characteristic as "mutant" depending on whether it appeared in the standard type. The standard, they decided, would be the Marglobe, which thirty years after its release by Pritchard was still widely grown and typical of the general concept of what a tomato looked and acted like.

Every year, the cooperative published new updates of the genetic dis-coveries of its members. Some of the genes were highly deleterious to the plant: *Btl*, or brittle, was a gene that caused growth to cease after the first flowering, with progressive defoliation; *cm* caused a mottling and distor-tion of the leaves and abortion of flowers; *imb*, "imbecilla," caused a weak plant with few branches. Other mutations produced freakish plants, like *d2*, a dwarfing gene that caused the plant to grow extremely slowly, or *gq*, "grotesque," in which the pollen-carrying stamens were twisted and interwoven. But there were dozens of genes of economic interest that breeders could try to pull into the plant, such as *bg*, which produced fruit resistant to bursting, or the cracking-resistant gene *cr*. Many of the most important discoveries were disease resistances. By 1995, more than forty-two major resistances had been discovered in exotic species, and twenty had been bred into commercial varieties.

Two other early discoveries of vital importance were *sp* (self-pruning) and *j* (jointless). The *sp* gene was apparently discovered by a Florida physician in 1914; A. F. Yeager, a North Dakota agronomist, brought the trait into commercial use by breeding it into a standard Midwest tomato, the Michigan Forcing, in 1927. Self-pruning tomatoes, also known as determinate varieties, send off a shoot that flowers at the end and then stops growing. The traditional vine tomato, meanwhile, will keep growing and flowering until the cold comes. Its growth habit is known as indeterminate. The *sp*, or determinate, gene turned the tomato vine into the tomato bush. More than any other, it created the processing tomato industry.

For the breeder, it wasn't a matter of simply picking the genes you wanted, like shopping at a grocery store. Some of the genes weren't really genes at all, but rather sections of DNA that had an impact on when or how a gene was expressed. And genes in nature as the breeder worked with them were rarely discrete qualities. Even Rick's most commercially relevant single discovery, for jointlessness, wasn't something you could pop into the tomato like a battery, as Canadian breeder Jim Dick recalled.

Rick's discovery was christened *j-2*; the first jointless gene, *j*, had been discovered in 1936. Although both genes produced jointless stems, the first *j* gene was tightly linked to another gene, one that caused the stem to be tightly attached to the fruit. Seeds with the *j* gene also produced a plant whose flowering time was less concentrated than was the case with *j-2* tomatoes. This characteristic, known as "concentrated set," is avidly sought by tomato farmers and processors. The more a field of tomatoes fruits at the same time, the less labor is required to harvest them. For all of that, Dick initially preferred the fruit that he got from *j* cultivars. With *j-2*, the tomatoes were rough-looking and had to be cored, at a time when the canneries were no longer hiring women to core the fruit before they were cooked. "It took a heck of a lot of work to get a *j-2* tomato that was right," he recalled. The key breakthrough was the discovery of a gene for ovate shape, which when bred into the *j-2* line resulted in a smooth, coreless tomato.

The breeders who took advantage of this gene pool are tremendously grateful to Rick. "Most academics are just trying to publish and get ahead. Most geneticists are greedy and want to hoard whatever they find," said Kanti Rawal. Rick charged $1.50 for the annual report from the TGC. All the literature about tomatoes was listed there, with contact information for members, who lived all over the world. Breeders listed their new creations in the report. New genetic discoveries and techniques were published in brief by the TGC, often before they appeared at greater length in journals. And the genetic material collected at Davis became an indispensable reservoir for breeders.

Beginning in the late 1960s, Rick's gene-hunting technology grew more sophisticated. Working with graduate students like Steven Tanksley, Roger Chetelat, and Daniel Zamir, he developed a system that introduced individual chromosomes, and later chromosome snippets, from wild species into *L. esculentum* varieties whose traits were well established. By comparing these hybrids with the "controls" and using early DNA-tagging technology, he and his colleagues created the first molecular linkage map—mapping genes of interest to small areas of particular tomato chromosomes. By 1983, they had detected in the genome 233 markers that indicated whether a tomato line would have certain traits. This was of huge value to commercial breeders, many of whom now use a more sophisticated map of trait markers to select which tomatoes to use for developing new varieties. Zamir and other Israeli scientists who passed through Rick's world were among the global leaders in breeding sophisticated tomatoes.

By the time Charley Rick died in 2002, academic tomato breeding had moved into the background. In the 1970s, after a change in intellectual property laws allowed seed companies to obtain clearer ownership of their new plants, commercial breeders began using hybrids, which made their work inherently more secretive. Gradually, universities stopped hiring and training plant breeders as the work shifted to business laboratories with expensive, high-tech gene marking technology. Nowadays, growers and processors look to the seed companies rather than university breeders for their varieties. Rather than creating new crop varieties, the dwindling number of breeders at agriculture schools are doing more basic science—work that is "upstream" of the actual crop products.

Rick's heirs at Davis continue to do important work and to maintain his collections. They still get plenty of requests from the seed industry— they mail out five thousand seed packets a year—but they rarely hear back. "The seed companies don't keep us up-to-date about their doings," said Chetelat, now a professor of genetics and director of the Charles M. Rick Tomato Genetics Resource Center at Davis. The center may need to change its business model in light of dwindling USDA funds to maintain the collection, Chetelat told me recently. To keep a tomato collection viable, you need to generate new seeds with a round of plantings every ten years or so. "We're getting very nervous about our future."

For all that, one still gets an intense sense of wonder touring the Davis greenhouses, where the collections maintained by Rick and his students and collaborators are a treasure house of botanical wonders but also historical markers in the progress of breeding. During a tour, Chetelat showed me an *L. peruvianum* specimen from a collection made at Nazca, Peru, of a type that provided a virus resistance gene present in most hybrids today. We looked at feathery *L. cheesmanii* plants, whose seeds Rick had painstakingly and memorably removed from turtle feces. Chetelat showed me an *L. hirsutum* that grows at ten thousand feet in the Andes. This drought-resistant plant bears hairy-looking fruit and contains plentiful terpenoids—the highly aromatic component of plants like eucalyptus, clove, and ginger—in its skin. It has few insect predators in the wild and is resistant to the thrips and whiteflies, tiny insects that plague tomato cultivars, feeding on the leaves and inoculating them with damaging viruses. In Ecuador, people eat the softened fruit of *L. hirsutum* to treat intestinal disorders and use them as a salve for skin diseases.

I also got to examine a *Solanum ochranthum* from Cajamarca with bright yellow flowers and hard fruit the size of golf balls, and an *S. lycopersicoides* from Tarapaca, Chile, with greenish purple fruit with purplish casks that grow in the high desert and produce fruit with only two or three seeds, which must remain on the plant up to six months to mature. Perhaps the weirdest plant I saw was *S. juglandifolium*, which grows with its roots in the rivers of Amazonia and spreads its vines high into the jungle canopy. Its leaves are shiny and have the shape and arrangement of walnut leaves.

It's getting harder to collect species in the wild as developing countries grow suspicious that their national heritage is being robbed. "They have this misconception that there's a treasure trove of wealth in each new variety, and that the seed companies will develop them and then sell them back to South America," Chetelat said. "It's good we got there before access became difficult, because city growth, modern agriculture, and overgrazing have wiped out a lot of populations. The host countries are doing little to protect them."

Luckily, the Tomato Genetics Resource Center remains intact, packed with knowledge, painstakingly gathered, and tenderly curated for the benefit of tomato fanciers everywhere.

CHAPTER TWO

The Flavor Cravers

When you eat the supermarket tomato that tastes terrible, it is
"terrible"; when you bite into the heirloom tomato that happens to
be tasteless and watery, you adjust it to taste "real."

—Mark Greif, *On Food*

 I LOVE THE SMELL OF *CIS*-3-HEXENAL IN THE MORNING. It's
that smell, that tomato smell, that gets us out in the fuggy
summer mornings in our pajama bottoms and slippers, coffee in hand, to check on what miracle God, or whatever, has
performed in the garden overnight. The tomatoes are a shaggy confusion of intertwining vines, despite our best-laid tidy May plantings.
We can't tell the Big Boys from the Tasti-Lees, the Small Fry from the
Sun Golds, but we don't care, because the smell is all around us and,
as we wade in, searching for a morning treat, it comes off on us, that
"loathsome stink," as the English gardener Charles Stevens described
it in 1601, that does not, to the modern nose, smell loathsome at all. It
smells tangy, borderline sour, but bracing, vegetal, pleasantly suggestive

of the jungle. In parts per million, the tomato is sending out a chemical invitation to the animal kingdom: Eat me, carry off my seeds, enable me to carry out my accidental destiny.

In the haze of that distinctive chemical, we observe the miracle of vascular transport, which takes the sucrose made in sunlight in the hirsute, bitter, green leaves, and pulses it hydraulically into the reddening berries, some tiny as peas, some big as softballs, that hang in such lovely clusters or all on their lonely own.

In March 2008, I planted a couple hundred seeds in trays of peat moss and potting soil in my basement, put my grow-lights in position, and waited to see what would come up. I had heirloom varieties—Speckled Peach, San Marzano 2, Green Zebras, and Black Plums. I had some commercial prototypes, including Tasti-Lee, a new slicer that the University of Florida's Dr. Jay Scott had sent me. And I had a lot of old cultivars, some weird, some classics, ordered from the USDA's massive (5,700 varieties) tomato seed collection in Geneva, New York—ribbed Marmandes from Israel, yellow Biisky Zhelty from Siberia, Rutgers from New Jersey, something labeled Geng Dgon Xiao-jang, which a Swedish seedsman had collected in China during the Great Leap Forward, wild cherries and currant tomatoes from Puebla state in Mexico. I had VF-145A, the father of the modern canning tomato. And I had Kanti Rawal's tomatoes, cherry hybrids mostly, along with the yellow Roma that is his signature, patented line.

On a rainy Sunday in May, I invited about twenty friends to lunch on the condition that they take the plants off my hands, but although the barbecued chicken and sausage all disappeared, there were still dozens of seedlings left when the guests cleared out. So a few days later, I put them in my kids' wagon and made my way through the alleys behind the house, looking for neighbors with space in their yards and a yen for homegrown tomatoes. As the summer went on and I watched my tomatoes grow in a dozen gardens, I felt like Johnny Tomato-seed, sowing the city with flourishing plants. It was a wholesome diversion to a midlife crisis. I was expanding the biodiversity of the neighborhood with my strange fruit, each with a story of its own.

Diversity is probably the key to the excitement and controversy that surround tomatoes. When epicures complain about food in America, one of the first items they mention are supermarket tomatoes, the kind the stores used to present in militaristic pyramids. Yet we're learning more all the time about the nutritional benefits of eating tomatoes. They are high in vitamins C and A and in lycopene, the red pigment that seems to protect against prostate cancer and possibly heart disease. They rank high among fresh fruits and vegetables in potassium, magnesium, zinc, and iron. So people keep eating fresh tomatoes—average per capita consumption increased from twelve to twenty pounds over the past thirty years—although, according to surveys, people don't usually enjoy the experience. Tomatoes are a fresh vegetable that people hate but eat anyway.

In recent years, the rainbow colors and unruly shapes of the heirloom have arisen as a defiant response to the industrial tomato. There are "black" heirlooms (mottled olive-green, actually), which arose from a single mutation somewhere and are popular in Russia and Ukraine; heirlooms in shades of pink, orange, green, and pale yellow; "zebras" with different-colored stripes; heirlooms shaped like strawberries, beef hearts, plums, pears, and apples; and deeply ribbed or fasciated tomatoes with wrinkles like the muzzle of a bulldog. Farmers such as Doug Gosling, the master gardener of the Occidental Arts and Ecology Center in western Sonoma County, California, are passionate about heirlooms in part because they represent a way of life in which the farmer can maintain and cultivate his or her own varieties, instead of relying on seed companies. The opposition to hybrids has intensified among lefty back-to-the-land types because the seed industry is increasingly—though not entirely—concentrated in a few hands.

In a few instances involving corn and soy crops, food-and-chemical conglomerates like Monsanto have criminally prosecuted farmers for replanting expensive hybrid seed instead of buying it. In the first decade of the aughts, as Monsanto began buying up vegetable seed companies, including some of the leading tomato producers, heirlooms began making a comeback. The thousands of old tomato types out there, each of which you can grow in your own garden, are a dramatic embodiment of the biological cultures of yesteryear. Heirloom tomatoes are nostalgia come to blooming life. They've become a mainstay of foodie culture, a testament to authenticity, and a strike against monotonous, chemically dependent produce. I think that heirlooms, like all products of nostalgia, don't quite live up to their ideal, which is to say that they aren't quite what we wish they were. But no one can deny that they're awfully beautiful.

Gosling told me, "The pursuit of heirloom tomatoes is the biggest symbol there is of the growing appreciation of biodiversity." In fact, as diverse as heirlooms appear, they're the product of only a handful of mutations. Compared with the germplasm available in all the wild species, heirlooms contribute little to expanding the diversity of the tomato crop. There's far more genetic diversity in hybrid species that have made use of this wild germplasm. When heavy June rains sent late blight racing through the farms of the Northeast in 2009, many farmers lost as much as three-quarters of their heirloom tomato crop. Those who grew hybrid tomatoes—and especially, those who used fungicides—fared better. But let us not belittle the value of aesthetics.

In mid-September, I visited with Gosling on the verdant, rolling five-acre gardens where he and other members of an intentional community grow as many as three thousand varieties of every imaginable fruit or vegetable. Gosling doesn't grow for the market, but has trained dozens of organic gardeners and preserves seed as a member of the Iowa-based Seed Savers Exchange. The property, a few miles from the Pacific Coast, also includes seventy acres of redwoods and meadows in a temperate piece of California's northern coastal range, where the average yearly precipitation is a whopping sixty-four inches. Gosling, who at fifty-five was wearing a gold earring, a long beard, and half-moon glasses that made him look a bit like the French anarchist Pierre-Joseph Proudhon, has been farming this land for twenty-five years. He's also an inventive cook who's always got his senses working at ground level, searching for interesting new flavors. There were plenty of other foods growing in Gosling's garden—many varieties of basil, dozens of squash, a dozen different potatoes and their relatives, Iranian mulberries, and Central Asian apples—but like so many organic gardeners, Gosling's heart is in his tomatoes. Although the wet climate poses challenges, Gosling couldn't help planting what he called "162 of my favorite varieties" every year.

Gosling explained his approach as we sat in the north garden with Tussy, his normally shy, orange-and-white longhair mouser. Since we were ignoring Tussy, she was extremely ardent and bothersome until a cricket drew away her attention. Gosling grew up in Toledo, Ohio, where gardening was limited to helping his mother with her roses. At the University of Michigan, where he got a B.S. in botany, he discovered his passion. "I didn't want to stay in academia, because I had discovered how much I liked to grow food." In 1981, he came to California looking for an internship in organic gardening and got hooked up with the disciples of Alan Chadwick, an English gardener who brought biointensive gardening to the States. Chadwick used a combination of French methods and those of the Austrian mystic Rudolf Steiner, who believed that the health of the soil was paramount to good farming and good nutrition. In 1982, after the main gardener left for graduate school, Gosling found himself in charge of the gardens at Occidental.

He is a modest, inquisitive, friendly sort—still a midwesterner by temperament, perhaps, for all the distance he's traveled from Ohio. With the assistance of his partners and generations of interns, he created a beautiful, edible landscape traced by paths and heaps of healthy compost, where children can wander among a tangle of fabulously shaped and aromatic food plants, plucking and picking and popping unusual, healthy things in their mouths as they go. Frogs make vaguely embarrassing sounds in the pond, squash vines curl up and over everything, pale green tomatillos burst from their papery husks amid sheaths of chard, kale, and other greens that I don't recognize. I can't think of a more beautiful place to grow tomatoes.

"This is a difficult place for tomatoes," he cautioned me before we plunge into the patch. "It's cool at night. And there are fogs, and unseasonal rains. We get into all kinds of trouble, especially with fungi." Usually he sprays with Serenade, an "organic" fungicide that's composed of a strain of bacterium, *Bacillus subtilis*, that works by outcompeting other bacteria and fungi on the tomato leaf. But this year he had decided to try something new: sheet composting. He grew a cover crop of beans over the bed, cut the crop and then laid it on the bed, top-dressed with manure, and added straw. This was several months before planting. "When we pushed away the straw to plant, the soil was friable. We added oyster shell flour for calcium, wood ash for potassium, bone meal for phosphorus, and earthworm castings. They have everything compost has in it, but more bioavailable, concentrated. The worms transfer kitchen scraps into a fine manure. The idea was that all these ingredients would make the plants stronger, more resistant to wilts."

It seemed to have worked. Gosling waded into the thicket and began snatching fruit off the vines for my delectation. We tasted Japanese Black Trifeles that looked exactly like ripe Bartlett pears but burst with intense sweet flavors that were not at all pearlike, delicious dark Brazilian Beauties, and sweet Roses de Berne—small, seed-heavy tomatoes with orange shoulders and tiny golden spots. An acquaintance's father had brought seeds over from Poland, preserving them in a roll of toilet paper, and this tomato, which Gosling had named Andy's Polish, was a noble, smooth-skinned, deep pink monster shaped like a cow heart, its flesh creamy like watermelon (secret admission: I found it a bit insipid). We tasted marvelously sweet Green Grapes and pale Coyotes and beautiful crimson Marmandes.

Gosling is skeptical of hybrids because they've made farming more expensive and reliant on multinational corporations and led to the neglect of wonderful food crops. Yet he grows a few—the tangerine-colored Sun Gold is very popular, as is the Sweet 100. He does no breeding of his own, but is always on the lookout for genetic mutations, or "sports," in his plants. Once, a Red Montserrat plant produced pink tomatoes. Doug saved the seeds and now has his own Pink Montserrat. Another variety, which he called Farallones Orange Beefsteak, sprouted mysteriously from a compost heap.

Gosling has helped fire up the enthusiasm for heirloom tomatoes in the San Francisco Bay Area by holding two plant sales every year at which he sells thousands of tomato and other seedlings. "The variety of these tomatoes overwhelms people," he said. "Ninety-nine percent of those coming to the sales are home gardeners. Some are pretty serious students of diversity. One of the wonderful things about doing the sales is that over the past decade, the level of sophistication has risen noticeably. People come back and say, 'I have to have my Coyotes.'"

After I bit into a dozen or so varieties, I started to lose interest. As always happens to me when I'm invited into these garden havens, taste fatigue had set in. The tomatoes started to taste, well, like tomatoes. Here's a dirty little secret: In general—and there are lots of caveats and exceptions here—I don't especially like the flavor of a plain tomato. My fellow citizens, I believe I am not alone in this. Whether they be part of a salad, adornment to a hamburger, cooked and tarted-up with onions, garlic, and basil, or as minority, industrially processed partners in Heinz's emulsification of corn syrup, vinegar, spices, and paste, the tomato needs friends to win a continuous welcome to my palate. And I am not alone.

Gosling has noticed that however delicious his tomatoes are, few tasters can describe their flavor in a way that distinguishes one type from another. "We've had tastings here where we give people cards to write down descriptions. But people don't have the language to describe tomatoes. I'm not sure whether they lack the adjectives, or the sensitivity."

Not that it hasn't been tried. Perhaps no one has done more to broadcast the wonders of heirlooms than the food entrepreneur Gary Ibsen, who has held a festival since 1991 in Carmel, a hundred or so miles down the coast from Occidental. Ibsen has sought to do for the heirloom what an earlier generation of California vintners did for the wine industry. His festival, which had more than three thousand visitors the year I attended, is a mecca for sybarites of the central California coast. In a greensward by a golf course on the outskirts of Carmel, musicians play at a bandstand while chefs, restaurateurs, and caterers distribute samples of lush tomato-centric cuisine under tents. With precocious vineyards freely dispensing their wines, there's no better buzz for the $90 admission price. The cool field is full of gloriously good-looking, tipsy Californians.

Ibsen and his friends lay the tomatoes out under a big tent. On plastic plates they present the platonic ideal example of each idiosyncratic tomato, surrounded by chopped-up pieces for sampling. The Russian Limes are yellow, with nipples. The Wapsipinicon Peach is a tiny, leathery, persimmon-shaped yellow fruit with canal-like veins under the skin. The Speckled Roman is elongated, with streaks in different shades of orange. The Black from Tula is dark green-and-red with a mottled appearance. There are also black cherries, black princes, and black zerpas, each with skins of dark olive-green and muddy orange. A big, striated Dinnerplate looks like a nectarine. The Farbo is a yellow grape, while the German Red Strawberry is shaped like a giant strawberry. There are big hollow stuffers, and green tomatoes, sliced and dipped in corn batter.

I start out trying to taste each of the varieties, which are laid out in alphabetical order. That turns out to be a big mistake. I start noticing that the names don't necessarily tell me anything about the content of their character. Take Abe Lincoln—very mushy. In contrast, Amana Orange is juicy and sweet, almost like melon, and not at all like a household appliance. Andrew Rahart's Jumbo Red turns out to be watery, while Angora Super Sweets taste like cherries. Aunt Ginny's Purple is a bit bitter—was Aunt Ginny? In general, the blacks have a winey flavor. Black Plum, one of the most popular, tastes like it grew in its own marinade. Sweet Pea Currants are sour. The Early Girl, which hasn't been watered much, is also tangy (and isn't an heirloom). Named after one of Ibsen's Carmel neighbors, and the town's former mayor, Clint East-wood's Rowdy Red is very sweet, unlike its namesake. Says Ibsen, "Clint always drops by, usually unannounced."

Again, taste fatigue sets in early for me, but Ibsen says I have to think about the tomatoes as I would about wine (not good advice in my case, since I have only three wine descriptors: "really nice," "goes down, stays down," and "bluccch—vinegar!"). He tells me the yellow and orange tomatoes are less acid, and a good place to start. "The greens are sweeter, the blacker ones have more acids and complexities. They're my favorites—a good balance of acid and sweet. The blacks are cold-weather varieties. Similar to wine, more complex, with more of a varnish. They're the Bordeaux of tomatoes." For some reason that no one seems to understand, the pieces of DNA that cause the dark coloring seem to be linked to early ripening, which explains why the dark varieties became popular in the short growing seasons of northeastern Europe and Russia. Where and what was the original "black" sport that started this branch of the tomato family? No one knows.

Kids are clustered around the sample table, gobbling up tomatoes. The Speckled Peach is very popular in this demographic. "It tastes sooo good," enthuses Emma Morgan, a nine-year-old from Salinas. "Really fresh, tangy, and sweet." Her pal Hannah Grogin says the Red Peach is "very sweet too, but it's too sweet. Not enough tang." For Regina Greel of Sebastopol, "the peaches taste melon-y. Well, like peaches, fruity, but not like a tomato. The orange ones are like a combination of cantaloupe and peach." A Santa Cruz woman favors the peaches, too. "They cling. They stay with you. Speckled Peach is sweet like peach, tangy like tomato, but it's a pure tanginess."

William Foerster, chef of the fabulous Post Ranch Inn restaurant at Big Sur, has used Lemon Boys and Marvel Stripes to make a killer

Thai-spiced gazpacho; he's passing out ten gallons of the stuff in paper cup portions, along with six hundred crostini. But he says the varieties aren't so important. "It's really a question of choosing the tomatoes at the right time more than anything else. It's the soil, the right conditions, harvesting at the right time. In the winter, I don't even use tomatoes, though I'll use canned Romas as a stew base." The famed chefs of the Google cafeteria are serving a tricolor sorbet made of salmon and Green Zebra and Brandywine heirlooms, with candied onions on the side. Ya gotta love California.

Ibsen is a lean fellow with mischievous eyes. He wears a big straw hat and a carefully trimmed, pointy beard. He was a wine and food trader who ran restaurants like the Bayou Café in Carmel before he got into the heirloom business. "I started out as a backyard gardener like everybody else. I bumped into a retired Portuguese farmer. He said, 'I've got something for you.' He gave me six spindly heirloom plants. I figured, 'These are all going to die.' But within a year everything else was pushed out of the garden. I fell passionately in love with the different flavors of the tomatoes that I had never heard of before. Eventually I had ten plants of each variety. I called some chef friends and said, 'I've got flavors you've never tasted before.' I held a potluck, kids and all. We tasted their food and my heirlooms. That was the first Tomatofest: forty people in my backyard. This year we have three hundred and fifty varieties, three thousand one hundred visitors, and sixty vineyards. My restaurant friends weren't really into heirlooms at the time. Back then you'd see 'such and such with tomato sauce.' Now you see 'reduction of Black Prince.' It's just like the wine industry. The additional information takes the dining guest a little further in the enhancement of the meal."

Where are the seeds from? "Italians around the world send me varieties. English people in China. South Americans, seeds stuck to napkins from the Ozarks." A UC Davis agronomist provided him with lots of varieties from Charley Rick's collection twenty years ago. Sometimes they come in without names. "I met Julia Child and said, 'If I was a songwriter I'd write you a love song.' We had a tomato from Iowa that a family farmer had sent in—'Our favorite tomato,' he said. I named it after Julia." At the 2007 event, the favorite of a panel of chefs and winemakers was the Paul Robeson, a black Russian cultivar, named for the Russophilic opera singer.

Everyone in the tomato business seems to have been to Ibsen's event at least once. One year, I met Chris Rufer, whose gigantic tomato processing company, Morning Star, is the direct antithesis of heirloom gardening. "Tomatoes are really a small business, you know," he told me. "And I'm always curious about what different people are up to." The head of Campbell's Soup's food division was there, too. So were a lot of corporate executives and organic tomato farmers.

Larry Jacobs of Del Cabo Farms had been to the festival, and so had Kanti Rawal. I was surprised to hear their somewhat jaded view of it. "Heirlooms are like motherhood and apple pie," Kanti said. "You can't say anything bad about them. They're a status symbol. Of course, life is more fun when there's diversity, and I admire guys like Gary Ibsen who do these things."

"Some taste good," Jacobs said. "Others are just curiosities, and I don't understand why anyone would want to buy them. It's important to conserve seed diversity. The number of varieties at Tomatofest was amazing; it blew my mind. But I didn't find anything that I really liked." He had experimented with heirlooms—he grew Peaches, but they didn't do well. He grew Purple Cherokees at his own farm, in Pescadero, California, and they were delicious, but in the sandy soils of the southern Baja Peninsula, they turned out too soft; they could never have been

trucked to the United States. "There's a big difference between growing
in your backyard and growing as a business venture," he said. "Getting
the consistency is difficult, because you're dealing with the vagaries and
variability of nature."

So, it turned out that not everyone who cared about tomato flavor
believed in heirlooms. To get a sense of a hybrid flavor farm, I spent a
week in southern Baja visiting the Jacobses and their operation in April
2008. One afternoon, we drove out to Kanti's big test garden near the
village of Miraflores, under a striking cleft in the mountains known as
the Boca de la Sierra. Kanti pointed to some big, juicy-looking Zapotec Pinks—strikingly ridged heirlooms that are among the most popular varieties. He was experimenting with these and other heirlooms
to see if he could get the same shapes and colors into hybrids with
decent commercial characteristics, like disease resistance and reasonably firm skin and flesh that could tolerate the trip to the markets. It
wouldn't be easy. "Frankly, the taste of these is awful," he said. "They're
mainly a curiosity."

With the blessing of Larry Jacobs and Sandra Belin and their company, Kanti was using hybrid breeding techniques to bring new flavors
into his tomatoes. And he was far from the only tomato breeder who
had turned with interest to breeding varieties that were more flavorful.
Around the world, many seed companies—mostly Dutch and Israeli, but
also Monsanto, which had a big test garden in Woodland, California—
were increasingly producing seed that yielded durable, good-tasting
fruit, smashing the paradigm of the cardboard supermarket tomato.
Del Cabo was going a step further. It was striving to produce tomatoes that would remain tasty and intact all the way to the consumer
while sustaining the soils they grew upon—and the nobody Mexican

farmers who grew them. Kanti's quest was to bring these goals together—to hybridize them, in a sense.

Kanti explained it to me: "I found Larry and Sandra's point of view, their lifestyle, appealing—I respect their feeling about preserving the lives of their farmers so their kids don't have to wash dishes in the U.S. I like this principle of the Gandhian simplicity of existence: keeping your own needs small so that others will benefit from your knowledge." Larry and Sandra's pursuits were singular. When they lived in Guatemala, they would sometimes ride bicycles from their home near Quetzaltenango all the way to Lake Atitlan—a distance of maybe thirty miles—to go swimming. "Their idealism got me feeling, 'I want to find that what I'm doing isn't a waste of time, and contribute to something positive,'" Kanti said. "I realized, if I can get Fabiola and others and train them to be plant breeders, my experience and the materials I developed will be my legacy.'"

That day, we'd brought along Claudia, an intern in Kanti's breeding program. She was in her early twenties, pretty, petite, and just out of a Mexican agriculture school in La Paz, further north on the peninsula. It was easy to see that Kanti was blowing her mind, as he cornered her like a friendly ogre and began to ply her with knowledge. The first thing she had to do, he explained, was to learn English—she'd need it to read the literature and talk with other breeders. "Let's start. Say, 'Good morning!'" With Kanti, the teaching never stopped and everything was personal. If you let him, he'd take you into his extended family, which had branches in California and even in Tian, China, where his seeds were produced by a woman he called his goddaughter—Kanti had convinced her to leave a Dutch operation and start her own company.

Kanti and his assistant, Fabiola Rodríguez, had a competition going in which they'd taste a tomato in the field and guess its brix—the measure of soluble solids in a tomato's juice—a number that is often a good measure of flavor. When Fabiola got back to her office, she'd test it on a refractometer, a gadget that measured the suspended particles in a liquid. Usually she was closer to the correct number than he was. "Fabiola," Kanti would say, "you're a genius. Remember—it takes a genius to recognize a genius."

In the test plot—16 rows with 632 tomato lines and thousands of plants—Kanti wore a light blue polo shirt, sunglasses, and a black baseball cap with a red bill. We went down the rows, tasting as we walked. "Even when you are reluctant to eat tomatoes," he warned, "I'm going to feed you tomatoes, my friend."

He handed me a yellow pear—sweet, with a tangerine note. But there was something wrong with it that an heirloom grower would never think about, and Kanti wanted to show his new pupil. "Claudia, *ven.*" Though the tomato was tasty, it came to a point at the bottom, forming a sharp nipple. "Put that in a container, and a whole lot of tomatoes will get pocked. In transit, within thirty minutes, you develop a bruise, all the water in the tomato will collect, that tomato will spoil from fungus or bacteria within a day or two.

"OK, let's give Art a chance to taste something really bad." We encountered a plant with dead brown leaves, ravaged by *Alternaria solani*, a fungus also called early blight. Kanti forced me to take a bite from one of its yellow fruits. The flavor was interestingly awful—acrid, putrid, ruined. "The by-products of the fungal metabolism completely destroy the fruit." He turned to Claudia with a giggle. "See, now I'll test Claudia to see how obedient and subservient she is. Will she taste this and say, 'This is excellent?'" Fabiola translated. Claudia laughed nervously.

We moved on down the row. "When you walk through here, you can taste cantaloupe, honeydew, mango," Kanti said proudly. The brix of some of these tomatoes was probably 10 or 11. Your average supermarket tomato might be a 4. Kanti pulled something red off a vine—"Try to harvest this fruit like you were going to put it in a basket." The tomato wouldn't come off the stem. "We call that sticky stem . . . We know that the sticky gene is dominant, so if you're developing a commercial hybrid for cherries that will be packed singly, you don't go for the sticky stem." He swung a raceme of the tomatoes around his head. "But if you're selling them as tomatoes-on-vine, it may be useful, see? *¿Eh, Fabiola, tú tienes navaja?*"

Fabiola whipped out her pocketknife and we cut open a cherry that contained *t*—the tangerine gene. The color, inside and out, was egg-yolk-orange, which launched Kanti on an explanation of the lycopene pathway. All tomatoes contain a substance called phytoene, which is yellow. One enzyme converts the phytoene into lycopene, which is red. Another—present in this tangerine-gene tomato—converts the phytoene into orange-colored beta-carotene, a precursor to vitamin A. Kanti handed me a yellow cherry. This fruit didn't contain either enzyme; the fruit was full of phytoene, "and therefore, it has no so-called nutritional value," Kanti said.

So phytoene has no nutritional value? I asked. "We don't know of any yet," Kanti said. "Call me back in a couple of years, during the phytoene craze. When new scientific information comes out, people have a knee-jerk, Pavlovian response." Lycopene was the big one as of this writing. Beta-carotene, it's well-known, also had value as an antioxidant. "But if you're looking for vitamin A, you're better off with carrots or sweet potatoes," Kanti explained. "You'd have to eat two pounds of tangerine tomatoes to get what you get in a carrot or two."

The bulk of Kanti's varieties were small fruit, but he had some "beefsteak" types as well, and one of his lines had mysteriously developed a peculiar characteristic. While most tomatoes had two or four or six or eight locules—the cavities that hold the gel-covered seeds—this tomato had no visible locules at all. In fact, its locules were broken up and distributed throughout the fruit. He thought McDonnald's might like it because of its consistent internal structure and uniform sliceability.

Another cultivar, containing a gene called *puffy*, looked like a yellow bell pepper, and all the seeds were at the bottom of the fruit, too, just like a pepper. Tomatoes and peppers share most of the same genes and have DNA sequences that are about as identical as those of a chimp and a human. But at some point in their shared prehistory, an accident occurred during recombination and the genome got flipped around and inserted on different chromosomes. And then there were two different vegetables—tomatoes and peppers.

Over the past four decades, hundreds of plant breeders, food technologists, and biologists have tried to isolate the chemicals and other factors that make a tomato taste good. They've boiled it down to three essential components: sugars, acids, and the fleeting scents known as volatiles—as well as a fourth, elusive component, which is the balance of these three building blocks. When they talk about sugars, the flavor experts are referring mainly to glucose and fructose; some of the sucrose produced by photosynthesis converts into these two sweet-tasting sugars. The tomato is rich in citric, malic, and oxalic acids, and at least four hundred measurable tomato volatiles, of which perhaps twenty can contribute significantly to flavor. Most volatiles are evanescent molecules created by the enzymatic digestion of acids in the fruit during ripening, or even as the tomato is sliced open, or chewed. As their name suggests, volatiles lead a fleeting existence and are often sensed in the nose rather than the tongue. The hundreds of taste tests that have been conducted to try to correlate the balance of different volatiles with consumer judgment of "a good tomato" have yielded a tangle of data.

There are many other factors besides flavor that go into making or breaking a tomato's sex appeal—color, texture—in the mouth and in the hand. Our associations with tomatoes can also affect how well we like them. The pleasure of growing your own weird-shaped tomatoes can predispose your brain to form a welcoming appreciation of the sensations coming from your taste buds, whatever they happen to be. Cultural expectations can kill a tomato for us—or make it something grand.

But the role of biochemistry can't be underestimated. In a little booth at Tomatofest, I got a simple explanation from Teresa Beck-Bunn, a plant breeder for the seed company Seminis. Although her employer is a conglomeration of old seed companies and had itself recently been bought by Monsanto, Beck-Bunn was just as humble a practitioner of her trade as the other breeders I met along the tomato trail. "What is good flavor? Everyone has a different perception. You can do things to boost sugars and acids, but different people want a different balance. Volatiles are subtle. It's hard to get a taste panel and get people to agree on the same thing," she said. Then there was the issue of how sight affects the perception of flavor. "Blindfolded an orange tomato may be good, but a lot of people won't buy an orange tomato."

One thing could be said of heirlooms that distinguished them, as a class, from hybrids. The lower yield of the heirloom plant, in general, meant it would produce a tomato with more flavor. "Think of a tomato as a factory," Beck-Bunn said. "Sugar, acid, volatiles have to be made in the plant. Heirlooms produce fewer fruit with more factory. That gives more perception of better and more intense flavors. On the commercial side, farmers are paid for yield. They want as many fruit as they can get. A lot of times it's perceived that heirlooms are better-tasting, but it could be that they just pack more (as opposed to better) flavor into them than a typical tomato. Just because it's an heirloom doesn't mean it's a good tomato. You breed for different things. In the past, roses were more fragrant. Hybrid tea roses were bred for the number of buds but not the aroma. Now breeders are going back to the old ones to get the aroma back. It's the same with tomatoes. The industry has to decide they're going to pay for flavor. Right now, flavor is not the priority."

While flavor has not been a priority for the tomato industry in general, industry, academia, and even the federal government have their share of flavor fanatics. In an industrial-looking building off Interstate 80 in Albany, California (Berkeley's northern neighbor), an Australian-born chemist by the name of Ron Buttery had been exploring the imponderables of tomato flavor for half a century at the USDA Agricultural Research Service's regional center. After completing postgraduate studies at Yale and working at a couple of Canadian universities, Buttery came to Albany in 1958, and since then had been using gas chromatography, human noses, and other tools to analyze the chemical components of food aromas. In some cases, he figured out how to duplicate them artificially. Though retired long before, Buttery was one of those graying emeriti who still haunted their old workplaces, when I turned up at his cubbyhole on the Albany campus in 2008. But the USDA wasn't funding much flavor chemistry work anymore, he told me—all the focus was on food safety, terrorism, and nutrition. "They don't like us flavor people anymore," he said.

In his time, though, Buttery had re-created a number of odors, including one for cooked tomato flavor. That flavoring, which Buttery and his colleagues patented in 1991, consists mainly of four chemicals: dimethyl sulfide, beta-damascenone, 3-methylbutanal, and 3-methylbutyric acid. Later, some more sophisticated testing also turned up furaneol, an extremely fleeting odor that is usually associated with sweet strawberries. One drop of Buttery's soup, whose ingredients can all be procured from chemical supply houses, is enough to flavor five gallons of tomato sauce. Stand downwind of a cannery in season, and you'll experience the contents of Patent #5064673, "Cooked tomato flavor composition." In isolation, the ingredients are singularly unappealing: To be sure, beta-damascenone is a sweet contributor to rose scent, but dimethyl sulfide is a flammable liquid whose odor, in a brewery, indicates bacterial contamination. The taste panels that Buttery ran out of a corner of his laboratory described 3-methylbutanal as "sweet, malty," when they got it in small doses. In larger amounts, it was an unpleasant skin irritant. The odor of 3-methylbutyric acid is generally described as "sweaty." The individual chemical notes of the tomato could be sweet or dissonant. The symphony of tomato flavor came through only when they were played together.

The compounds in Buttery's patent were all things found in nature, so you could call them "natural flavors" on a label, even if the compounds in that particular jar of tomato sauce had been created in a factory. A large tomato company showed interest—Buttery won't say if it was Heinz—but the deal fizzled over licensing disagreements. He was fuzzy over whether his compound was currently being used in any product. But if you see "natural flavorings" on your next jar of tomato sauce, you'll have an idea of what it is.

In the 1960s, Campbell's Soup was trying to figure out which components of its best-tasting tomato accounted for its flavor. It awarded a doctoral fellowship to M. Allen Stevens, a bright, young agronomist who was working with the Oregon state extension service, to study flavor chemistry and genetics at Oregon State University. In 1967 it hired him to analyze the tomato at the company's Camden, New Jersey, laboratories. "Campbell's had a gold standard tomato, the Campbell 146," Stevens said. "It had big old soft fruit, and few resistances. I was hired to figure out what gave Campbell 146 its flavor, with the idea that you could transfer those genes to a heartier tomato." The main compound responsible for the excellent flavor of the 146, Stevens found, was 2-isobutylthiazole. "To this day, I can tell the tomatoes that have the higher levels of that compound," he said. "It's a green note. Not a viney green, but a unique note that a lot of people find very desirable in a tomato. Most of that is olfactory. It's very difficult to describe." As far as Stevens knows, nothing came of his work. Tomato breeders were so busy breeding for yield and disease resistance that they never focused on a characteristic as fine-grained as the level of 2-isobutylthiazole.

While it went hunting for the secrets of its successful soup, Campbell had already figured out a way to enhance its flavor. One of the big secrets of the tomato business, very hush-hush until recently, was an evaporative process Campbell developed in the 1960s. The process captured the volatile compounds from the tomatoes as they were cooked. The company then returned these flavors—at least the ones that hadn't been destroyed in the cooking process—to the paste it used for its soup.

Later, Morning Star used a similar machine, but it was said not to work as well for preparing "hot-break" paste—the high-temperature process used to make the paste that goes into ketchup, spaghetti sauce, and pizza sauce, the majority of Morning Star's business. Tomato juices and soups are typically prepared using a lower-temperature "cold-break" process. The "break" refers to the deactivation of enzymes that break down pectin in the tomato. If you "break" at a higher temperature, you deactivate the enzymes more quickly, more pectin remains in the paste, and it is thicker. Cold-break pastes are runnier, which makes them inappropriate for ketchup or pizza sauce—they're also brighter in color and maintain more flavor. Americans prefer chunkier, hot-break spaghetti sauces—Europeans like simple, bright red cold-break sauces.

Campbell sent one hundred gallons of its essence to Buttery and asked him to figure out what was in it. In his view, Campbell's essence machine was only partially successful, because there was no way to replace the most important ingredient in tomatoes that's lost when you cook them: *cis*-3-hexenal. "We've made this substance synthetically, but it was never practical. When you heat it, it changes to *trans*-2-hexenal, which has a much weaker odor." You couldn't add it to a finished sauce, either, Buttery said, because you'd still have to sterilize the bottle at 120 degrees, enough to change it. In the end, Campbell figured it didn't really want fresh-tomato flavor, anyway. Cooked tomato flavor is different—some of the chemicals that characterize it actually *form* during cooking—and this flavor has its own associations. Tomato soup with saltines when you're home sick from school; the marinara sauce at the red-checked-tablecloth Italian joint in your hometown; red pizza in all its variety. Canned tomato flavor is entirely different from fresh-tomato flavor.

Work on tomato flavor is challenging because the tomatoes are in a state of metabolic change as they ripen, with different flavor balances from day to day or even hour to hour. "Fresh flavors are just too unstable," said Buttery. Many tomato volatile compounds aren't even formed until you chew the tomato. Enzymes in your mouth degrade the carotenoids, the source of tomatoey flavors such as the "fruity" note of beta-ionone. The same goes for *cis*-3-hexenal. "You don't get *cis*-3-hexenal to the fullest extent," said Buttery, "until you chew up the tomato, or cut it up." One group of scientists fed tomatoes to a subject with a tube stuck up his nose to extract volatiles from his mouth, then pumped the vapors into a mass spectrometer. They found that cherry tomatoes released higher amounts of *cis*-3-hexenal than do larger tomatoes. But these ingredients varied from tomato to tomato—even in fruit gathered from the same plant in the same plot.

There's ten times more *cis*-3-hexenal in the vine than there is in the tomato. Eugenol, a component that contributes to the odor of cloves, bay leaf, and cinnamon, is also a big component of the vine and, to a lesser extent, the fruit. Both chemicals are commonly found in the vines and leaves of edible plants, but tomato fruit contains more *cis*-3-hexenal than does any other food crop. Before I left his laboratory, Buttery pulled two small bottles out of the refrigerator and opened them for me. The first was pure *cis*-3-hexenal, and it was overpowering and uninteresting, a chemical smell like any other. The other was diluted at 1:10,000. I took a deep sniff, and that was what I was after: "Green," or "cut grass," was how the flavor books described it. For me it was the smell of the tomato vine. The smell of summer.

CHAPTER THREE

No Hands
Touch the Land

We need our economic pragmatists—they feed us well. But we
also need our social critics—they keep the dream alive.

—O. E. Thompson and Ann Scheuring,
From Lug Boxes to Electronics

 ONE AFTERNOON IN 1959, A GROUP OF PROFESSORS AND
agricultural extension agents from the University of Cali-
fornia, Davis, stood around a funny-looking machine in a
tomato field near the town of Clarksburg while their clients—
farmers, seedsmen, cannery executives—milled around in the hot
sun, joking and spitting tobacco juice. The existing accounts of that
day don't indicate whether there was a Mexican field hand somewhere
on the edge of the picture, a worker with his own thoughts about what
was about to transpire. The center of attention was a hulking olericulturalist (food-crop breeder) with a big, farmer's face, C. Gordon
Hanna—Jack to everyone who knew him, which was everyone in the
California tomato business. Hanna was a professor on the faculty of

the Department of Vegetable Crops, but he didn't spend much time in his office. UC Davis was an Agriculture, or Ag, school—even the sports team was the Aggies—and Hanna was there to help the farmers and the food processors. Period.

He had been preparing for this moment for many years—though he didn't expect to have such an audience. Hanna and his colleague, Coby Lorenzen of the Department of Agricultural Engineering, had been working together for a decade on two intimately related projects: the first mechanical tomato harvester, and the first tomato that could be mechanically harvested.

The lopsided prototype of the machine stood behind them, a funky conglomeration of hand-shaped and hand-soldered metal pieces, canvas, and wooden parts. It had a long blade that ran parallel to the ground and was designed to lop off the tomato plants just below the surface of the dry California soil as the machine rolled forward. A belt with metal spikes would carry the tomato plants up to a vibrating platform designed to separate the fruit from the vine by shaking. Several grad students and postgraduate research fellows, pressed into service as field workers for the afternoon, stood on either side of the machine on raised platforms, waiting to sort out the green tomatoes, dirt clods, and ruined tomatoes from the good ones as the tomatoes passed by on their way to the end of the conveyer, where they would flow into big crates. If all went according to plan.

Since 1942, Hanna had been trying to breed the perfect tomato for machine handling. He wanted a tomato plant that fruited all at once, and fruit that wouldn't fall off the vine when the machine cut it, but that could be shaken off a few minutes later without getting damaged. He wanted tough-skinned tomatoes that could withstand a long trip to the cannery packed in a truck bed with thousands of other tomatoes.

A third UC Davis professor stood off to the side, a little detached from the others, quietly watching the birth of this new machine. That was Charley Rick, who also had a role in the experiment. The *j-2*, or jointless gene, contained in the tomatoes came from *L. cheesmanii*, the winsome, furry little tomato plant with tiny orange fruit that Rick had collected on the Galápagos Islands some summers before. With the jointless tomato, all other things being equal, the tomato would come cleanly off the stem at the right time. God and Darwin both were looking after Jack Hanna's obsessions.

"Fire it up, Coby!" Hanna shouted. The machine began shuddering down a row of ripe tomatoes, cutting the stems just below the surface of the brown earth, then lifting them on the conveyer and neatly depositing them in the crates. That was the idea, anyway.

"Hey Coby, I think your machine's gone haywire!" someone shouted. As the farmers doubled over with laughter and Hanna watched with dismay, the machine sputtered, stopped, started again, and then came to a tremulous halt. It had torn a deep trench in the earth and deposited a slick mess of broken tomatoes and dirt on the conveyer belt. After some tinkering, Lorenzen had it started again. But as the conveyer belt coughed the tomatoes into the crates on the back of a tractor running next to the machine, what came through looked more like sauce, the tomatoes smashed and bruised and dirty—"nothing but cores and juice by the time they got to the cannery," an onlooker would recall.

Many of those same farmers wouldn't be laughing a few years later—especially those with smaller farms, who couldn't afford $25,000 for a new tomato harvester. Within five years, the harvester would represent an abrupt new direction in their lives and that of the industry. Within a decade, the harvester would pick nearly every processing tomato harvested in California, and the number of tomato farmers would fall from roughly three thousand to six hundred.

In the 1950s, most Americans innocently enjoyed the abundance of fresh, canned, and frozen fruits and vegetables they were newly able to buy in variety at supermarkets. Since the late nineteenth century, the tomato had been a growing part of the American diet. By 1890, railroads were shipping green Florida and Mississippi tomatoes to northern markets. One 1892 guide to commercial tomato growing sold ten thousand copies in its first few years in print and was reissued in 1906. By 1910, there were hundreds of greenhouses devoted to providing winter and cool-weather tomatoes, and the value of the U.S. crop was nearly $14 million. Few questioned technological progress in the food processing industry or in agriculture itself; such advances fed the bounty of an American food supply that was "unsurpassed in volume, variety and nutritional value," as the U.S. Food and Drug Administration (FDA) said in a 1959 pamphlet. Hanna, Lorenzen, Rick, and their colleagues fiddled with their machines and plants in pleasant obscurity. Davis, with its cows and cornfields, wasn't exactly an ivory tower, but these men would have been happy in an ivory stable as long as no one cared what they did inside it.

They had no concept of the scale of demonization they would face within a decade or so. They would be vilified by social critics and impassioned foodways aesthetes, cursed by young back-to-the-land farmers, sued by farmworkers, and held out as examples of everything that had gone wrong with the American way of eating and farming—the homogenization of food, favoring quantity over quality, the replacement of a way of life with a machine. And as the tomato fields grew ever more mechanized, computerized, and controlled, the unorthodox, wrinkled, fragile heirloom would symbolize the food snob's florid repudiation of Hanna and his dreams.

Within a few decades, many Americans would become remarkably demanding about what they considered a good tomato. They'd want the tomato farmer to employ a lot of workers, providing them with good wages, health insurance, and decent living conditions. They'd want tomato farms that didn't damage watersheds, wetlands, or the ozone layer. The tomato, for starters, should be highly nutritious, organic, and tasty; have a minimal carbon footprint; and reduce our dependence on Middle Eastern oil. Its cultivation should feed the soil, make farmers prosper locally or in developing countries, and be free of germs and chemical residue. And they'd want it cheap, and they'd want it now—whether it was July or January.

The mechanical harvester—and in particular, the electronic sorter that was mounted on it a few years later—tipped the scales in the nation's ambivalence over the industrial intrusion into its food supply. The interface of machines and tomatoes, somehow, bothered neo-Luddites and the milieu that fully or partly shared their views to an extent that centuries of agricultural progress had never done. People got used to the plow and the tractor, the cotton gin and the wheat harvester, quickly enough. It was OK to till the dirt with a machine. But picking tomatoes with it was somehow beyond the pale.

Jack Hanna was working on processing tomatoes—and this is a distinction worth drawing out a bit. The tomato world has a dividing line of which the average mortal is unaware. Among farmers, table tomatoes—the kind you buy in their original, uncooked form—are an entirely different crop from the processing tomato—the type that gets cooked after picking and goes into commercial sauces, pastes, salsas, juices, and everything else you might buy in a can or jar. From breeding to cultivation and harvest, these are entirely different industries, although there is some cross-fertilization from time to time. They may look and smell and even taste similar, but they aren't grown or processed the same way.

Around the same time that Hanna was doing his experimentation, Florida farmers were revolutionizing the table tomato as well. They were starting to use ethylene gas to ripen tomatoes that had been picked green and that were destined to be sold in the produce section. When they were picked ripe, the tomatoes were rotten by the time they got to faraway markets. Green-harvested fruit, at the other extreme, often would not turn red at all unless exposed to ethylene. Though they were two entirely different things, the green-gassed tomato and Hanna's mechanical harvester fused into a single cultural enemy. The crunchy left confounded them and condemned them, equally and bitterly. "Better they should have canned him," *Boston Globe* columnist Ellen Goodman wrote of Hanna in 1975, "for producing those red, tasteless tennis balls mass-produced and marketed in nearly every supermarket produce department in the country." She would add in a later column, "We all know how the innocent *Lycopersicon esculentum* has had its hide toughened, how it has been pushed around, squared, even gassed to death. Every year the tomato becomes less of a fruit and more of a metaphor for our dissatisfaction with limits."

Though Goodman and many like her got their facts wrong, the harvester undoubtedly touched a deep nerve, even if there were advantages and disadvantages—for the workers as well as the bosses—to mechanization. "The mechanization issue," wrote historians O. E. Thompson and Ann Scheuring in a 1980 study, "may be viewed as a metaphor for at least two very central human concerns: man's relationship with the earth itself, and the distribution of economic and social power among human beings. Far from being only an economic issue, the controversy has philosophical overtones dealing with human values. The currents in present-day criticism of mechanization may be compounded of nostalgia for bygone days, when life was supposed to have been simpler, slower, more satisfying (was it ever, really?)—some private resentment against 'rich farmers,' uncertainty in a fast-moving society, which leads to a grasping for simple answers—and a need for a visible adversary, the machine, in a world that seems somehow intangibly threatening."

The harvester didn't have nearly as much to do with the aesthetics of the tomato as people thought, though. The harvester was for canned tomatoes. It picked them ripe and it picked them fast, which meant they were cooked and packaged for eating a lot more expeditiously than in the days when they were picked by hand. In other words, they were fresher. If the machine-picked tomatoes weren't particularly tasty, they weren't "cardboard," either. Some pretty straightforward economics went into the decision to use the machine. Still, a lot of the impulse behind it came solely from Hanna, who clung to his vision of a harvestable tomato despite the ridicule of his peers and the downright disapproval of his bosses in academia. The same mystique that made the tomato sacred to many people got deeply under the skin of Hanna, who was all about progress and efficiency. "We took a lot of the backyard garden philosophy with us out in the field," he said in 1975. "We never considered the vegetable industry as a field venture like the grains, which became mechanized rather early. It's rather difficult to get rid of these traditional concepts of growing and handling fruits and vegetables. That's been really the great drawback to the whole mechanization program."

To realize how ridiculous the idea of a mechanically harvested tomato seemed in 1947, it's enough to run a search in a newspaper index using

the word "tomato" for the first seven decades of the twentieth century. Do this, and you'll find that a large number of these articles are
about people throwing tomatoes at politicians and others they disliked.
Whether you were the Beatles or Nixon or Henry Wallace, getting
tomatoed was a sure sign you were touching a nerve. The 1940s tomato
was a soft, mushy fruit that looked great, from the tomato thrower's
perspective, on a freshly pressed suit. It worked much in the same way
as an attack ad: Supply your loyal rabble with a box of ripe tomatoes,
and they'd create a smear that even dry cleaners couldn't remove.

By the end of the twentieth century, by contrast, there's a dearth
of tomato-throwing episodes in the news. Perhaps the political dis-
course has grown more refined after all. More to the point, though,
tomatoes have gotten a lot harder. If you examine a typical heirloom tomato in cross-section, you find large cavities filled with jelly-
covered seeds and liquid that contains sugar and acids and aromatic
compounds. These cavities are called locules—the flesh surrounding them, meanwhile, is the pericarp. Most of the flavors that make
a tomato a tomato are located in the locule. Brix—the percentage of
soluble sugars, based on a refractometer's reading of the cloudiness of
the liquid in the tomato—tends to be higher in larger-loculed tomatoes. Brix is a shorthand measure of flavor, though high-brix tomatoes are not always better. Brix is also higher in the older tomatoes
because they have a higher leaf-to-fruit ratio. Cherries, pears, and
other small tomato types also have higher brix, because they have a
higher locule-to-pericarp ratio. This has First Amendment implications as well. There's a lot more of the hard, fleshy parts in a modern
tomato, a lot less of the gooey stuff in between. Throw a tomato at
a politician these days, and you could be doing serious felony time.
In modern campaigning, if you want to despoil a Neiman Marcus

dress or a Brooks Brothers suit, it's more tactical to use rotten eggs or cream pies. Or YouTube.

When Hanna started his work, no one but he and his closest friends could imagine that the soft, juicy tomato would ever be something you could run through an assembly line with the sincere conviction that it would emerge intact. The whole project seemed ludicrous until it became a necessity.

"We were kind of the laughing stock around here when we mentioned that we were going to work on harvesting tomatoes," Roy Bainer, the dean of engineering at UC Davis, recalled of Lorenzen's activities in a 1975 interview. "It was very evident that if you were going to do this job, you were going to have to have a different tomato." Lorenzen and Hanna were deeply skeptical of each other. Each of them "did his utmost because he felt the other was crazy and, unless his part was perfectly executed, the whole experiment would founder. Hanna thought Lorenzen's machine was ridiculous and Lorenzen thought Hanna was crazy."

Born in Quannah, Texas, in 1903, Hanna had spent a single year studying at the University of California at Berkeley, washing dishes to pay his expenses, and then moved to Davis, where he got an undergraduate degree in science in 1928. He started doctoral studies in genetics but moved to Ryer in 1929, and never received the Ph.D. Hanna's adventures in tomato technology began in 1942, when a farmer known as Fum Jongeneel told him that he didn't have anybody to pick his tomatoes, and challenged him to create a mechanical harvester. At the time, Hanna and his wife were living on Ryer Island, in the delta formed by the San Joaquin and Sacramento rivers. Hanna was working unsuccessfully on an agricultural extension effort to mechanically harvest asparagus.

California had depended on waves of immigrants to harvest the tomato and other crops. The Mexicans were only the latest in a series that started in the 1850s with the Chinese, who were replaced by Japanese, Filipinos, Turks, Arabs, and Indians (Indians from India, and later from Arizona, and even later from Oaxaca). The low wages paid to these immigrants kept the produce cheap and ensured a large market for it. But "it looked to me like we were running out of nations to import to do our work," Hanna said in an oral history published by Avrom Dickman in 1975. "I felt we had to somehow or other start in and develop a tomato that could be harvested mechanically." Although in the 1950s there were Mexican immigrants around, they weren't always available to harvest the tomatoes, though farmers were being offered good prices.

Sometimes, farmers imported Navajos from Arizona or rounded up crews of hobos from the railyards in Stockton or Hayward, or poor whites or former sharecroppers from the deep South. But the farmers found these workers to be an unreliable labor force. The tramp workers were put up in tents with straw pallets. "The men would all get drunk on Saturday night. I'd take the bad ones in and throw them in the pokey and go bail them out Monday morning again," said one farmer. College students wouldn't pick tomatoes—at least not enough of them. Housewives took up some of the slack during World War II. But soon they were replaced or supplemented by Mexicans, who came over in what would be called the Bracero program. Launched to deal with emergency labor shortages during wartime, the program (which came from the Spanish word for arm, *brazo*) brought sixty-two thousand Mexicans to work in U.S. fields in 1944. The original law expired after two years, but was repeatedly extended.

Hanna started out by looking for a tough tomato. He did this by dropping different varieties of tomatoes. "I had one tomato . . . I found I could drop it from a height of about three feet out in the field on the ground without it breaking. I could drop it once, but the second time it usually broke. And it always broke on the third time. As far as firmness was concerned, this was quite superior to anything else that we had at the time." The next step was to find a tomato that fruited all at once. Hanna set about finding such a tomato by using selection—the time-tested tool of the olericulturalist. Selection meant getting some seed from a tomato, planting a couple hundred plants, and picking the one that seemed to have the most desirable set of traits. Then you took a few fruit from that plant and planted their seeds, and selected the best plants from that generation, and chose their best offspring, and so on down the line. In any generation of tomatoes, there is genetic diversity; the more you select, the more likely you are to isolate the so-called segregating trait you're looking for and produce it consistently in your tomatoes. Despite repeated selections, the firm tomato Hanna found didn't contain the genetic components of "concentrated set"—the term breeders use for a plant whose tomatoes all ripen at or near the same time. "By the end of 1947, after I'd really been looking at this for some five years, I hadn't arrived anywhere at all with it," Hanna said. In one early experiment, Hanna bred a short-vined plant and kept boosting the soil with nitrogen to improve the yields. But he ended up getting all fruit and no factory. Finally, the last leaf fell off, leaving the fruit sunburned and moldy.

Despite lacking formal approval for his project—Hanna never paid much attention to his department chair, anyway—that year he got a six-week leave, which he used to visit with people growing or preserving a range of different tomato types. After talking with at least two dozen breeders around the United States, Hanna found what he was looking for in Geneva, New York, where the USDA kept an enormous seed bank. The cultivar he settled upon was called Red Top, a cross between the Gem and San Marzano varieties that the Meckler Seed Company

of Metamora, Ohio, had provided to the USDA. When he first saw the
Red Top, Hanna thought the plants looked like "little pine trees with
two or three tomatoes on each of them." It grew on poor soil, producing
a few tomatoes that fruited all at once.

Red Top was susceptible to verticillium, a fungus that thrives in
California, where it is carried from field to field in irrigated water.
Hanna found a Red Top selection that was resistant to verticillium. He
crossed the resistant plant with the main Red Top line and called the
cross Red Top-9. When he got back from Geneva, Hanna approached
Coby Lorenzen for the first time. With the approval of his department
and the sympathy of a handful of farmers, Lorenzen got to work. After
fooling around with a potato digger, which managed to harvest 80 percent of the Red Tops but deposited them in a sodden, muddy mess in
the harvester, the two sat down together and drew out the specifications for the tomato.

"Coby gave me a concept I never would have gotten from any
horticulturalist or geneticist," Hanna recalled. "A tomato wasn't necessarily a tomato with him. It was merely an object that had certain physi-
cal properties." Said Lorenzen, "We decided there were certain things
the machine would have to do, and certain things the plant would have
to do." Lorenzen would become frustrated as he learned, as Hanna put
it, that "it takes a long time to develop something new in a plant." Even
after you got a decent variety to work with, it tended to mutate and
change, "whereas a machine you can walk away and leave for months
and come back and find it exactly as you left it."

Lorenzen concurred. "I really had an education in all the physiolog-
ical factors that are involved in a product like a tomato," he said. "When
you mess around with one and get something you want, you get something else you don't want—maybe the color might be good, but doesn't

taste any good, or the solids aren't any good, or you can't get it off the vine with a ten-ton truck."

For a while they worked on a device that had fingers mounted on chains that cradled the vine and lifted it upward and backward. It picked the vine and the fruit, but there was no way to get the vine off the back of the machine. "Over the years from 1950 to 1958, we must have investigated thirty or forty different systems or combinations of systems," Lorenzen said. Eventually they settled on the model that would set the standard for years to come: a single blade that cut the plant about an inch and a half below the ground. It made the cut underground because the stem became woody and tough as it matured, while the part below the ground had enough moisture in it, and was held firmly in place by the soil, so that a blade could cut through the stem without jarring the plant so hard that it knocked off the tomatoes.

Red Top was an elongated tomato, like its San Marzano parent, and Hanna was enthusiastic about its shape because it seemed to handle much better than a round tomato. The tomato engineers took a high-speed movie of the Red Top coming off the belt and found that, with the vibration of the machine, the fruits oriented themselves at right angles to the direction the belt was moving and landed on their sides, which gave them a greater area of contact to absorb the shock. Hanna found he could drop a long tomato onto his desk two-and-a-half times more than a round one before it broke.

By October 1959, Hanna and Lorenzen were ready to try out their system. They planted the tomatoes on land owned by a farmer named Les Heringer. When the day for the trial arrived, "we told Heringer we'd bring the machine down but we didn't want an audience," Bainer recalled. "This was just a prototype; if it failed we didn't want a lot of witnesses." But when they got down to the field, there was a crowd waiting. The farmers, in particular, got a kick out of watching the machine. At the time, they didn't see the Bracero program ending. The economy was going strong, Americans were hungry for canned tomatoes, and the harvester was a big joke. "Some of the early contraptions they tried out," Charley Rick noted mildly, "were highly amusing, to say the least." One witness said the machine "will never work because you can't find that many PhDs to sort tomatoes on a machine." But there were a few farmers who showed interest, and some canners as well.

One of them was Flotill Foods, which was run by a brash New Yorker named Tillie Lewis, one of the most extraordinary American businesswomen of her time. Lewis was a charismatic redhead from Brooklyn— "a petite, Titian-haired woman with a razor-sharp brain and the courage and determination to put it to work," according to an *American Mercury* magazine profile. Born Myrtle Ehrlich in 1901, she married a wholesale grocer at age fifteen and became preternaturally obsessed with the San Marzano tomato or *pomodoro*, as the Italian imports were known at the time. Lewis thought San Marzanos had more tang, and she was always puzzled by the fact that American farmers didn't produce them. Her husband said they couldn't be grown in America. She didn't believe him and didn't appreciate his telling her to shut up already about it; they were divorced after five years. The story goes that the summer after leaving her husband, Lewis was on a vacation cruise to Italy when she met Florindo del Gazio, one of the biggest Neapolitan tomato canners, who exported seven hundred thousand crates of San Marzanos a year to the United States. Or maybe the trip over was an assignation to begin with, since Lewis eventually became del Gazio's *innamorata*. Whatever the case, when Congress slapped a 50 percent tariff on imported Italian tomatoes in 1934, Lewis was ready with a serious proposition for del Gazio. With money fronted by him and his brother, she created Flotill

Products, combining their first names. Lewis started canning tomatoes in Stockton in 1935 after winning over farmers who didn't want to grow her freaky San Marzanos. Two years later, Florindo died and Lewis took over the business. Within a decade she had the country's fifth-biggest canning business. In some postwar years, it was also the largest supplier of army C-rations, which were assembled at another Stockton plant. Flotill Products helped transform the San Joaquin Valley into the center of tomato production in the United States.

In 1939, when the American Federation of Labor threatened to strike her canneries, she invited Meyer L. Lewis, the union's western director, to examine the plant and its working conditions. He was apparently impressed—the union decided not to strike Flotill. The next year, she hired him as her plant manager, and they were married in 1948. In the early 1950s, nearly half the tomato fields of Southern California produced San Marzanos. And Italian delegations were visiting Tillie Lewis to get tips on improving their canning businesses.

Tillie Lewis had shown a lot of interest in Hanna's harvester. During the harvester trial in Clarksburg, bins of the mechanically picked tomatoes were trucked to Flotill's Stockton factory, where workers the next day raised one of the bins on a hoist, tilting it to make the tomatoes roll out. "But they didn't roll out," recalled Bob Hartzell, Flotill's chief of operations. "The fruit flies flew out in droves. The tomatoes came out as a huge glob—all at one time, about a thousand pounds of tomatoes. It was a horrible-looking mess and I remember Mrs. Lewis was quite disappointed. But it was a first." By tinkering with the machine, Heringer eventually was able to harvest 1,200 tons of muddy Red Tops. He ran the machine all day and spent the night adjusting it.

Red Top-9 was a provisional cultivar. It didn't yield well, and despite Lewis's enthusiasm, few canneries wanted a pear-shaped fruit. While the Red Top's spin off the conveyer was good for absorbing shocks, it required the worker to twist his or her hand to grasp the fruit. More importantly, the canneries had by this time switched back to the round tomato. "This is where people come in," Hanna said. "A tomato is supposed to be round. Why? Because it's always been round."

Hanna was working on a new tomato even as the Red Top was field-tested. In this breeding program, he used the Santa Clara, a large, wide, irregularly shaped canner tomato in use in California since the 1900s, and the Pearson, a 1936 cultivar named for Hanna's predecessor at UC Davis, Oscar Pearson, who had developed it using the Santa Clara, the Fargo, and a line of *Lycopersicon pimpinellifolium,* the currant tomato. The Fargo possessed *sp,* the critical gene for mechanical harvest. As noted earlier, *sp* resulted in a tomato vine that stopped growing after it flowered, producing a compact, bushy plant whose tomatoes tended to fruit simultaneously.

To be a good breeder, you need to know a smattering of genetics, but most breeders describe the process in decidedly unlettered terms. "We get as many varieties of tomatoes as we can, look them over, figure out what's in the varieties and how you can improve them," said Jim Dick, a tomato breeder in Ontario. "Say I want to make them a little firmer and bigger. You select those characteristics out in field tests. Sometimes you can see it. Other times you weigh them, do chemical tests. My best tool is this"—he pulls out a jackknife—"I see how thick the walls are, the firmness, the colors. I squeeze them. I use my taste buds. Generally you're looking for sweetness with some acidity. I can't identify a particular chemical variation in the tomatoes. I just say, 'It's got a more tomatoey flavor to it.'"

"It depends on the eye and the skill of the breeder," said M. Allen Stevens. "We used to say that we'd never known a successful breeder that did it on a computer. You had to get out into the field. Most of the breeders I've known who've been successful are artists. Looking at something and recognizing that it has potential. You're looking at huge populations and selecting the few that are going to be successful."

Hanna and Lorenzen were not the only agronomists who were working on mechanization—there were groups at Purdue and Michigan State designing harvesters around the same time, and several private companies later developed models. And of course, Hanna was not the first person to breed tomatoes—but his was the most ambitious undertaking up to then. As of 1930, 90 percent of the tomatoes grown in the United States were one of nine cultivars: Earliana, Bonny Best, Gulf State Market, Globe, Marglobe, Early Detroit, Greater Baltimore, Stone, and Santa Clara. The Gulf State Market was the most important tomato in Florida. The Marglobe, a cross of the Marvel and the Globe, two Livingston tomatoes, was exceedingly popular in the United States and the leading Mexican export tomato.

The first California tomato cannery had opened in 1859, when Francis Cutting set up a shop in San Francisco using Mason jars. A few years later, tin cans replaced the jar; workers packed the tomatoes into holes in the lids, then sealed the lids with hand-soldered tin plate and sterilized the cans in boiling water. Through the 1930s, the popular cultivars were the Trophy, developed by a farmer in Sing Sing, New York, in the 1840s; and the Santa Clara Canner, brought over from Italy. Most of the canneries—including the Del Monte factory, now a museum on Fisherman's Wharf—were in the Bay Area. As late as 1964, Del Monte had tomato canneries in Oakland, Sacramento, and San Leandro. Tomatoes and other canning crops were grown in the coastal valleys north and south of the city, and in the Delta area, especially as levees expanded the acreage under cultivation there. Still, in 1925, Indiana was the leading processing tomato state, with 67,340 acres of tomatoes; California had about half that number.

At UC Davis, Hanna was working partly with materials gathered by Pearson, who had left the campus in 1933 to work for private seed companies. Pearson had helped breed in resistances to verticillium, fusarium, and root-knot nematode, a microscopic wormlike parasite that stunts and kills tomatoes. Around the same time, the USDA experimental station in Beltsville, Maryland, developed the Roma tomato by selecting progenies of crosses involving the San Marzano, Red Top, and Pan American (a cross between Marglobe and *L. pimpinellifolium* that was also the parent of the famous Rutgers) varieties. The Roma would eventually become the best-known American cooking and canning tomato.

To the extent that Hanna's name became known to the public, he was inevitably associated with a half-truth called the "square tomato." The story began as a joke. Every January since 1956, UC Davis and the tomato industry have held a Tomato Day to celebrate the campus's historic role in developing the crop and its centrality to the surrounding Yolo County (neighboring Sacramento was long known as "The Big Tomato"). In the early 1960s, colleagues of Hanna displayed one of Hanna's products at Tomato Day, describing it as a "square tomato." The term was somehow relayed to a San Francisco radio station, which broadcast the achievement. A wire-service reporter chanced to speak with a USDA breeder named Ray Webb, who thought the reporter was referring to his own breeding efforts and was apparently all too happy to let them be called "square tomatoes." The story went out with Webb's name in it, and soon the U.S. government was bombarded with requests for the seeds.

Hanna, typically, celebrated the mistake by making it the subject of jokes told to his friends and drinking buddies, the breeders from private seed companies who routinely stole his creations and gave them their own names. In August 1968, Hanna wrote a letter to Paul Thomas of Peto Seed Company and other friends with a photograph of an angular, though not square, tomato. He described it as a "picture of a square tomato which I have developed." He called it the Paul Thomas.

Hanna's research was prodigious, but his research publications were practically nonexistent. Though his letters display humor and verve, he apparently hated to write. His annual report for the department chief was typically one or two paragraphs, and he stubbornly resisted requests to publish. "He'd say, 'I'm not going to write anything. I'm going to go out and do it,'" a colleague recalled. As a result, the university tried to block Hanna's promotions, but his friends at the canneries and seed companies—which funded much of the research at the Department of Vegetable Crops—would make threatening noises until the administration caved in. "Jack doesn't like rules," said Bob Hartzell. "He'd much rather be doing something with his hands in the field than writing a manuscript."

He also worked weird hours. On the Texas farm where he'd grown up, Hanna's father woke Jack and his brothers with a shout at 3:00 A.M., at which they were expected to tumble out of bed into their clothes. Hanna hated this routine, but it was apparently etched into him so deeply that he couldn't shake it. He'd get up every morning at 2:00 and head out to his greenhouses or his fields, eat breakfast at 6:30, lunch at 11:00, take a nap until 1:30, work until 5:00, and be in bed by 7:30. Others described him as an insomniac whose sleep was unpredictable. When he wasn't out in his own fields or visiting plantings that friendly seed companies made for him in Mexico or Puerto Rico, he'd invite the boys around for a drink at the shed behind his house.

"Hanna developed close relations with some of these guys from industry and they'd come up and sit in what he called his doghouse," said Stevens, who replaced Hanna at UC Davis in 1970. "They'd sit and drink whiskey and go look at tomatoes. They'd spend a couple days doing this." It was with the help of one of his doghouse buddies, Barney Wilson of Castle Seed Company, that, in 1961, after many crosses and selections—149 in all—Hanna was ready to roll out his new machine-harvestable tomato, the VF145. Wilson, who had a good nose for varieties, chose plant number 7879 in a field of VF145s. The "square" VF145B-7879 would dominate the California processing tomato industry for the next decade.

Hanna enjoyed goading his commercial friends about their reliance on his seeds. "Thank you for your letter informing me that you had finally gotten around to planting my material," he wrote in one letter in the late 1960s. "I know there is great reluctance on your part to planting any of it down there because it is bound to make yours look very bad." The breeder replied, tongue in cheek, that this was "not true at all. Every year I look forward to receiving your material to include in our trials. We have a certain novelty type trade with little old ladies and crackpots who are always on the lookout for the odd and unusual type."

In a May 1968 letter to Thomas, Hanna joked about his academic status. "We who have attained eminence and dwell in the ivory towers devote considerable time to profound thinking for the benefit of mankind," he wrote. "This may seem strange to many people in your class who devote so much time to the pursuit of the filthy lucre. You, of course, not only soil your hands but also soil your minds, so that it is difficult for you to appreciate the realms of higher learning and our delicate thought processes." The self-deprecation was revealing of how Hanna really felt about academia.

Hanna was never really satisfied with the VF145. The longer tomatoes, like the Red Top and the San Marzano, handled better. More importantly, the VF145's lackluster flavor didn't escape notice indefinitely. "Not so long ago, tomatoes were soft, juicy and tasted of tomato," the respected journal *Science* opined in 1974. "Several varieties available in today's supermarkets are rubbery gobs of cellulose that taste of nothing. They are bred that way for mechanical picking." In fact, the lofty journal had made the cardinal error of tomato critics—confusing the hard market tomato of Florida with the mechanized tomato of California. Still, it had a point.

Even Hanna acknowledged that his tomatoes weren't paragons of flavor. "The Red Top and the VF145 didn't taste as good as the Pearson, and in my view the Pearson wasn't as good as the Santa Clara Canner," he said. But flavor didn't count much in Hanna's view. "At least 80 percent of the canned tomato products are mixed with condiments and spices to the point that you don't know what the tomato underneath tastes like anyway," he told the *Los Angeles Times* in 1977. And what the public had to sacrifice in flavor it got back in economics. "If people were willing to pay $1 or $2 for a can of tomato sauce, we could come up with a very flavorful handpicked variety. But people won't pay that, so the alternative is to reduce the cost. We did that by taking out most of the hand labor. The flavor is not bad at all," he added. "But even if it were nonexistent, I think that a poor tomato is better than no tomato at all."

More than simple indifference, Hanna could sometimes express a kind of cynicism about the blandness of his products. His opinions echo jarringly today, when overeating and obesity have replaced high prices and scarcity as the source of our worries about food. "People don't notice the taste once you've put sugar and salt and the vinegar and the rest of it in with them," Hanna said. "Anyway, the blander a food tastes, the more of it people want to eat."

As Hartzell, whose Flotill Foods was an early enthusiast for Hanna's tomatoes, put it, "Jack has the ability to think far ahead. We tend to eat potatoes and rice in large quantity. We can eat two helpings if we want to and still want more. On the other hand, you take a freestone peach and a cling peach. Freestone peach is more highly flavored. You'll eat more cling peaches than you will freestone peaches. The first taste of freestone is better, but your taste buds become saturated rapidly because of the high flavor. The same is true of tomatoes. They are modestly flavored. We eat more of a modestly flavored thing, in total pounds, than we will of something that's highly flavored, where we want one mouthful and maybe two, but after three or four we don't want too much more. Hanna observed this and I think he's absolutely right."

Hanna's preoccupation at the time was winning acceptance for his tomatoes and the machine that harvested them. But processors were initially reluctant to go to mechanical harvesting. They had millions of dollars invested in the big, open-ended crates used by the workers, and no way to handle the 1,000-pound bins that the harvester filled. That was just the beginning of the challenge. In the early iterations of Hanna's tomato, up to a quarter of the tomatoes were damaged by the time they reached the cannery. The mechanical harvester required more systematic agriculture: Sorters on the machine worked on its time, abandoning the piece-rate rhythms of handpicking. Fertilizer and water were applied carefully to make the crop ripen thickly and uniformly. The harvester didn't work well with wet land or fruit softened by extra water. Planting was on even, raised beds so the harvester's cutting blade could easily get under the soil. Irrigation stopped early so the vegetation died back, reducing the vine clutter that slowed the harvester's march down the row. Less water changed the composition of the tomatoes, concentrating the sugars and other solids. This was better for the product, but it required adjustments in the cannery and angered farmers, who were paid by the ton.

The new tomatoes were smaller than the old beefsteak variety, and coreless. Tillie Lewis, whose San Marzanos had never required coring, appreciated that it was no longer necessary to have women—they were always women—core the round tomatoes before they went in the can. Her company, which had canneries in Antioch, Modesto, and Stockton, was indebted to Hanna, who'd bred a disease-resistant strain of the San Marzano back in the hand-harvesting period. But most of the canneries had employed corers as long as anyone could remember, and it wasn't easy to drop traditions. The transition was tough even for Flotill. "I have a lot less hair now than I did in 1961," Hartzell said in 1975. "I could never seem to go to lunch and come back and the harvester would still be running."

As late as 1964, the California Tomato Growers' Association was still skeptical of mechanization, but because of labor shortages and rumblings from the labor movement, increasingly viewed it as a necessity. Growers recruited workers in Mississippi and Puerto Rico that year to replace the braceros. Fears that their industry would move to Mexico were real enough. In May, a group of growers and canners visited one of Hanna's field trials in Sinaloa, Mexico, to see if the new variety would be ready for use by the harvester. While there, they saw five hundred acres of tomatoes being grown by a U.S. company for processing. "If harvest labor is not available in 1965, the only way California can remain competitive in tomato production is to mechanize," an industry publication said.

The university was fully in accord with this assessment and determined to help speed mechanization. "There can only be two solutions to the problem," said C. F. Kelly, director of the University of California Agricultural Experiment Station: "find another labor source or mechanize." The university was working on mechanization of thirteen crops as of 1965. Faculty members were also investing time in technology that would be used, starting in the early 1970s, in the electronic tomato sorter, a machine installed on the conveyer belts of the harvester. The sorter would shoot out a metal finger to discard green tomatoes, dirt, and other unwanted material from the tomatoes as they rushed past. Incorporated during a period in which labor unrest had hit the tomato fields, the new technology would provoke an immediate political outcry.

The controversy came to a head gradually. In the mid-1960s, UC Davis officials met with Secretary of Labor W. Willard Wirtz to ask him to phase out the Bracero program, rather than ending it immediately, as some members of Congress were suggesting. By 1961, Tri-Valley Growers, the largest tomato-growing cooperative, was talking about building a plant in Mexico. Heinz already had one there, and so did Cal-Pak (which later became Del Monte). Some of this may have been a bluff to keep the Bracero program going. But it was clear the program's days were numbered. The cotton harvest was mechanized between 1948 and the early 1960s in Texas and California, which made tomatoes the most labor-intensive crop. Reform-minded Democrats felt the program held down wages for poor Americans and exploited Mexican laborers. There was an element of truth to this. The elimination of the Bracero program would not eliminate Mexican immigration, and illegal immigrants were somewhat easier to exploit. But you could only exploit them if they were there in the necessary numbers when it was time to pick tomatoes. That was never guaranteed, and besides, most growers preferred not to hire illegal labor.

In 1964, some thirty thousand braceros had worked on the tomato harvest in California. By mid-August 1965, only twenty-five hundred had been allowed in. The federal government had hoped that a program to enlist native labor, including high school and college students, would fill the gap, but it didn't. Tomatoes were rotting on the vine, and canneries were paying $35 a ton, up from $25 a year before. Wirtz, fought by organized labor at every step of the way, eventually authorized the entry of an additional sixteen thousand braceros to work the harvest. In 1966, he authorized an additional six thousand—and an additional ten thousand domestic workers stooped to pick tomatoes at wages that were considerably higher than in years past. By then, the writing was on the wall: Smaller farmers were ditching the tomato; the machine was taking over.

The social response to agricultural mechanization has followed a curious pattern. The first wave of mechanization took place before the American Civil War, when mechanical wheat reapers drawn by animals replaced people with scythes. In the early 1900s, the tractor came into general use, and then the various implements that it dragged behind it. While there were certainly those who rued the advent of these machines, these tools did not immediately transform the structure of American farms. The tomato harvester was part of what some historians have called the third wave of agricultural mechanization, which also included machines to shake orange and peach and almond trees and the mechanization of seeding and transplanting operations. The capital requirements to buy these new tools, and the economies of scale in land that these investments required, had a major impact on the size of farms and the number of them. More than 1.2 million farms were lost in the 1950s and 1960s, along with 2.8 million farm jobs.

In California, 24 percent of the canning tomato harvest was done

by machine in 1964; in 1966, 80 percent was done by machine, and by
1968 virtually the entire harvest was mechanical. The professors and
extension agents never asked the laborers what they thought of the
machine. "Since we were only guests on these growers' ranches, there
by permission only, we avoided labor contract as much as possible," said
Melvin Zobel, cooperative extension agent in Yolo County in the 1960s.
"When we wanted to do something with labor, we worked through the
owner or the labor boss."

Ostensibly, mechanization of the farm was no different in its dislo-
cating effects than was industrialization in general. It cut jobs, but they
were often crummy, dirty, low-paying, backbreaking jobs. It changed
the landscape, but fewer and fewer people lived in this landscape, and
efficiency cheapened the price of the food they ate. Perhaps there was an
inverse relationship between proximity to the land and nostalgia for it.
Starting in the early 1970s, changes on the farm produced an upwelling
of sorrow over a disappearing way of life and sympathy for those whose
lives were upturned by the transformation. This was partly due to the
rise of the United Farm Workers, who organized boycotts of grapes
and other produce to protest treatment of workers who picked them.
The story of Cesar Chavez, told in his memoir *Sal Si Puedes*, resounded
in a middle-class audience drawn into the lives of deprived poor and
people of color. Concentration of land and production in fewer hands
made people suspect that the entities producing our food had less and
less of a relationship with it or with us. Gone were the milkmen and
the little green grocer on the corner. Milk was in cartons, steak in red
Styrofoam, and they came from enormous herds of dung-covered cows
on huge feedlots, or antibiotic-fed heifers on ever more industrialized
dairy farms. The reduction of field labor seemed to strike at an intrin-
sic, if sentimental, feeling of disconnection from the land.

The controversy over the harvester, as Thompson and Scheuring wrote, "contains all the elements of some high drama: epic acreage, hard-working farmers, dedicated scientists, brilliant businessmen, struggling workers, union organizers, millions of dollars and a well-favored adaptable, bright red product." In addition to provoking a major lawsuit, which dragged through the courts into the 1990s, the tomato harvester sparked activism among consumer, labor, and student groups and protests on UC campuses. In 1974, the United Farm Workers (UFW) called a strike on cannery tomato growers in the Stockton area, and the strike later spread to Stanislaus and the Delta. Another strike began in Yolo County in September, with five hundred workers leaving the fields. Growers conceded a fifty-cent-an-hour wage increase, but they also started looking for ways to stop paying many of those workers.

The UFW's timing was exquisitely bad. If it had struck earlier, it might have put a severe pinch on the growers. But it chose to take action just as farmers were toying with a labor-saving device that would significantly reduce their need for workers. After 155 of his employees joined the strike, Yolo County farmer Bernell Harlan fitted his five harvesters with electronic sorters, cutting his harvest workforce to forty-four. "One of the big advantages of these machines is you can keep the people you want, and get rid of the troublemakers," he said. At the time, only 9 percent of California growers employed the sorters. The percentage grew to 56 percent by 1977. In 1961, the harvester had allowed twelve people to do what sixty had done in the past. With the sorter, five could do the job. The new sorter probably eliminated another twelve thousand jobs.

In a 1977 pamphlet, written two years before it sued the University of California, a group called the California Agrarian Action Project charged that UC Davis agriculture professors and extension agents had, with their inventions, added misery to the hard lives of field laborers. The group charged that the Board of Regents had conflicts of interest—and it was entirely correct. Several of the board members held important positions in farming corporations, compromising their ability to steer the university's research in directions benefitting all Californians, and not just the wealthy. At least two regents were on the board of Del Monte Corporation, then the world's largest fruit and vegetable processor. Another was a director of Miller and Lux, an enormous agribusiness concern. James B. Kendrick, director of the experimental station, was on the board of Tejon Agricultural Corporation, a wine grape and tomato producer located on the biggest chunk of private land in California—owned by the Chandler family, which also held the *Los Angeles Times*.

The pamphlet described an immigrant worker named Flavio Martínez, who made his living picking cannery tomatoes in the area around Woodland. In previous summers, he had worked as a sorter on the mechanical harvester, but in July 1974, when he returned to the ranch where he had worked for eight summers, "the ranch foreman told him there was no work. The harvesting machines had been outfitted with electronic eyes which could sort out the green tomatoes. The sorting crew was being cut from twenty workers to five."

In 1976, three hundred unemployed farmworkers demonstrated on the Davis campus to protest the use of public funds for mechanization research. The electronic sorter had thrown so many people out of work that emergency food banks were being stretched to the limit. At a regents' hearing on mechanization in 1978, activist Tom Hayden, carried away with his rhetoric, compared the farmworkers to Vietnamese peasants. "Their cry for justice splits the very heavens," he said, declaring the university's work on the mechanical harvester "an absolute perversion of the humane potential of automation." Activists like Hayden and Cesar Chavez demanded that the university, as a party responsible for job loss, find ways to help those who had lost their jobs. In step with the radical social climate of the times, Robert Bergland, President Carter's secretary of agriculture, declared in a 1979 speech that he would "not put federal money into any project that results in saving of farm labor." At the land-grant colleges, this declaration set off a chorus of dismay that dulled the administration's appetite for more confrontation on the issue.

In September 1979, the California Agrarian Action Project filed suit against the UC Regents on behalf of nineteen Hispanic farmworkers. The lawsuit came at a time when many social activists were criticizing the underpinnings of industrial America. Activists were increasingly mindful of the concerns that Rachel Carson's *Silent Spring* had raised in 1962 about the potential hazards of pesticides. The 1979 nuclear meltdown at Three Mile Island raised questions about the reliability and safety of technology and the authority of those who oversaw it. "Concern about the social costs of industrialized farming with its reliance on chemicals and heavy machinery," Al Meyerhoff, an attorney for the plaintiffs, wrote in *The Nation* in 1980, "reflects the growing credibility gap between science and society." William H. Friedland, a UC Santa Cruz sociologist who testified against the university, argued that Hanna and the engineers who worked on the harvester were "social sleepwalkers," clueless about the impact of what they were doing. Public institutions, including the university, Friedland said, needed to concern themselves with the social results of their inventions. Friedland asked why greater productivity had to come at the cost of the rural community. "Although it was not their original intent, the developers of the tomato and the machine facilitated the process of grower concentration," he said.

The university was on the defensive. Charles E. Hess, dean of the UC Davis College of Agriculture and Environmental Sciences, acknowledged in 1981 that small farmers were going out of business—the number of farms had shrunk from 1.3 million in 1959 to 400,000 in 1974. Agricultural consolidation in the United States followed what he called the "treadmill and cannibalism model." As new technologies improved yields, the bigger farmers jumped in. In a normal market, this would drive prices down. But when the government supported farm prices, the larger farmers instead expanded their operations by "cannibalizing" their smaller, weaker neighbors. Hess offered no suggestions for how to reverse this trend.

Others felt that protests against the harvester were symbolic and naive. "Given a choice, nearly all employees will opt for equipment operation over manual labor," one farmer testified at the UC Regents' hearing. "They will normally opt for an air-conditioned cab rather than an open tractor. And almost no one who works on a farm wants to go back to the good old days—forking bales by hand, hand milking cows, hand picking and carrying tomatoes, hand knocking and poling of almonds or walnuts. All hot and dirty work. I wonder, just who it is we are saving these jobs for?"

Economists Philip L. Martin and Alan L. Olmstead, in a 1984 paper supporting the university against the lawsuit, argued that harvesting tomatoes was so exhausting that few stayed at it more than fifteen years. Eliminating a harvesting job wasn't like removing an autoworker from a lifetime job and pension. "Older workers gravitate into lower-wage but easier irrigation or hoeing jobs in U.S. agriculture, or they return to Mexico." (Critics contended that many out-of-work migrants ended up in the slums of Los Angeles or other cities.) Martin and Olmstead also denied that machine harvest diminished the nutritive value of the tomatoes, since "machines permit the harvest to be accomplished quickly, when the commodity is at its peak quality."

The public, meanwhile, gave few signs of really giving a damn. It "reads condemnations and defense of the industry, and goes on eating tomatoes," Scheuring and Thompson wrote.

As for the farmers, even those operating smaller farms, they were happy to have a machine that limited their labor difficulties. "We can't operate with a union, so we have to eliminate as many people as we can to keep the work force down to our steady employees," Robert Button, a farmer from Winters, California, said at the 1978 hearing. "Our steady crews are well taken care of as far as compensation for their work, health and accident insurance, retirement and bonuses." Button, inventor of a mechanical harvester, was hopeful that a fresh-market tomato harvester could be made. "If the consumers don't know the difference they'll never be able to tell the difference, but if you tell them it's harvested mechanically, it will make a difference."

But the success stories couldn't hide the destructive power of mechanization. The mechanical harvester did throw unskilled laborers out of work. It also transformed the tomato farm and helped remake the urban landscape by leading to the closure of urban canneries, while opening the south lands to tomato farming. In the 1950s, Fresno was a sparsely populated county that hadn't previously attracted large numbers of braceros, because there was no water. When the California Aqueduct reached the area in the late 1960s, there were no braceros, but the mechanical harvester opened the area to large-scale cultivation. West Fresno County growers added tomatoes to their rotations of cotton, sugar beets, and wheat. And the new tomato canneries were built directly in the tomato-growing areas of the valley.

Tomato growing was being concentrated in the hands of fewer and fewer farmers. Tomatoes had always been temperamental, subject to more microorganisms, pests, and weeds than most other crops. Farmers were paid for the crop they delivered to the cannery after it had been graded—measured for mold damage, color, and soluble sugars. A load that was too green could be rejected, while if the wait was too long, the tomatoes started to fall apart. Exposure to sun created white spots and flattened areas on the tomato that bred mold, while a late rain—especially in September or October—caused the tomatoes to swell, burst, or attract other microorganisms. It was a risky business, but one that paid well. Increasingly, only larger farmers could afford the risks—and enjoy the benefits.

By 1975, the number of California tomato growers had shrunk to 595, from 2,200 in 1962. "Today you can't stay in the farming business on less than 800 acres in California," the farmer Les Heringer said that year. "It used to be 100 or 200 acres. This is just a change in the way of life. The small tomato operations have been bought out." There were new economies of scale, and the machine required different cultivation practices, too. You had to change how you irrigated. Weeds and mud clogged the machine. "Marginal farmers are no longer growing tomatoes," Heringer said. They faced the same choice they'd always had: Change or die.

As the number of farmers fell, production increased—from 1.3 million tons in California in 1954 to 3 million in 1964, 6 million in 1974, 8 million in 1990, and 12 million in 2007. Acreage doubled, and yields went from an average of 17 to 40 tons per acre. Tomatoes earned $153 million for California in 1972, second in vegetable production only to lettuce, which earned $182 million. The number of workers in the tomato harvest had dwindled from about one hundred thousand in 1958 to thirty thousand in 1972, and seven thousand five years later.

Mechanization of the tomato industry occurred a decade or more

later in the eastern United States, but when it did, the conflict with labor
was more direct and immediate. A bold Hispanic organizer named Bal-
demar Velásquez and his compatriots on the Farm Labor Organizing
Committee tried everything from strikes to boycotts of the Campbell
Soup Company to raise wages and improve living conditions for Ohio
tomato pickers.

In 1971, when California's tomato crop was entirely mechanized,
only 11 percent of cannery tomatoes were machine-picked in Ohio. In
1968, major unions had struck Campbell's Soup canneries, and hundreds of thousands of tons of New Jersey, Pennsylvania, and Maryland tomatoes were ruined. But in the early 1970s, tomato processors
developed sterilized tomato paste packing methods that allowed them
to store the stuff for months or even years. Campbell and other big
food companies would soon be able to purchase as much industrial
paste as they needed—California paste, Canadian paste, it made no
difference—to tide them over periods of bad crops or labor conflict.
A 1968 strike against farmers in Lucas County, outside Toledo, drove
many small farmers out of the tomato business. As it became evident
that the wages farmers could offer depended on the shifting price paid
by producers like Libby, Campbell's Soup, Hunt-Wesson, and Heinz,
Velásquez's organizing committee started targeting the canneries
instead. The movement was met by replacement labor, bloodshed, and
arrests. Ohio's churches supported a boycott of Campbell's Soup products, which included Swanson frozen dinners, Pepperidge Farm cook-
ies, Godiva chocolates, and Vlasic pickles.

Rather than winning better conditions, the conflict sparked mod-
ernization that put more people out of work. The food companies
increasingly prescribed how their tomatoes were to be grown, cultivated, and harvested. The percentage of machine-harvested crop in

Ohio crept to 22 percent in 1978 and jumped to 60 percent in 1981. Once the big eastern food companies decided they could live with a mechanically harvested tomato, they switched quickly, and many of them soon refused to buy tomatoes from growers who did not use the harvester. Thus, the food companies took power out of the workers' hands while driving small farmers out of business. As in California, the Ohio State University extension service took little interest in preserving the handpicked tomato.

But the harvester was more difficult to use in the East, and this would have a major impact on the geography of the tomato business. Button, who took one of his harvesters to Ohio in 1966, described the problem: "Working in the mud was a real eye opener to me." East Coast farmers don't grade their fields the way California farmers do; theirs are often sloped. "We sold some harvesters to Libby, and they were running in fields that had four inches of rain Sunday. We were working Wednesday. The harvesters were sinking down a good foot into the ground." In the decade after the harvester came on line, nearly all the cannery tomato business shifted to California. About 10 percent remains in the eastern states of Ohio, Indiana, and Pennsylvania, with a small amount in Ontario, Canada.

In interviews with the trade press and the newspapers, Hanna was happy to be portrayed as Mr. Brave New World of the vegetable. He was unsentimental about food, uninterested in food traditions, and firmly convinced that what American grocery shoppers cared most about— and always would—was convenience. "The vegetable crops industry of this country has developed from the backyards of our people," he said in 1977. "Unfortunately, we've taken too much of the backyard philosophy along with us . . . Who says we have to leave the capstems on strawberries—does the housewife enjoy standing at the sink picking them off? Why do we keep worrying about how to mechanize the lettuce industry? Maybe we ought to plant Romaine type varieties, run through the fields with mowing machines and put the leaves in plastic bags ready to use." And finally, "Who says we have to have a round tomato—why not a long one that will cut up into attractive, uniform slices? No, we don't change things because everybody thinks that's the way they're supposed to be . . . that's the way they came out of the backyard and everybody's afraid to change." Mechanization of the tomato harvest was easy, he said. The hard part was figuring out "why didn't we do it a long time ago."

Hanna had plenty of reasons to feel proud. He'd saved the tomato business for California, and it was growing. As it expanded to the south, there were new breeding requirements. Don May, a UC Davis extension agent, was working with tomato growers in the Fresno area in the early 1960s when the harvester was coming on line. The hot, dry area was ideal for tomatoes once irrigation water reached it. Among the families that jumped into the tomato business were the Boswells, whose crusade to drain Mono Lake and introduce vast cotton acreage is chronicled in the 2005 book *The King of California*. Planting early, the Fresno-area farmers could harvest in early July. For these growers, the biggest problem was that when summer temperatures got too hot, the tomato plant shut down. Flowers would fall off, fruit would abort, and they'd end up with a leggy plant and few tomatoes. These farmers turned to a new generation of UC Davis plant breeders—in particular, M. Allen Stevens, Hanna's successor.

"Davis came after me because people were claiming the mechanical harvest varieties didn't have any flavor and so on," Stevens told me in an interview at his rural home near Davis. "That turned out to be a bunch of BS in my opinion. But the university was kinda sensitive about that." Based on Stevens's work with Campbell, his new bosses at the university figured, "'here's a guy who thinks he can do something about tomato quality—let's see what he can do.'" He thinks the university was eager for Hanna to leave because of the mechanization dispute, which Stevens, too, was unable to sidestep. One of his worst moments, Stevens said, was when he was deposed for the lawsuit. "They were trying to find out what we were doing to make life better for the farmworkers. Frankly, we weren't thinking about it. The suit never went anywhere. But it made the university uncomfortable for a while."

Stevens and Hanna overlapped for several months before Hanna left to work for Peto Seed. The relationship was tense, because Hanna was either unable or unwilling to help. "He had a lot of information but he was an insular, terrible teacher," Stevens recalled. "I followed him around like a little pup my first summer here. He left at the end of that growing season. I don't think he had much regard for what I was going to be able to do. He was the Tomato God; there was no doubt about it, as far as the industry was concerned. I had to scramble pretty hard to convince people that I was going to be worthy of their support."

Hanna didn't publish and didn't want graduate students. Stevens wanted to be successful in the university system. When Hanna was asked once to calculate how much it cost to develop his harvestable tomato, he gave a figure of $42,000—adding that it was padded. "I wanted a lot more than that," Stevens said. He wanted graduate students and an ambitious research program, but he had to find a way to pay for all that. "I was feeling pretty insecure, and he wasn't much help." Hanna had moved on to breeding sweet potatoes.

Stevens's goal was to continue his research into tomato flavor and quality while creating a big germplasm development program. "I'd have field days, where people could look at the varieties and request the seed if they liked it. After a couple years, I could see that it wasn't working well with industry. They couldn't tell if any of my stuff was making a difference, because once it got into their hands, they'd never admit that they'd used my varieties as parents to develop something. It dropped into that black hole of trade secrets that was their main protection. I was doing a lot of developmental work for these people, but I wasn't getting any credit for it. So I decided to do something different—breed finished varieties." The main variety that came out of this was the UC82, which was released in 1976.

Stevens's breeding program incorporated improvements that a number of breeders had been making. Heinz had provided firmer tomatoes to Oscar Pearson, Hanna's predecessor at Davis, for some lines that Pearson was developing for a private company back East. Stevens's UC82, drawing on the Pearson material, contained more "wall" and less juice than the traditional tomatoes. The greater firmness and pliability of the UC82 allowed growers to harvest a field with a bigger percentage of ripe tomatoes and reduced broken tomatoes and juice. This all increased "paid yield" to the grower. In other words, by providing more "field storage"—the ability to keep ripe tomatoes on the vine for a longer period, allowing later tomatoes to catch up—UC82 ensured that a large percentage of tomatoes gathered by the harvester would be right for canning or paste-making. The Heinz breeding lines that made their way into UC82 contained genes that helped tomatoes survive nippy eastern springs; these genes also conveyed resistance to extremely hot weather.

Ironically, for a breeder who had specialized in flavor, Stevens had not come up with a tomato that had particularly good postharvest qualities, as he was the first to admit. "What it mainly had was yield," he said. "It set like crazy when conditions were not ideal. If there was stress during fruit set—heat, cold—a lot of varieties would completely poop out. The flowers dropped off. UC82 would set. That's what made it a winner. It became the dominant variety in California and a lot of places around the world."

As for Hanna, who died in 1989, a conference room in Asmundson Hall at Davis bears his name and honors his work with plaques and tributes from friends and colleagues. He and Stevens were the last important breeders at Davis. As hybrid tomato seed started to take off, it taxed the relationship between academia and private companies. Whereas everyone had been happy to share their knowledge when they were using open-pollinated varieties, which could be duplicated anyway, once the companies had hybrid seed, they became more secretive about what they were doing.

In 1989, the lawsuit against the UC Regents was finally settled. Most of the case was thrown out, but Judge Raymond Marsh ordered the university to evaluate how its research contributed to family farming, as laid out in the 1887 Hatch Act that originally established federal funding for agricultural extension programs. Indirectly, the suit led to the creation of research programs at UC Davis for small and sustainable farming operations. While laudable and interesting, neither program had much to do with the plight of the migrant farmworker.

CHAPTER FOUR

Destino Cruel

We can always do better in terms of the food we buy.

—Chipotle Corporation

 IT'S LONELY IN A BIG TOMATO FIELD IN THE MIDDLE OF THE Everglades just after dawn. A filigree of lime-green plants stretches endlessly through an unshaded, monotonous field, while birds flit through shrubs around the margins. Jet trails crisscross a vast, purplish sky. It's always humid in Florida, and already it's hot. And there's nobody here but a truck driver, two guys who catch the tomato buckets, and twenty-four frightened, destitute, illiterate men and women, picking tomatoes at a breakneck pace. And me, trying to keep pace. The crew chief, a big guy with a mustache, a guy who looks ready to handle any trouble, is barking from the top of a 2.5-ton truck that's slowly moving down the row as the workers stream to and from it as ceaselessly as ants, pulling tomatoes out of the bushes, heaving thirty-five-pound

buckets onto their shoulders, jogging to the truck to the bucket catchers, jogging back to start picking again.

Entrale al trabajo, señores!

Abre la mata, ábrela, ábrela!

Faster! Faster! Less talk and more work!

A tomato field near Immokalee, Florida, is like a hellish, outdoor version of Las Vegas, with no clocks and no clear idea of how you'll end up at the end of the day. If anything nasty happens here, it stays here, most likely. You could always lodge a complaint with the Florida Department of Labor. And good luck with that.

You hear the steady *clunk* of hard tomatoes bouncing into the *cubetas,* the plastic buckets that are filled with tomatoes and carried to the truck. The tomatoes are the size of Granny Smith apples, and they feel and sound like them, too—*tock, tock, tock, tock*—cascading into the buckets, like money coming out of a one-armed bandit. These are the famous Florida "mature-green" tomatoes. From here they'll be sorted and stored in rooms full of ethylene gas that kick-starts the ripening process so they're all the same color when they reach the next destination, the repacking operation, where they'll be sorted and reboxed again to meet the demands of Safeway or ShopRite or Chipotle or Burger King or a thousand other buyers.

Up close to the row, I hear the rustle and snap of hands darting into the vine, grasping tomatoes and letting them fall into the bucket. Sometimes you hear men humming, bantering, the crew chief ordering them to work harder. *Tock-tock-tock-tock.* Lift the bucket. Shuffle to the truck that keeps moving down the rows to keep pace with the harvest.

One of the Mexican guys gives a singsong refrain each time he tosses his bucket up to the catcher on the truck bed:

Destino cruel.

He pauses between the two words.

To the guys on the truck, the pickers have no names, only crude appellations that refer to their provenance or size.

Dale, Caballo: "Horse" is a big, gentle Haitian guy.

Vera Cruz: A Mexican with a pencil mustache.

Órale, Chiapaneco: A wiry guy from Chiapas, with Indian features.

No me lo tires, Cuba.

That's me. At six-two, they figure I have to be Cuban, since Americans don't do this kind of work. "You should pick oranges, *Cuba*," one of the *dumpeadores* helpfully suggests. "You're the right height for it."

Destino cruel. A good name for a new Florida tomato cultivar. By most accounts, the industry of the state was doomed to a cruel fate. The workers complained of being virtual (and sometimes real) slaves, of paying exorbitant rents to live in miserable trailers, and of receiving wages that hadn't changed in thirty years. The growers bitched about the seemingly infinite number of insects and microorganisms that attacked their crops; the endless upward spiral of costs for seed, fertilizer, pesticides, machinery, and land; the hell of unpredictable hurricanes and freezes; the devious instincts of their Mexican competitors; the lack of respect from consumers and columnists alike; the incessant need for new safety inspections against rats and insects and salmonella. The breeders sighed that whatever innovations they came up with were pointless, because all the growers cared about was yield; they were indifferent to how their tomatoes tasted.

In 2008, tomatoes were the number three Florida crop, behind oranges and sugar, but acreage has been shrinking. It started from 6,500 acres in 1900, went to 66,000 in 1957, and was down to 31,500 in 2008. Half the state's 150 packinghouses have closed since 2000. "I find it very sad that we're going to be the state that gets rid of agriculture," said Jan Risi, who headed Subway's independent purchasing cooperative out of Kendall, Florida. "We're going to be driving by five years from now, and in the place of tomato fields there's going to be big McMansions and golf courses." Unlike processing tomato growers, who sign contracts with canneries in January to deliver a crop in August, fresh-market tomato farmers are at the mercy of a roller-coaster market. In the 2005 season, for example, the average price paid Florida farmers was 41 cents per pound, but it varied from 18 cents in May to $1.07 in January. With all those swings and risks, the rule of thumb is that for every ten years, the grower makes it big three years, loses big three, and breaks even the rest of the time. That doesn't add up to a lot of profit.

If California has the perfect climate for tomatoes, with its long, hot summers in which irrigation can be applied and withheld on a scientific basis, Florida is all topsy confusion at the mercy of a thousand human and natural curses. "We see more disease in a single season than they see in California in thirty years," a plant pathologist told me. "We're subtropical. We're an ideal environment for microorganisms."

In 2004, Hurricane Charlie roared up from the Caribbean—a huge disaster for the Ruskin-Manatee-area farmers, south of Tampa, who harvest typically in September and October, and a bonanza for the growers around Immokalee, at the southern tip of the peninsula, who missed the storm. As their tomatoes were ripening at the start of November, the market was going nuts, with the unprecedented price of $35 to $40 per carton. By the end of December, it was below $4. The break-even point was $9. To survive these kinds of conditions, you needed to have a farming operation with plantings around the state, so you could hedge your bets. "Consolidation happens with every crunch in the market," Fritz Roka, a University of Florida economist, told me.

"The bigger companies are the ones that survive because they have diversified in terms of production areas. If fields in Immokalee aren't productive, maybe they have something in northern Florida, or even North Carolina and Virginia."

It has taken plenty of politics to keep the fresh-market tomato industry of Florida from going under. It's the last surviving off-season tomato-growing area in the country, unless you count greenhouses. At one time, winter tomatoes were grown throughout the South—always in Florida, but also from Tennessee to Texas.

As consumers started showing an interest in fresh tomatoes for their salads a century ago, farmers around the country started growing them. Railroads put out flyers urging farmers with lands along their lines to get in on the act. "There is a large territory along the line of the Nashville, Chattanooga, and St. Louis railway which is well adapted to the tomato," one such tract stated. "There is no reason why the farmers of West Tennessee should not be reaping some of the golden harvest ... [I]n order to get the benefit of the lowest freight rates and the best of service it is necessary to plant sufficient acreage to furnish loading for a car or more per day."

Vestiges of these tomato-farming cultures exist in places like Warren, Arkansas; Crystal Springs, Mississippi; and Rutledge, Tennessee, in the form of annual tomato festivals. In some places, like Avery, Texas, the festival tomatoes are shipped in from somewhere else nowadays. Texas had many winter tomato farms once, but at a hearing in McAllen, Texas, on June 12, 1961, a congressional subcommittee on small business heard the death rattle of these south Texas tomato growers. Florida and Mexico were both expanding their season to try to corner the market on spring tomatoes—a market that had been controlled by the Texans; supermarkets were consolidating and bargaining harder to drive producers' prices down. The farmers described begging retailers for a break. Ruin was stalking them. "We're not asking for the world with a fence around it, but just from one to two cents per pound extra for our commodity," one grower said. "The small farmer doesn't want to get rich," said James Griffin, who farmed five hundred acres around Mission, Texas. "He would like to stay on a small farm, instead of having to go to Dallas or San Antonio and drive a taxi . . . Whenever you run a small farmer off the farm, he is going to show up some place. You are going to have to let him work or you are going to have to find a way to feed him."

The same story has repeated itself thousands of times. Most of the surviving operations in Florida are still family-run, but they're much larger and more sophisticated than their failed cousins of the past. I interviewed one big grower, Tony DiMare of DiMare Fresh, at his 131,000-square-foot warehouse. Tractor-trailers hauling thousand-pound bins of green tomatoes were emptying their loads onto an assembly line of sorters. Most of the tomatoes were Florida 47, a mainstay of the gas-green industry for a decade or more. Developed by Asgrow, which is now part of the expanding Monsanto seed industry, they have good firmness and size and contain the crimson gene, which gives them added lycopene and a bright red color when ripe.

In a warehouse staffed by about 250 men, tomatoes went through chlorine and fungicide baths and were lightly waxed, which produced a sheen that also prevented abrasions that can discolor or ruin the tomatoes. Fresh-market growers in Florida operate under an extremely precise market order, an industry arrangement that establishes how much and what type of a particular commodity gets produced. Florida tomatoes are classified, with a small overlap, as medium or No. 3 grade ($2^9/_{32}$ to $2^{19}/_{32}$ inches), large or No. 2 ($2^{17}/_{32}$ to $2^{29}/_{32}$), or extra large or No. 1

($2^{25}/_{32}$ and up). The day I visited DiMare Fresh, they were throwing out anything smaller than $2^{17}/_{32}$ of an inch. The No. 2 grade would go to wholesale and ethnic markets and restaurants, the big ones to supermarkets and to fast-food chains, which bought 60 percent of the Florida crop. The No. 3s and smaller dropped out through holes in a belt as they passed down the line, destined to become cow feed. The market was pretty strong that day—$14 per twenty-five-pound box of extra large No. 1 grade tomatoes, $12 for large.

After the tomatoes were boxed—the general rule is that for each thirty-two-pound *cubeta* picked in the field, a twenty-five-pound box will leave the warehouse—they're forklifted into the ethylene shed, where they'll sit for four to six days (the smaller the tomato, the less mature, and therefore the longer it needs ethylene exposure to turn red). After one night sitting in an ethylene-rich environment, the tomatoes are starting to blush. They ripen from the inside out. Depending on where they are and where they're going, they may be stored at temperatures as low as 58 degrees Fahrenheit. From DiMare Fresh they go to repackers, who'll take apart the boxes and repack them by size and color for individual customers—retail, food service, fast food. There are five or six major U.S. repackers. "It's a cutthroat business, all on price," DiMare said. "The margins are extremely tight and getting tighter all the time."

DiMare is a muscular, forceful guy with a goatee, graying hair, and blue eyes. He was forty-five years old when I met him, one of three brothers working in the family business. There were four electronic screens open in his office—e-mail, CNBC, security footage from the warehouse floor, and the Weather Channel. The glass cabinet behind the desk had a Michael Jordan–autographed basketball and other sports paraphernalia. A framed article on the wall told a happy story about the DiMares and their college sports careers. Tony, the oldest, played football for Boston University for a year before graduating from Miami University. Paul ran the farm in Homestead; Scott was in charge of the company. A fourth brother, Gino, was a baseball coach at the University of Miami, Florida. "He's the smart one, stayed out of this aggravating business," said DiMare.

I asked for his idea of the perfect tomato. "We have good attributes," he said. "Good size, firmness, smoothness, ripening qualities. We're continually looking at new varieties, trialing them all the time ... We could probably improve tomato flavor," he conceded. "It's easy to produce a vine-ripe backyard fruit, but to do it commercially is so difficult. When you breed in enhancements for large fruit size, you sacrifice smoothness." Nevertheless, Tony disputed that his tomatoes lacked flavor. When he brings home fresh tomatoes, his neighbors all rave about them. The problem is the processing these tomatoes go through—repackers, slicers, retailers, and so forth. There's a lot of opportunities for bruising, and worst of all—and don't get Tony started on this, or if you do, stop him pretty quickly—"people don't know not to refrigerate tomatoes. You walk into a restaurant. The tomatoes are in with the lettuce at twenty-two degrees. So no wonder people say our tomatoes taste like shit. Probably because they were mishandled."

Talking about quality spiraled Tony into a dismal fret about the enormous difficulty of his business. "They tell you there's no inflation? Bullshit. I don't care what I'm buying, the price is going up." He ticked off his rising costs: food safety supervision, fuel, fertilizer, seed, pesticide, mulch, twine, land, labor (the minimum wage went from $5.15 to $6.79 between 2005 and 2007). Immigration enforcement has tightened the labor market, so he has had to go out of state to hire workers. Many of the guys working in the warehouse that day are from Brownsville, Texas. DiMare is putting them up in a local motel. Hurricanes meant more construction work, which paid better than picking toma-toes, adding to the labor crunch. The company's packinghouses on John's Island, South Carolina, used to hire six hundred people for six weeks. They'd have two thousand applicants. Now those people work at McDonald's or Walmart.

All his problems and hopes got mixed together: "When we plant our fall crop in early August, it's very hot and humid. We have a lot of diseases, fungus pressures. Lately we've had virus problems—yellow leaf curl—due to whitefly. Drought during the summer makes the whiteflies multiply, and they have tens of thousands of hosts. We spray on a regular basis, but it's hard to control. The whitefly feeds on the undersides of the plants. It's hard to get stuff under there. Every time the wind blows, it can blow more whiteflies into a field . . . The chemicals we're spraying are not even controlling them as far as I can see, and believe me, if there were ways to get away from these sprays, we'd do it—the costs are eating us alive." Methyl bromide, a fungicide that farmers are phasing out because it destroys ozone, had gone from $0.90 to about $4 per pound, $200 to $800 per acre. As more land went to build golf courses and developments on Florida's coasts, farmers moved inland. That meant higher transportation costs. The inland environment was different, too—four or five inches more of rain, and more potential for frosts. And as the farms piled up on each other in smaller areas, fungi, bacteria, and viruses spread freely among the tomato, orange, malanga, green bean, and nursery crops. Whitefly came to Florida in imported poinsettia plants. Another species came in with Chinese figs. DiMare was growing tomatoes in the dead of winter, on the shortest days of the year, in coral-rock-based soil that lacked good organic material. The mornings were wet and foggy.

And then, of course, the hurricanes: "No way to plan around that."

In 2004, Charlie ripped out the mulch and the irrigation tape. A few weeks later, Frances hit at transplant time. Then Ivan knocked the tomato plants off their vines.

On top of all this, the industry has had to spend millions to improve monitoring of safety from the field to the market. "Food safety is important to everybody in the industry," DiMare said. "Our food is the safest it's ever been. But you've got enhanced technology such that you can detect things you didn't find before. The media has publicized it to the level of panic and alarm that spreads all through the food chain, from the consumer to the middleman to the grower. I think we're in an overboard mode." In 2007, tomato growers persuaded the Florida legislature to create a law governing growers and packers, to avoid dealing with dozens of requirements from McDonald's, Safeway, and other purchasers. And all for nothing. In April 2008, the FDA announced that salmonella-contaminated tomatoes were sickening people. Hundreds of millions of dollars in tomatoes had to be destroyed or left in the fields. The true salmonella vector turned out to be Mexican chili peppers, but it was too late to help tomatoes. Demand sank and hadn't fully recovered in 2009.

Was it any surprise, then, that Florida tomato farmers fought dirty sometimes? In the late 1960s, after watching their Texas brethren go under, the Florida tomato farmers began operating under a marketing order that allowed them to set guidelines as to size and grade, production quotas, inspection procedures, and means for settling trade disputes. Florida farmers have wielded their marketing order to keep innovators from trying anything too fancy. Or tasty. In 1999, a Philadelphia-based vegetable entrepreneur named Joe Procacci introduced the UgliRipe, a curvaceous relative of the old Rutgers type. He grew them in Florida and had them picked ripe by hand and shipped north by air. Some food critics, and especially Procacci himself, said the UgliRipe had a particularly delicious taste; panels run by the University of Florida horticulture department felt it was sour and tasteless. The Florida cartel put up with the UgliRipe for a couple of years, but panicked when its sales picked up. In 2003, the Florida Tomato Committee ordered him to stop exporting UgliRipes. Procacci, who already had seven hundred acres in the ground, had to feed $3 million worth to the cows. "I guess the cattle were eating better tomatoes than humans," he said. In 2007, the Florida Department of Agriculture relented and allowed Procacci to sell the UgliRipe under a program that protects unusual varieties. By then, lots of other niche tomatoes—many of them grown in greenhouses—were sucking oxygen out of the Florida retail market.

Exports from Mexico have increased steadily since the 1960s—tripling from 246 million in 1964 to 749 million in 1973, and to 2 billion pounds in 2007. Florida wasn't about to accept that. In the 1970s, its growers sought federal legislation that would have forced Mexican growers to use the same packing boxes they did. Ostensibly, the bill was intended to eliminate disparities in fruit size and grade. In fact, it meant to shut the Mexicans down. The "vine-ripe" tomatoes that Mexican growers picked were several days riper than the Florida gassed-greens, which meant they had to be packed tighter to make the thirteen-hour trip from the Culiacán area to Nogales, Arizona. To comply with the Florida standards, Mexican growers in effect would have had to switch to the Florida system, with its ethylene and hard green tomatoes. A major grower at a Florida Tomato Committee meeting delivered the bottom line: "We're trying to eliminate our competition. Let's face it. That's what we're trying to do."

At an October 1977 hearing of the U.S. House agriculture committee, the Florida delegation faced blanket opposition. Rep. Morris Udall of Utah said the bill was gross protectionism that would have raised prices for the "thick-skinned, gas-ripened tomato, which has become a symbol of consumer discontent. Many consumers are growing their own tomatoes rather than buying this tasteless product." The Florida delegation moaned that unless the regulations were changed, their growers would go out of business. In fact, the market was growing for both Florida and Mexico. Roughly 85 percent of the areas east of the Mississippi were served by Florida tomatoes in the October–June months, with about the same percentage in the West buying Mexican products. Arizona shippers and packers were tied in to the Mexican industry, which also bought most of its pesticides, fertilizer, and farm equipment from American dealers.

Following the North American Free Trade Agreement of 1993 and the subsequent crash of the Mexican peso, Mexican tomato imports again jumped, and Florida again brought out its lobbyists, legislators, and lawyers to try to damp down the competition. This time, they accused the Mexicans of dumping tomatoes at an unfair price.

The basic problem remained that the Florida tomato industry had shrink-wrapped itself into mediocrity. As supermarkets expanded to five or six or a dozen varieties of tomatoes of different shape, color, and flavor, Florida tomatoes were often the least desirable. The era in which the consumer notion of a beautiful tomato was a uniform one was over. But the flawed Florida tomato still had one loyal customer: the fast-food business, which wanted big, firm tomatoes that could be sliced thinly, maximizing the tomato-to-hamburger ratio. To meet those requirements, Florida growers were all about increasing their yields of big, heavy, firm tomatoes. But firmness and size, unfortunately, are genetic strangers to flavor. Breeding for firmness means more pericarp and less locule. The more the Florida growers catered to the fast-food industry, the less their product interested any consumer with taste buds.

"There's a disconnect in this bizarre Florida system," said Harry Klee, a plant geneticist at the University of Florida in Gainesville. "The farmer is paid for size, and the marketing order says they have to be round. So there's no incentive for producing a better-tasting tomato. McDonald's specific demands drive production in Florida. McDonald's doesn't care about flavor. They want a round slice that fits on a burger. I don't want to give the impression that the farmers are deliberately trying to deplete flavor. But they could care less what the tomato tastes like because it's irrelevant for them in the system. They're paid to produce tons to ship around the country, and that runs counter to good quality flavor. Because, the bigger the tomato, the more the plant is maxed out—it only has so much photosynthetical capacity. The breeders have exceeded the capacity of the plant to pump carbon and nitrogen into the fruit."

This heartless logic was squeezing the Florida tomato industry, and the further you got down the food chain, the more suffocating the squeeze. At the bottom of the food chain was a sprawling, charmless town near the southwest tip of the Florida peninsula called Immokalee (rhymes with broccoli). Immokalee was forty miles northeast of Naples, one of the wealthiest cities in America. As for Immokalee, it resembled a middling banana company town in Honduras except that it lacked any public parks, gardens, or itinerant food vendors. The center of town was several square blocks of leaky trailers where workers lived ten or twelve to a room, trying to squeeze a few savings from their meager wages. There were a few convenience stores and places to wire home a few dollars at loan shark rates.

For many of the tomato pickers, the day started at the Fiesta Food Market, a shop on the corner of the gravel parking lot that's as close to a town square as you get in Immokalee. On a typical morning during the harvest, the place was bustling at 4:30 A.M., with three checkout girls and a bunch of people in the kitchen throwing tortillas on the griddle and pulling tamales out of boiling water. The $1.50 lunch they prepared for the tomato pickers consisted of a couple of thick tortillas, a container of beans, and a *tamal* in a paper bag. At 5:00 A.M., it was time to climb into one of the yellow school buses parked in the lot, where I found a dozen or so other guys already slumped in their seats. Half an hour later, the driver—a chain-smoking bruiser with facial scars and bad teeth— showed up with a chest full of ice and sodas. He revved up the motor and drove off into the darkness, headed east on Route 846. Twenty minutes or so out of town, the bus turned down a dirt road, through a metal gate, and past orange groves and fields. It stopped for a while at a storage shed, and the workers milled about aimlessly in the dawn light. By the time they reached the work site, a vast tomato field of 150 acres or more, it was 7:00 A.M. No one was being paid for the transit time.

The harvest that day was for 6Ls, a big shipper owned by a family that's known in Fort Myers for its philanthropy. But the benevolent owners were far away that day. The boss was a labor contractor, Yzaguirre Brothers Trucking, and brother José was giving orders. As the sun came up, he passed out orange plastic *cubetas* to each of the twenty men and five women on the bus. He picked up a single whitish green tomato, about four inches in diameter. "Nothing smaller than this," he said. Then he pointed to the fields, and the pickers trotted out and started picking.

Certainly there are more difficult jobs than picking tomatoes. Hauling bloody sides of beef up a slippery metal staircase in a Nebraska stockhouse, maybe. Using your bare hands to scrap oil tankers on a beach in Pakistan. Even so, I'm glad I don't have to pick tomatoes for a living. I wonder whether those who perform this backbreaking labor wouldn't be grateful if mechanization forced them to get another job.

The machine harvest of table tomatoes, as opposed to the canning tomatoes that Jack Hanna worked with, has so far been impossible—not that it hasn't been tried. Florida agricultural extension agents started experimenting with a mechanical harvester in 1966, and a few years later, the Johnson Farm Machinery Company adapted its processing tomato harvester for table tomatoes by putting rubber tubing over the metal parts and polyurethane strips on the side walls to prevent bruising and shaking. Clemson University professors designed a machine specifically for fresh-market tomato harvest, and in 1971, Florida breeders developed the MH-1 for machine harvest. This tomato, a hybrid of the Walter and the Heinz 3, a processing tomato, had the *j-2* jointless gene and good firmness. In taste trials, consumers couldn't tell the difference. But the machine performed well only when the tomato vines were first cut and allowed to dry a few days before they were harvested. In California's Central Valley, where the skies were clear and irrigation was stopped before the harvest, the plants were usually shriveling, the ground dry when the harvester came through. In Florida, rain could come at any time. The precut plants were drier and less bulky for the harvester, and cutting the plant stopped osmosis and thus weakened the bond holding the fruit onto the stem.

In the end, the losses in Florida were too high to convince farmers to replace their field hands with machines. While the MH-1 produced a fairly concentrated set, the yield of a single machine harvest was still much lower than what the vines could produce in three, four, or even five hand harvests—with market prices going up and down all the while. And there was a lot of damage to the mechanically harvested fruit. Florida tomatoes were grown on rocky or sandy soils. Wet sand scuffed the tomatoes on their path through the harvester.

By 2009, low-wage stoop labor continued to occupy thousands

of people in the tomato industry. In Florida, nearly all of them were first-generation immigrants, Indians from southern Mexico and Guatemala who barely spoke Spanish, let alone English, some right off the boat or the smuggler's van, working to pay off the extortionist debts charged by the notorious *polleros*. Some were slaves kept in trailers by the *polleros*, chained up at night and permitted to leave only to work. Over the decade ending in 2008, police, aided by worker activists, freed more than one thousand workers from seven slavery rings. A peculiar twist in the evolutionary history of humans and their cultivars had brought these grunts of the tomato industry up from places where indigenous people had been growing tomatoes on their ancestral lands for millennia.

They were not entirely defenseless. A remarkable grassroots labor organization, the Coalition of Immokalee Workers, has been fighting since 1993 to end the worst of the exploitation and has made some headway. But progress is painfully slow. Since the late 1970s, workers in the Florida tomato fields have received an average of 40 cents per thirty-five-pound pail of tomatoes. Although yields have gone up since then, which makes it easier to pick more tomatoes in a given period, real wages have been stagnant. But low wages are only part of the tragedy of the tomato fields. The coalition, which started when eight workers started meeting with two labor lawyers, came into its own in the winter of 1996. Fed up with beatings and scumbag labor contractors who stiffed the workers on their wages, the coalition found a simple principle to bring together thousands of uneducated workers who normally competed against each other in the existential, Hobbesian fashion. "We decided," organizer Lucas Benitez told me, "that a blow against one of us is a blow against us all."

One afternoon in 1996, a hulking labor contractor busted a scrawny

Guatemalan guy's nose for the crime of stopping work to get a drink of water without permission. That proved to be the spark that catalyzed worker solidarity. The blow wasn't anything new; there were a dozen cases like this every season. But this time, five hundred workers descended on the labor contractor's house that night, with Benitez and other coalition members leading the way. They waved the worker's bloody shirt over their heads. The contractor didn't come to the door; the next day, he couldn't find anyone to get into his bus to pick his tomatoes. "The bosses and contractors noticed," Benitez told me in 2008. "Since then, we haven't had a single incident like that. We used the people's power. We're poor and we don't have any government support. The only power we have is our own."

Benitez, when I met him, was a muscular, handsome, brown-skinned thirty-two-year-old with spiky black hair cut in a fade and dark, alert eyes with deep creases under the brows. His neat beard and mustache recalled old photographs of Pancho Villa, though he wore a T-shirt bearing the likeness of Emiliano Zapata. As students of Mexican history know, Zapata was the selfless peasant revolutionary who remained loyal to his constituents. (In keeping with the tragic bent of Mexican history, he was also the first to be betrayed.) Benitez grew up in the town of Arcelia, a six-hour bus ride from Mexico City in the *tierra caliente* of lowland Guerrero state. At sixteen, he chased the tomato harvest to Immokalee, following three generations of his mother's family. While his sister and parents continue to raise corn, beans, and squash on a small piece of land back home—his grandfather still speaks Nahuatl—four of his brothers are with him in Immokalee. Their campaign has generated a lot of publicity for Benitez and his partners, and while engaging with outsiders is an important part of the task they've set for themselves, they give off an impassive, Zapataesque air.

Though courteous to visiting journalists and the like, they don't seem overly interested in pleasing them.

The coalition operated out of a sprawling storefront next to the central parking lot. It ran a small grocery, whose low prices have forced other stores in town to cut theirs, and its carpeted hall with couches, folding chairs, and reading material was open to anyone. At Wednesday night meetings, the coalition might play a Marxism-tinged Mexican TV documentary about the North American Free Trade Agreement, followed by a discussion about how NAFTA was relevant to their lives. Then they'd discuss upcoming collective actions, and the humblest workers there could talk about conditions in the fields. Haitian, Guatemalan, and Mexican workers mingled with do-gooder twenty-somethings in an atmosphere resembling a college dormitory or a political campaign office. The coalition ran a radio station out of a trailer in the back, broadcasting in languages like Creole, Popti, and Canjobel. Everyone was friendly and open and vague about how they got to the United States. "Same way as everybody else," a coalition leader told me. "Like a feather in the wind."

The coalition was very focused on its constituents. It had its ear to the ground, ready to take action whenever it heard about abuses, and its activists weren't shy about calling in the authorities when laws were broken. Working in conjunction with sheriff's deputies and FBI agents, the coalition had broken up three slave rings. One November night, I made the rounds of town with Gerardo Reyes, a tall, scraggly-bearded Mexican with big ears and a sweet face. Work hours were over, and we found men resting side by side on bare mattresses on the concrete floors of their trailers. The buildings were unpainted and the wooden trim was rotting; it was slum housing of the worst kind, much of it owned by a single Anglo family. A dozen guys might pay $150 per month each to live in a twelve-by-ten-foot trailer with cold-water plumbing. The advantage, since they couldn't afford cars or even bicycles, was that they were a short walk to the morning pickup spot. "You leave home at four A.M., work all day, get home, and sleep piled up in a tiny room with ten or twelve people you don't know. It's very lonely," a Mayan from Guatemala told me. Guatemalan Indians, whose culture tends to low-key introversion, had to share close quarters with brassy, profane Mexican guys. "You hear things you don't want to hear," he said. "I had a hard time dealing with the Mexicans at first. They're different from us."

As we walked through the trailer park, one guy was stripped to the waist outside his trailer, shaving with a hand mirror. Another sat in a folding lawn chair listening to the radio. Reyes handed them pink cards inviting them to the weekly meeting. It promised free juice and a discussion of what free trade meant to poor folks like them.

In 1997, the coalition organized a hunger strike that got local media attention and forced one company to rescind a pay cut. But it soon became clear that strikes would not bring growers to the bargaining table. At a strategy meeting, a worker named Virgilio Hernández came up with the idea of taking their plight directly to American consumers through the tomato retailers and restaurants that served the consumers. The workers would launch an attack on the brands. It was a long, frustrating campaign, but within a decade, it had started to blossom and gain momentum. The plainspoken eloquence of Benitez and his comrades attracted the sympathy and involvement of hundreds of liberal church members and student activists—as well as the ear of progressive congressmen like Senators Dick Durbin (D-Ill.) and Bernie Sanders (I-Vt.). After a series of protests and letter-writing campaigns, in 2005, Yum Brands, which owned Taco Bell, KFC, and Long John Silver's, agreed to pay a penny a pound more for Florida tomatoes. It would

pay the workers directly through a third-party administrator who veri-
fied which workers picked whose tomatoes. In 2007, McDonald's caved
in to the protesters, signing an agreement to pay the extra penny and to
help ensure humane and decent working conditions. In late 2007, when
I visited the coalition, the organization was locked on to its third target,
Miami-based Burger King.

The coalition hoped that when enough big-name brands agreed to
their demands, the action would catalyze an across-the-board increase
in the piece rate. "It's the first time in the history of the world that a
company has paid directly out of its pocket to the lowest position in its
supply chain," Benitez told me. But the coalition's enemies were fighting back. Burger King and the growers were telling reporters that the
farmworkers made $12 to $18 an hour, which seemed wildly inflated. In
the first few days of the "crown harvest," when the plants were heavily
bedecked with fruit, a very good worker might make $12 an hour, but
to get that, you'd have to haul in three tons of tomatoes in an eight-hour
day (from what I saw, a really strong picker could pick two tons).

As he spoke to the hundred or so guys who showed up at the coalition's headquarters that night, Benitez asked how many planned to stay
in the United States for a year. Everyone raised a hand. "I came here
thirty years ago for a year," said an older guy in a cowboy hat. "I've still
got nothing, and I can't find work." Benitez asked, "How many of you
make twelve dollars an hour?" Nobody budged. They had a laugh over a
guy who used to be paid $12 an hour gutting chickens. He fought with
his wife, and now he had nothing—"no chickens, no *gallina*, no job,
and no money." Turning Burger King's claim on its head, the coalition
asked the workers to collect their old shoes to ceremonially dump them
on the steps of Burger King's corporate headquarters in Miami. "These
aren't twelve-dollar-an-hour shoes," Benitez said. "They smell, sure. But

the smell is evidence of the honest work you did to put food in front of your families. If we don't show our reality, who's going to do it for us?"

Although the coalition wasn't asking them to pay anything more, the Florida growers bitterly resisted its campaign. The growers have complained for forty years that low-cost Mexican growers were threatening their livelihood, and the squeeze had clearly intensified in recent years. "The costs are eating us alive and we can't pass them along," said Tony DiMare. He ticked off a list of major producers who'd left the business in the past two years: Taylor and Fulton, Big Red Tomato, Thomas Produce, Ruskin Vegetable Corp., Mecca. "All of our purchasers want assurances. Nobody wants to pay for them. Everything is scrutinized for the bottom line."

DiMare had no sympathy for the coalition, which he described as a "small faction." Their campaign against the restaurant industry was "a farce," he said. "Their agreement with Yum hasn't had an effect. But they've been smart about publicity, going after churches and universities that aren't knowledgeable about the issues." The October day I visited DiMare at his company's warehouse in Apollo Beach, he handed me a news release from the Florida Tomato Growers Association announcing that the members would not cooperate with the coalition's penny-a-pound agreement. Not only that, but they also threatened $10,000 fines against any of their members who took part in it. They'd hired a public relations firm—one with experience combating Cesar Chavez in California—which advised them that the agreement violated antitrust laws.

"We can't have restaurant chains negotiating on behalf of our employees," DiMare said. Besides, the checks the workers got from Yum Brands "were smaller than what it would cost to cash them. We're talking two fifty, a dollar twenty-five. Taco Bell didn't give a shit; they just wanted to get the coalition off their backs. The bad publicity was affecting their sales."

In other words, the coalition had been smart enough to figure out how to exact better wages in a very different environment from the one that, say, Cesar Chavez had operated in: Unions had less power, but corporate image could be leveraged. The tomato industry's response was something it called the SAFE program (Socially Accountable Farm Employers), which promised safe produce and safe working conditions, DiMare said. "For the most part, our industry has always done the right thing. We've contributed to a lot of causes that go back to the workers and their families." He cited charity golf tournaments. As for the coalition's strategy, he clearly saw it as threatening. "The wages we pay," DiMare said, "are none of your business."

Of course, gigantic buyers like McDonald's did have the power to get into the growers' business. They could in effect ban the use of certain pesticides, require highly demanding safety audits at repacking plants, specify tests to check for salmonella. Indeed, DiMare told me that some of his operations were subject to seven separate audits. When I spoke with Benitez and his colleagues at the coalition, they inverted the argument. How was it that a company like Burger King or Safeway could pressure its suppliers to make sure their products were organic, pesticide-free, or humanely treated if the products were animals, but couldn't force its suppliers to certify that the workers who picked their fruits and vegetables weren't enslaved or treated like dirt? Chipotle, the high-end Mexican-fast-food chain, promised to humanely treat its free-range chickens and pigs before it slaughtered them for burritos. But its "food with integrity" program did not include a guarantee of decent labor conditions.

By 2008, pressure was building on Burger King and the tomato growers. At a Senate hearing in March, Dick Durbin called conditions in Immokalee "a national disgrace." Ted Kennedy noted that his brother Robert had made the conditions of the rural poor a focus of his 1968 campaign for president. In the 1950s, Edward Murrow had drawn attention to the conditions in Immokalee with his famous documentary *Harvest of Shame*. "Too little has changed over the years," Kennedy said.

That April, I returned to southern Florida to witness another demonstration at Burger King. But I wanted to see for myself what the coalition was protesting about, which is how I found myself getting dressed in a room at the Immokalee Inn one morning at 4:30 A.M.

Late April is pretty much the end of the season around Immokalee. The first harvest is the best, from the worker's perspective, because the tomatoes ripen from the top of the plant, which means the first crop is right in front of you. They are big ones, too, because, depending on market conditions, the farmers wait to harvest until the first tomatoes are big (which means that some of the later tomatoes are also *big enough* to be No. 1s). It takes fewer big tomatoes to fill a bucket, so the work is faster and you get paid more. We were the fourth crew to work this field. There were still plenty of tomatoes, but most of them were smaller, and you had to reach deep into the lower part of the bush to get them. Luckily, it was an overcast day.

As we set out into the field, no one I asked could say with certainty what we would be paid. As far as I could gather, the labor contractors had created a sliding pay scale that mixed piece rate and hourly wages in a way that was guaranteed to keep wages as low as legally possible. When you worked the crown harvest, the wage was 45 cents per bucket, period. But today, we'd get $50 plus 45 cents per bucket, one of the guys told me. Others said we'd get the flat rate plus 10 cents per bucket. The boss didn't tell us anything, and no one asked.

Sensing right away that I didn't know what I was doing, Yzaguirre assigned an older guy to watch over me. Fabiano, who was from Mexico City, had kind, world-weary blue eyes and dark, leathery skin. Like the other practiced pickers, Fabiano worked by stooping from the waist and jamming his hands into the bush. He seemed to know by instinct where to feel for the biggest tomatoes, pulling them off with a twist that freed the tomato from the stem. Fabiano would place his bucket underneath the vine on the raised bed, shoving it along the bed as he moved, so the tomatoes fell into the bucket as it filled up and he didn't have to move it more than a time or two. All of that was easier to do when you were barely five feet tall. I found it worked better if I got on my knees.

After I'd turned in a couple of buckets that contained tomatoes with stems attached, José came over to yell at me: No stems, *Cuba*. But I never perfected the brisk movement required to snap a green tomato off the vine without taking stem with it. To pinch off the stem, I sometimes had to dig my nail into it. By the end of the day, my cuticles were black and bleeding. My clothes and face and hands were also black, from chlorophyll and other substances in the vine and tomatoes.

Fabiano was fifty-eight years old. He'd worked as a file clerk in Mexico's National Archive, but the pension wasn't enough to support his family. He told me he'd been in Florida for seventeen years and his wife had ditched him in the meantime, but still he sent her and their children money sometimes. He moved fast, filling his bucket, bending over, and, with a single fluid motion, hoisting the container onto his shoulder, the other hand lightly slung over the top to keep the overflowing tomatoes from spilling out.

Then he'd jog to the truck—during the first pick, when they're working straight piece rate, they run—skipping over the raised beds, sometimes a distance of fifty feet or more, and toss the *cubeta* up to the catcher on the truck—the *dumpeador*—who immediately dumped it into a plastic crate that would be filled with one thousand pounds of tomatoes. The same catcher put a small, yellow plastic ticket into each empty bucket and tossed it back down.

The work never stopped. Tossing, catching, emptying. Sticking the ticket in your pocket. If you had a hole in your pocket, you lost your tickets and your pay.

A guy from Chiapas with gold teeth and a little ponytail was covering the row across from me. He worked fast, and his hand was always feeling and snatching the tomatoes before mine did. I tried to kid him, calling him an *acaparador de tomates* (tomato hoarder). He barely cracked a smile. I asked him why he filled his bucket so full every time. "They want it that way," he said. And that was it.

I made it to lunch without much difficulty, but after that, I started to slow down. By 2:00, I was starting to stagger. I had to stop twice to buy a soda off the bus driver. He charged $1 for each. There was water available, but I needed sugar. It became obvious that the bosses were going easy on me because I was a tall, bearded white guy who might represent someone who could give them trouble. Surrounded by a squad of small, brown men with worn clothes and hands, I alone got charity. Eventually, I gathered that the other pickers were glad to have me there, as a buffer against abuse.

Sometimes, when their own buckets were full, they'd take pity on me and toss a couple of tomatoes into mine.

The last two hours I couldn't think of anything except one question: "When is this going to end?"

Ya merito terminamos, somebody told me. "We'll be done soon."

A little while later: *Ya merito*—"in an hour."

Destino cruel.

At 4:30 P.M., eleven hours after the bus had left the Immokalee parking lot and nine-and-a-half hours after we started working, Yzaguirre called it an eight-hour day. Everyone sat down at the end of the row and counted his or her little yellow tickets. I had picked 59 buckets. Most of the men had 110 or 120. The women averaged around 90.

It turned out they were paying $50 plus 15 cents per bucket. Yzaguirre handed me a $50 bill and seven ones; I realized later that I'd been gypped out of nearly a dollar. Gold Teeth picked 120, and got $68.

Earlier in the day, when I was still compos mentis enough to count, I estimated that each of those buckets had about one hundred tomatoes in it. So I'd picked about six thousand tomatoes, roughly a ton. In a supermarket, if they ended up there, those tomatoes might retail for $3 per pound. Six thousand dollars' worth of tomatoes. On the bus ride back to town, I asked Fabio, "Why does everyone work so hard, when the guy who picked twice as many as me only got ten dollars more?" He raised his eyebrows. "Because they have to," he said. "You saw how they drove us. Some of these people have families. They can't afford to get in trouble."

"You coming back tomorrow?" he asked.

We got back to the parking lot twelve hours after we left it, and I bid farewell to a few of my coworkers. I stopped by coalition headquarters, bought a soda, and pulled up a folding chair. Benitez looked me over with a bemused air and deduced that I had spent the day in the fields. "How many buckets did you fill?" he asked. I venture that for a rookie, fifty-nine wasn't bad. He laughed. "Is that all? My first time I brought in a hundred." He tapped his fingers on the desk and furrowed his brow. "Will you be at Burger King tomorrow?"

Leaving Immokalee, I felt a little like the couples in those horror movies watching as the green highway signs of Salem, Massachusetts, fade in the rearview mirror. Economically, the trip hadn't really paid off. Out of the $57, I spent $31 on dinner at a Day's Inn in Miami that night. Filling the rental car gas tank finished off the rest of my earnings. It would take four days and a lot of soap to get the black stains off my hands.

The next day, I felt pampered as I drove in air-conditioned splendor through Miami traffic to Burger King's headquarters to watch the demonstration. The workers were getting off buses and vans, some people carrying a long, brown-paper petition signed by 84,952 people demanding that the fast-food giant pay another penny a pound for the tomatoes it bought. I couldn't have agreed more.

That morning, the *Fort Myers News-Press* had run a front-page story that outed a Burger King vice president named Steve Grover. It seemed that Grover, by day a mild-mannered flak who produced reassuring explanations for why a socially responsible company like Burger King couldn't pay a bit more for its tomatoes, by night transformed himself into a blogger who posted venomous attacks on the coalition's leadership, under an alias set up on his daughter's computer. In comments on various Web sites, Grover called the coalition "bloodsuckers" and claimed they were lining their pockets with the additional payments from Yum. "This is libelous, because he knew it was untrue," said Greg Abed, a bearded, low-key coalition attorney. (He picked watermelons with Reyes and Benitez a couple of months a year—the activists didn't want to get too soft and alienated from their roots by doing office work all the time.) As the marchers paraded in front of the headquarters on a small corporate side street off Highway 836, Reyes took the microphone. "Burger King has the obligation to clarify if the words of their vice president reflect the position of the company," he said. "They should come down and say it to our faces instead of hiding like cowards in the shadows of the Internet."

A month later, after a series of embarrassing revelations about the company's efforts to infiltrate an agent provocateur into the coalition, Burger King caved in, signing an agreement with the workers to pay the extra penny and require safe and humane treatment. Whole Foods and Subway followed suit a few months later. By early 2009, the Coalition of Immokalee Workers had started a "Chipocrisy tour" to win concessions from Denver-based Chipotle—which agreed to the coalition's terms in September 2009. The Immokalee workers had become a cause célèbre for foodies: *Gourmet* magazine ran a feature deploring their plight, and a delegation of anticorporate food activists (the type who would *never* allow a Florida tomato to pass their lips), led by author Francis Moore Lappé (author of *Diet for a Small Planet*), came to visit and hold a news conference.

The campaign was doing well, yet its ultimate success was in doubt. For one thing, it was not an easy time to be organizing poor immigrant workers in America. While no one was too agitated about the presence of illegal laborers in Immokalee—no one else would pick the tomatoes if these guys didn't—raids in nearby cities continued to strike fear in the hearts of immigrants. In 2006, a Fort Myers Unitarian minister, the Rev. Wayne Robinson, held a community meeting attended by five hundred immigrants and their children. "We told them, 'Call the police if you've been attacked, go to the hospital if you're sick.' Well, a week later, ICE [the Immigration and Customs Enforcement agency] came in and arrested 170 people, though they only had warrants for 26. When I tried to hold a community meeting again a year later, nobody showed up. Two children came, saying their parents had sent them to collect information. That was it. The fear was inordinate."

The coalition's work may have raised morale among the workers, but it hasn't necessarily improved their material conditions much. At the Burger King rally, I met a guy named Bernabe Morales who hadn't been able to work for five months because of illness. To make ends meet, he'd become a consignment agent for a nutritional supplements company that used multilevel marketing to push its products. Morales was paying $200 a month to live in a single room with twelve other guys, stacked in bunk beds. He'd come all the way from a tiny village in Chiapas to end up in this job, trying to separate his compatriots from a few of their hard-earned dollars in exchange for snake oil. "It prevents allergies, gut pains, any kind of illness. The guys I live with are constantly getting sick, cuz it's hard work and they're exposed to all kinds of chemicals." He'd become a postmodern *curandero*, selling mumbo-jumbo to people who had no health insurance or access to doctors.

Robinson, whose congregation included many wealthy vegetable growers, saw the situation as tense and likely to get worse. "Everyone's caught in a difficult spiral," he said. "Agriculture is very labor intensive. There are no machines to pick these tomatoes. Customers demand products at the cheapest price. But it seems to me that a penny a pound is a reasonable increase to pay for those who do this work. The only people who will do this stoop labor are desperate Hispanics from other countries." At the same time, "the whole immigrant issue has become a veiled form of racism. Lou Dobbs [the CNN commentator who frequently railed against immigration] has done a huge amount of damage and we're suffering consequences in so many ways—it's hard for them to get labor, all up the east and west coasts of Florida."

The immigration squeeze was also ruining mid-Atlantic tomato operations, some of which had been in existence for decades. "Let me tell you, there is no local labor that is going to go out and harvest those tomatoes in ninety-degree temperatures except our immigrant labor," said Keith Eckel, who was the last major fresh-market tomato grower in Pennsylvania to quit the business in 2008. Frank Furman, a fourth-generation tomato canner from Northumberland, Pennsylvania (the family's tomato cans have been sold since 1962 under the brand-name Furmano's, to make them sound Italian), said it was hard to find hands. "People are afraid to work," he told me during a visit to the cannery. "When ICE comes, even the legitimate people get their records run." Later that day, I watched a bunch of white guys on work-release from prison run a harvester through a field of Furmano's tomatoes. They were the only workers available.

Would the public want to pay more for crappy Florida tomatoes, especially when there were so many higher-quality alternatives? Unlikely. Or maybe Burger King would source more of its tomatoes to Mexico, where wages and working conditions were lower. And more Florida growers would fold their operations. "If I'm sitting at Taco Bell and can go to south Texas or Mexico and pay twenty-five cents less per box, what will happen?" asked Fritz Roka, a University of Florida economist. "How can you insist that a farmworker in Mexico or Ecuador or Vietnam get that extra penny? So the coalition has won a victory, but if production stops and goes somewhere else, the farmworker is left with nothing."

Thirty years ago, farmworkers organized themselves out of jobs in California. Now, according to Jay Scott, there were renewed efforts to develop a machine-harvestable table tomato for Florida. In a decade or two, there may be no tomato industry in Florida. Or maybe the machine will have taken over.

CHAPTER FIVE

Fried Gene Tomatoes

Rin changed the world of tomatoes completely.

—Kanti Rawal

 KANTI RAWAL TOLD ME HIS LIFE STORY IN A SERIES OF
conversations we had in Mexico and California. He'd been
a debate team star back in his village in India, and he knew
how to get good traction out of a yarn, which, coupled with
a genuine interest in other people and ideas, made him fun to be
around. When I asked why one tomato was sweet and another tasted
like gasoline, we'd end up talking about Darwin, Kant, and Galileo.
I sometimes had trouble following his train of thought, but it also
seemed to deposit me somewhere interesting. As an immigrant,
Kanti had had to fight hard for his education and professional standing, but being an outsider must have been liberating, too, because
other people withhold their judgment when they're not sure whether

an immigrant's idiosyncrasies are the products of brilliance, insanity, or a different culture.

Some years ago, Kanti said, he'd been in London with his family when he suddenly was fired by a desire to make a speech at Hyde Park Speakers' Corner. In a way, he was discharging an ideal of democracy that his father had instilled in him. Kanti had read as a boy about how Churchill and Nehru and Krishna Menon cut their teeth as crowd wranglers at Hyde Park. He didn't really have anything to get off his chest, but what the hell—he was an extrovert. So he got up on a box and began to harangue a few dozen people with a fire-and-brimstone rant. His family, in the meantime, had carefully ensconced themselves at a healthy distance. He began, "'Rejoice, you sinners of the corrupt universe! For I have arrived to retrieve your souls from eternal damnation.'"

Kanti is not a particularly religious person, but he knew he'd get a rise out of the Londoners, who generally don't take well to fundamentalists. He kept going on like that, infusing his speech with all the essential nonsense of dogmatic religion, with people yelling and calling him a wanker, until finally a Jamaican guy came up and said, "That's my box you're standing on." Kanti thanked him, got down, and then went to have tea.

Kanti was an intellectual hybrid—part revolutionary anarchist, part capitalist, and equal parts technology geek, flower child, and good-time Charlie. His approach to ideas and life in general bore the existential stamp of his life's subject. As in breeding, some of his ideas were good, some probably bad, and some were good but would never work.

He grew up in Unjha, a town of eight thousand in an area of Gujarat state that supplies the world with guar gum, cumin, coriander, and other spices. His father had returned from Karachi to Gujarat when Karachi became part of Pakistan in 1947. Having survived the mass murders and migrations of Hindus and Muslims, his father set up a fabric shop and provided free astrology readings. Local politicians also consulted this astute and mellow follower of Gandhi. The house was full of books by Poe, Emerson, Dickens, Hardy, and Shakespeare. Kanti got undergraduate degrees in chemistry and botany at colleges in Ahmedabad. In 1956, riots broke out as protesters, Kanti among them, demanded that Gujarat get its own state, rather than being part of Bombay. A guy standing next to Kanti was shot and killed. Kanti ran, was clubbed by a policeman, escaped, and went underground for four months. The experience left him with a suspicion of authority.

In 1965 he left for the United States, where he intended to go to graduate school. The first stop was his uncle's house in Stamford, Connecticut, where a cousin gave him a tour of the town that included the new car wash. "The latest technology! We had no car in India. But the whole idea of this was strange to me. Just wash the damn car!" His uncle's neighbors were Italian and made delicious pizza. Kanti, who'd eaten a lot of tomatoes in stews back in India, quickly became a fan. After a year in Oklahoma, he found a place at the University of Illinois-Champaign-Urbana, where he studied plant breeding and genetics under Jack Harlan. "He was like a father to me. He gave me the academic freedom to study anything I wanted." Kanti read anthropology, archaeology, history. In 1968, while he was on a summer fellowship at UC Berkeley, two of Kanti's friends died in Vietnam. Overnight he became a bitter opponent of the war. He had arrived in California wearing dark pants, white shirt, and tie, the uniform of the international student grind. "When I came back to Illinois I wore bellbottoms and purple shirts. I was transformed. I had long hair and was noncomformist." He read Thomas Jefferson and Henry David Thoreau and was fed up with war and U.S. belligerency. But he published his papers and completed his studies. "That's what I love about America. There may have been people on my committee who disagreed with my views, but no one tried to keep me from getting my Ph.D."

Still, Kanti was eager to leave the country. When the Rockefeller Foundation offered him a chance to work on agricultural projects in Ibadan, Nigeria, he jumped at it. "I went there with a fancy background and I ended up planting cowpeas right in the ground"—something he'd never done before. Cowpeas were a staple bean in many parts of Africa. Kanti collected cowpea land-races—varieties that had slowly been adapted from their wild forms for use in particular geographic locations and soils—from all over Africa. The Rockefeller Foundation was trying to make sure that the super-seeds it developed to create a Green Revolution in Africa didn't drive out valuable native crops. (The Green Revolution, though a mixed success in India and Latin America, went nowhere in Africa—farmers couldn't afford hybrid seed and fertilizer.)

"This was a transformative experience for me," Kanti recalled. "I'd pull into a village in my Land Rover with a guide. I'd stay with the Peace Corps or other volunteers. I carried a bunch of beer. I made lifelong friendships. When they came to Ibadan, they stayed at my house. I'd come home after a month on the road and there'd be thirty people and all their backpacks and their clothes and smells and everything lying around." He also brought Chef Boyardee pizza sauce to every flyspeck village he visited. "Whenever I came to someone's house, they got so excited. We made pizza on the spot, even if we didn't have yeast for the dough. They hadn't invented takeaway pizza then. Before takeaway pizza, the processing tomato industry had no scope. Did you know that even into the 1970s, 60 percent of the bulk tomato paste was sold to the U.S. military?" Kanti was bringing tomato sauce to the masses, and the masses liked it, something he'd remember later at Del Monte.

Kanti grew out four thousand varieties of cowpeas and cataloged them with the help of a computer program he developed that tracked all their variations. He met his future wife, Jeyamma Srinivasan, a Tamil-speaking mathematician who taught at the university. The cataloging project led Kanti to his first tomato-related job when the U.S. Department of Agriculture invited him to Boulder, Colorado, in 1975 to help computerize its plant genetic resources. "I couldn't do any breeding in Nigeria, and my wife was fed up with the country. She was a star mathematician and they treated her like shit because she was a woman. So I said, 'Let's go back to the States.'"

When Kanti was a graduate student in Illinois, IBM punch cards—the programming technology that preceded more modern computer languages—were still the norm. Kanti remembered winter nights when he'd bike to the computer lab. Once or twice, he slipped on the ice and scattered the cards in the snow. There'd be no choice but to start all over, arranging them in the precise order. By the time he got to Boulder, however, computer technology had advanced substantially. Kanti helped organize a database of tomato genes to help classify the thousands of varieties in the USDA's collection. Kanti's mentor, Jack Harlan, was a good friend of Charley Rick, and Rick gave his blessing to the project. But in 1980, Kanti's group lost its UN Food and Agriculture Organization funding. "It was time for me to move anyway. The five-year itch."

His next stop was San Leandro, California, where Del Monte had moved its agricultural research laboratory after shifting its tomato operations from the Midwest. The tomatoes were processed at a brand-new cannery in Modesto. Kanti joined Del Monte as a plant breeder but soon branched into research and development. Del Monte turned out to be a good place for an intellectually curious, entrepreneurial type to work.

CEO Robert A. Fox encouraged employees from different departments to mix it up in search of higher value-added products. This hadn't always been the case. In the 1970s, Del Monte breeder Bill Hepler had found a mutation that resulted in a coreless tomato, known as the Murieta, on a ranch near Fresno. In those days, before hybrids, the culture of the breeding world was candid and open. "Everyone from Heinz to Campbell to Del Monte told you what they were doing," Kanti said. Hunt's used the Murieta trait to save millions in canning costs, but Hepler couldn't convince anyone at Del Monte that the quality was worthwhile.

Fox liked new ideas and products, though a lot of the innovations he stimulated ended up leaving Del Monte, too. "Bob would say, 'Why can't tomatoes be like a Walkman? Nice and small and clean? We should breed small tomatoes, put them in a glass jar, and people could see them.'" Around 1984, Kanti had a grape tomato that he developed for the cannery, but it was too small for a harvester to pick. He gave the seed to a Taiwanese friend. A company in Taiwan liked these tomatoes, and eventually someone started growing them in North Carolina, where Joe Procacci bought them out. Since the late 1990s, Procacci has made a bundle selling the little grape tomatoes that he calls "Santa Sweets." They aren't any sweeter than many of the hybrid grapes that Kanti has developed since then. Such are the breaks.

There were some successes, too. At one point, Kanti went to the marketing department and said, "I use tomatoes to make tomato curry sauce. What do Americans make with tomatoes?" The company created a profile of Americans' use of tomatoes and figured out that in most parts of the country, people used Del Monte's stewed tomatoes to make tomato sauce; in the Southwest, they made salsa. "So that made a lightbulb come on—'Why don't we make salsa and spaghetti sauce?'" This was in the mid-1970s, before corporations had started marketing

Ragú and other cheap bottled sauces. Instead of making sauces, Del
Monte dropped some spices in the cans and sold them as "Italian-style
tomatoes," or "Mexican-style tomatoes." They sold out quickly. "That
was my claim to fame at Del Monte," Kanti said. "I got stock options. It
added to my fame as well as my security."

When Kanti visited his colleagues in the Midwest, they would
invite him to their homes and offer him beautiful cherry and plum and
pear tomatoes from their hobby gardens. "I'd bring the tomatoes home
and give my boss some. He'd say, 'Why aren't we canning this? What
about the winter—don't they miss it?' That kind of created a whole new
feeling. 'Why is everybody growing a Roma-type processing tomato?'"
Kanti thought. "Why not can pear tomatoes, cherry tomatoes, yellow
tomatoes, orange tomatoes?"

Kanti looked at it from an engineering perspective. How could he
take a typical processing tomato—a determinate fruit with concentrated
set—and breed more consumer-friendly traits into it? He went to Rick
and Stevens at UC Davis, and they explained the possible pathways. "I
wanted to bring in weird, abnormal shapes and size and flavors. Frankly,
flavor was the last thing I thought of. Because even today, I daresay
that those who want pure, unadulterated tomato flavor are few and far
between, and they don't want it daily. If you were served heirloom tomatoes every day for three months of the summer, you'd probably say, 'Put
rosemary on it, put some mozzarella on it.' After a while, the flavor is
so intense it becomes intolerable. So the main concern was, could I get
a size and a shape that could be machine harvested? I started breeding grapes and cherries and pears, but it didn't work—they weren't firm
enough to withstand the machine handling. They fell apart at full ripe
stage; they got squished. You couldn't fit it into the existing system."

That left Kanti with a single idea, which he would spend the following decade and a half developing, first at Del Monte, then on his own: the yellow processing tomato. Fox, who made millions developing new products at other companies, including Foster Farms, was in Kanti's corner. "I was a new guy—one Indian amongst many chiefs," Kanti recalled. "We became social buddies. He wanted to come to my field trial—unusual for a CEO; he put on a baseball cap and walked in the field." Kanti, with the help of Rick and Stevens, had a machine-harvestable, Roma-shaped yellow tomato all ready to go: It had yield, brix, and firmness. "I said, 'Well, Mr. Fox, this is something that's very mellow in taste, flavorful, yet different.' Fox said, 'It tastes good. Why aren't we canning this?'"

And they might have. But then in 1986, Nabisco bought Del Monte. Its new corporate rulers gave Fox an office without a secretary. Fox left, Kanti left, and the yellow processing tomato went out the window. Kanti went to work for the French concrete company Sojetel, which had bought a seed company and aimed to revolutionize plant biotech. That was a big bust, and he was fired two years later. "Biotech in those days was a conceptual cult," he said. "The hoopla was that we'd bring marvels to the American dinner table. It was flying without your feet on the ground."

In the meantime, Kanti created his own seed company. He called it California Hybrids, in honor of Henry A. Wallace, the socialist corn breeder and founder of Pioneer Hybrids who later became President Franklin Roosevelt's vice president and ran for president himself in 1948. Kanti got his breeding material for free, from Rick's collection at UC Davis. He got his farming and food industry friends to grow and ship his yellow tomatoes. Joe Carcione, a legendary greengrocer at South San Francisco's wholesale market, praised his tomatoes. But the project collapsed after the first shipment. "I didn't realize how long it takes to get from S.F. to L.A. Then came the news—these things don't work. They're overripe. Overmature. They rejected the whole crop. I didn't get paid. I lost $38,000. I called my wife from the Apricot Tree, out at Five Points. That was an awakening—I'll never get into the business of selling products I'd derived from my own technology."

Years later, Kanti filed a patent on a yellow processing tomato and licensed the technology to a company he'd formed, SunRoma. By then, he'd figured out a less time-consuming way to find a good tomato. Jim Dick pointed out that there were always yellow mutants in a field of red Roma tomatoes—perhaps one in ten thousand would have a mutation in a particular enzyme, changing the tomatoes from red to yellow. After finding his mutant, Kanti got Small Planet Foods to grow three hundred acres of his tomatoes, to can them, and to market them with a nice logo. Albertson's and Safeway started putting them out on the shelf. But again, there was a rate-limiting step. The tomatoes weren't terribly profitable in their own right, and Kanti lacked the capital to make a yellow tomato soup or a golden ketchup. He made a deal with Del Monte to grow the tomatoes and make them into paste. But Del Monte's technology turned them brown, not golden. Brown ketchup was not thrilling to consumers. Then suddenly, there was interest—Heinz wanted to make a yellow Classico spaghetti sauce. Mitsui, a Japanese food giant, offered to buy everything he could produce. But before any of these deals could work out, Kanti ran out of money. He closed down SunRoma in 2005. "I didn't suffer any consequence except the loss of hope. And I still have $200,000 worth of seed in my garage. It could have worked if we had $5 million to launch the product."

Now, Kanti's yellow tomato sales are limited to seed catalogs and the ones that Mexican farmers grow for Del Cabo.

Back in 1988, though, Kanti found himself in the middle of a hot new opportunity. A group of biotech entrepreneurs in Davis had created a company, Calgene, that filed a patent for a gene they figured would revolutionize the fresh-tomato market. The polygalacturonase antisense gene, which slowed ripening, would allow them to sell tomatoes that could be picked red and stay firm until they got to the consumer. One of Calgene's leaders was a fellow University of Illinois alumnus named Ray Valentine, who hired Kanti as its tomato breeder. His job was to find tomatoes suitable for insertion of the antisense gene and to evaluate them in the field. Calgene was so confident of its genetic property that it went on a wild spending spree.

The idea of using laboratory biotechnology to insert a gene that deterred the ripening of the tomato—or the ripening of any fruit, for that matter—was a new one in 1988. The idea of breeding a slow-ripening tomato was not new, however. In fact, by the time Calgene filed its patent, the gas-green tomato was already losing market share to a genetically modified, slow-ripening tomato. But this tomato's novel gene came from tomatoes and had been bred into the fruit using traditional methods. It was genetically modified in the old-fashioned sense.

To understand how anti-ripening technology was introduced, it's worth first taking a step back to explain how the gas-green tomato got its start. Ethylene, which occurs naturally in fruit and catalyzes a series of steps in ripening, has been applied externally to ripen different kinds of fruit since the nineteenth century. Companies using kerosene burners on trainloads of oranges being transported from California to the East noticed that the heaters, in addition to keeping the oranges from freezing, turned green fruits orange. By the 1940s, after isolating ethylene as the active ingredient in this process, producers started using it to ripen green bananas and then other fruits, including tomatoes.

Florida had begun growing winter tomatoes for the East Coast in the late nineteenth century. For obvious reasons, you couldn't pick a tomato ripe when it wasn't going to be eaten for two or three weeks. Into the 1940s and beyond, the fruit were crated in tissue paper and shipped by boat and train. But when tomatoes are picked green, it's difficult to know just how ripe they actually are; experts have four categories of ripeness in green tomatoes—M1 is for immature green, for example, and M4 is for tomatoes on the verge of turning red. Before the use of ethylene, tomato shipments would arrive at northern warehouses in a mosaic of colors. They'd have to be sorted out every day, and some would never mature. Ethylene changed that. While it won't ripen the most immature tomatoes, exposing a warehouse full of the fruit to the gas kicks off ripening in most of them.

The process required some serious tweaking. When a man named Dwain Gull arrived at the University of Florida in 1958 as a professor of vegetable crops, ethylene was still being used in a crude and dangerous manner. The gas is extremely flammable in air at concentrations as low as 3 percent. "What they'd do is load the tomatoes into the warehouse, bring a cylinder up, and through a port in the wall would blast this raw ethylene with such a force that it would go clear to the other end of the room," Gull told me in a telephone interview from his home in Florida. "If it came in contact with an electrical motor that was arcing, well then—*kabam!*" On a few occasions, Gull arrived at the smoking hulk of a packinghouse converted by careless gassing into a heap of charred timbers and fried green tomatoes. Sometimes eighteen-wheelers would blow up when ethylene was pumped into trailers with refrigerator motors running.

Gull set up a system to carefully meter the gas, blending it with outside air as it was pumped into the warehouse at a concentration of roughly 100 parts per million. He maintained that these gassed "mature-green" tomatoes were just as tasty as tomatoes picked vine-ripe. Florida growers have long made this claim, but scientists who speculize in ana-lyzing tomato flavor dispute it. Mature-green tomatoes never fully ripen after harvest, because the sugars, acids, and volatile precursors like fatty acids are continuing to move from the leaves to the fruit at least through the "breaker" stage—the point at which the fruit starts to turn red. And many Florida tomatoes are picked well before the mature-green stage. These younger tomatoes lack the ethylene receptors that allow the gas to trigger the ripening phase. Studies have shown that only about 15 per-cent of the tomatoes harvested in Florida are at the ideal stage. Roughly a third are so immature they'll never ripen at all.

Bigger green tomatoes tend to be riper. Yet even if tomato pickers and their crew leaders could tell whether a tomato was ripe, they're being paid for picking tomatoes, ripe or not. "When they go in to pick they grab everything that's the same size or location on the plant," said Gull. "They get a little happy and get fruit off the vine that shouldn't be taken off the vine, from the standpoint of the consumer. We used to have a saying down here, 'Garbage brings the best price.' When you gotta have tomatoes you gotta have tomatoes, so you take what you can. The bad years the tomatoes are not very good but the price is highest, because of supply and demand." Adel Kader, a professor emeritus at UC Davis who's been studying fresh-market produce for forty years, put it like this: "The only reason the tomato industry survives in Florida is because the fast-food industry doesn't care what tomatoes taste like."

The gas-green tomato started coming under intense pressure in the early 1980s, when Mexican farmers adopted varieties that could be picked closer to ripeness while remaining firm on the shelf. The new varieties were based on work done in the late 1960s by scientists at

Purdue University in the laboratory of geneticist Edward C. Tigchelaar. At the USDA's experimental station in Geneva, New York, these scientists found tomato varieties that contained mutations in two genes affecting the tomato's ripening rate. One Tigchelaar called *rin*, shorthand for the "ripening inhibitor" gene, while the other became *nor* ("never ripening"). The two genes blocked the synthesis of ripening enzymes, including polygalacturonase, which breaks down pectin, a major component of the tomato wall, and in the process releases other enzymes involved in the cascade of ripening.

Yosef Mizrahi, now a biology professor at Ben Gurion University of the Negev in Israel, was among those who took Tigchelaar's gene further down the road. In 1973, Mizrahi was a postgraduate student at another lab in Purdue's horticulture department. He was studying pectin methylesterase, another ripening enzyme, with the aim of producing a tomato that could hold its juice and remain firm after being sliced and put on a hamburger bun. Tigchelaar, Mizrahi told me, believed that the *rin* gene, which was recessive, would not work when introduced into a normal tomato. In principle, this seemed to be true, but in practice, Mizrahi found that when he crossed the offspring of a hybrid of *rin* and normal tomatoes, he got some tomatoes that ripened, but slowly. "We said, 'Hello, we have here a genetic way to slow down the ripening process, by crossing these mutants with the normal types.'"

Tigchelaar was skeptical. But when Mizrahi returned to Israel in 1975, his work drew the interest of a well-known tomato breeder, Nahum Kedar. He had a student, Ehud Kopeliovitch, who incorporated *rin* into a new, long-shelf-life tomato as his doctoral research. Kopeliovitch went to work for Hazera Seed Company, which sold its first long-shelf-life seeds in 1981, first in Europe and then in the United States and Mexico. The first U.S. customers were Howard Marguleas and Carl

Sam Maggio of SunWorld, an Indio, California, company that had been in the citrus business. After obtaining proprietary rights to use Hazera's seeds in Mexico, they created a company called Long Shelf Life to market the tomatoes, which they called DiVine Ripe Tomatoes. They made a bundle. DiVine Ripe grabbed an enormous share of the North American winter tomato market.

"This changed the world of tomatoes completely," said Kanti. "For some reason, the Israelis picked up on the gene, though the Americans didn't." The secret leaked out to other breeders and growers, and after much commercial wrangling, other Mexican growers started using them. "The fresh market today is based on *rin*," said Kanti. The tomato didn't have much flavor at first, because the inhibition of ripening also inhibited the creation of certain sugars and volatile substances that contribute much to the ineffable flavor of the tomato. But by using tastier parents and clever growing techniques—such as high-saline drip irrigation—growers have gradually mastered methods for creating reasonably tasty *rin* tomatoes.

Not Florida growers, though. For the most part, they have stuck to their old ways. While Israeli plant physiologists and breeders continued to improve the tomato at Hebrew University and Ben Gurion University, American breeders sniffed, and American growers for the most part did, too. Florida growers had nothing but scorn for the Mexican varieties, at least in public. "They cut like an apple and are crunchy, but they are called vine-ripened tomatoes and last a long time on the display rack. This makes them appealing to the retailer, regardless of how they taste," said Wayne Hawkins of the Florida Tomato Exchange, in 1998. Hawkins argued that Florida tomatoes tasted better. If Florida tomatoes were picked green mature and handled properly, consumers preferred them to the Mexican "vine ripes," he said.

In the late 1990s, growers from both countries started selling tomatoes with the "sticky" gene, which kept the vine in place so the tomatoes could be sold attached to it. This was a clever little maneuver because the vine was rich with *cis*-3-hexenal, a key component of "tomatoey" odor. The tomatoes were marketed as Tomato on Vine, or TOV. Even if they were picked green and hard as a rock, their stems would impart a farm-fresh aroma that was appealing to consumers. In the store, they still smelled like tomatoes—at least until you threw the stems away.

Instead of switching to new cultivation and harvest methods, Hawkins proposed a marketing effort to change the image of Florida tomatoes. "Gas-green" or even "mature-green tomato" was not an attractive name for something people ate. "The big secret is not what you have, but what you call it," Hawkins told a 1998 Florida Tomato Exchange forum. "In other words, no more 'mature greens'! Let's get our act together and start selling 'farm ripe' or 'Florida ripe tomatoes.'" One reason Florida growers opposed *rin*, according to a well-placed source, was more cynical: They worried that extending the shelf life of their tomatoes would reduce sales.

Calgene's 1988 patent application described the role of polygalacturonase, or PG protein, in tomato ripeness and claimed a method of silencing the gene by inserting a reverse transcript of it—a so-called antisense gene—into a genetically transformed tomato's DNA. The company thought that by silencing PG and PG alone, it could pick its tomatoes ripe and sell them at a premium to customers who'd pay extra money to have a tomato that tasted good even after three weeks on the shelf. Behind the patent application lay an expectation in the boardroom that the company could make inroads into the $4 billion fresh-tomato market, which was, pun aside, ripe for the picking. They would trademark their tomato as the Flavr Savr, and market it under the name McGregor, with a logo showing an old-timer hauling tomatoes in a wheelbarrow. High-tech promise and rural nostalgia, all in one tasty, red product.

At first, it was an idea that attracted partners. Campbell's Soup sponsored the research to the tune of about $1 million a year, and two of its cultivars, the CD3 and CD4, were used in the first PG transformations. But these were canning tomatoes. Campbell grew them back East, and Calgene planned to grow its crop in California. "They were compact, small, and not tasty," Kanti said. "I told the guys, 'You need to find varieties that grow well here in California.'" Kanti started experimenting with PG technology in varieties from Asgrow and Ferry-Morse, companies that had been breeding in California for decades. He used what he called a "Velcro system." Because the antisense gene was dominant, you could theoretically insert it into any commercial hybrid—like Velcro, the antisense gene could be stuck into any tomato. "Then you see if you've destroyed the tomato or enhanced it."

In the meantime, Calgene continued to spend and hire with abandon, despite the fact that it did not have an actual Flavr Savr tomato, and despite misgivings among some of its scientists about the safety of the genetic transformation. To remake the tomatoes, Calgene used a bacterial plasmid containing the antisense gene as well as a gene sequence that coded for a protein that gave the plant resistance to kanamycin, an antibiotic. This was a clever and commonly used tool in genetic transformation; plants that had been successfully transformed would grow well in a solution of kanamycin, thereby proving that the gene vector, including the antisense sequence, had been successfully spliced into their DNA. It was doubtful that the kanamycin resistance in the tomato was substantial enough to stimulate the creation of antibiotic-resistant bacteria in the people who ate it, but some of the scientists were a little dismayed at what short shrift the safety studies had gotten.

In Kanti's view, Calgene's management was blinded by visions of a quick buck. "'We'll make millions and walk away.' They had zero understanding of the fresh-market tomato business." Calgene brought on Tom Churchwell, a former Monsanto executive who'd gotten Coca-Cola to put Monsanto's NutraSweet in its cans and on its labels. But Campbell got leery of the business, fearing its brand might be besmirched, and dropped out. Management then tried bringing aboard Bob Meyer, a big grower in California and Mexico who was selling a lot of tomatoes to McDonald's. But Meyer embarrassed Calgene by announcing in the newspapers that the tomatoes produced by DNAP, a competitor, were better. To get back at Meyer, Calgene hired his production chief, Gary McKinsey. But the company was never able to convince any of the big fresh-market producers to grow its product. The big Florida growers were dismissive. A few flirted with Calgene, then backed out. Calgene was becoming the laughingstock of the tomato business.

On the financial end, things were moving fast. "Some idiot decided, 'We've got to build a mobile packing line.'" The focus was on impressing Wall Street. "I said, 'Great, but what are we going to grow?'" As Kanti recalled it, "They decided that taste didn't matter. The market would buy any piece of shit. They thought they could get away with murder. It was unexpressed but explicitly understood."

Kanti investigated growing out the seed in Chile, and then the Philippines. Nothing came of those deals—both countries were wary of contamination from "Frankenfood" seeds. The Flavr Savr had attracted a lot of publicity, and also the enmity of genetic-modification opponents like Jeremy Rifkin, who had threatened a boycott of Campbell's Soup products when it backed the Flavr Savr. "The middle class is moving in the direction of healthy, sustainable organic foods," he said. "The last thing they want to hear about is gene-spliced tomatoes." Rifkin said that while the tomato might be safe, it hadn't been tested enough. His followers organized Flavr Savr "tomato squishing protests."

None of the Mexican growers were interested in growing the McGregor without millions up front. Eventually the company found two packers who demanded $250,000 plus a contract, but they wouldn't plant until FDA gave permission to sell the tomato—which did not occur until 1994. Calgene ended up using the Pacific, a cultivar that didn't travel well, got soft, and bruised quickly. As soon as FDA approved the tomato, Calgene shipped the Pacifics in nice McGregor boxes from Guasave through Nogales to Chicago. When the company executives on hand for the big moment opened the trailer, it was full of mush.

"All hell breaks loose," Kanti recalled. Meanwhile, an executive had decided that Calgene had to monitor its product placement in stores. "So we hired all these beautiful women, who were walking around with laptops, in their high heels, and driving Ford Focus company cars. That didn't go over well in the stores. Produce managers are proud of their turf and they don't like being upstaged. And they were tasteless tomatoes selling for $4.50 a pound." As is his wont, Kanti griped about the business to everyone he met. "An executive told me, 'You're talking too much.'"

The tomatoes shipped for a while. There were a few enthusiasts, but not enough. Alice Waters, founder of Berkeley's famous Chez Panisse restaurant, sampled a Flavr Savr and declared that it "tasted like a seasonally ripe commercial tomato. Not bad," she said, but not good enough for Chez Panisse.

On March 23, 1994, Luis Donaldo Colosio of the Revolutionary Institutional Party, Mexico's presumed next president, was assassinated while campaigning in Tijuana. Kanti and McKinsey were in the bar of the Executive Hotel in Culiacán drinking beer. "The Mexicans were meeting their contract, but people were getting upset." An executive called, asking whether they should stop shipments. "I got home, my wife met me at the Sacramento airport. I flew to Chicago the next morning for an urgent meeting. They stopped shipping the tomatoes. We'd already lost $25 million. The dumbest thing we did was to ship a product no one had ever seen. The joke was, 'Flavr Savr could have been a great tomato if there was any Flavor to Save.'"

In 1995, Calgene sold the seeds and the patent to Monsanto, where they disappeared into a vault somewhere. There are rumors in the seed business that Monsanto has another genetically modified tomato all ready to go when the politics are right. But that seems unlikely, at least in the short term. With consumers showing enthusiasm for tastier tomatoes, Monsanto has gone aggressively into breeding programs that combine *rin* with high-brix fruit whose seed can be sold for a lot of money.

M. Allen Stevens, who witnessed some of the Calgene story as a breeder for Campbell, has a slightly more generous interpretation of the events than does Kanti. In his view, the Calgene fiasco says more about the pitfalls of tomato handling than it does about the relative advantages of genetic modification. "Calgene's tomato was not very good, but it was OK," said Stevens. All the company did was to take a tomato that had been around a number of years and put in a gene that didn't do very much for shelf life. What made the tomatoes OK was that Calgene harvested them almost ripe, handled them in a way that didn't ruin flavor, and got them to consumers quickly. The trouble with tomatoes today, said Stevens, is that they're picked too early, then refrigerated. "We at the front end are supposed to design a tomato that tastes as good as possible and if possible make it foolproof, resistant to handling processes. We can make improvements, but you'll never have the perfect tomato up north in the wintertime."

True, but the marginal steps toward perfection seem to be taking place everywhere but Florida. As much as Mexico challenges the Florida growers, an equally important player has moved into the niche left by the Floridians' inattention to flavor—the greenhouse growers. The demand for greenhouse tomatoes has skyrocketed in the past twenty years. As of 2008, they made up about 44 percent of the U.S. retail fresh-tomato market, according to the USDA. In 2006, about 652,000 metric tons of greenhouse tomatoes were produced in Canada, Mexico, and the United States. Greenhouses in Ontario, in particular, have stolen market share in the eastern United States from Florida, using tomato varieties that have better flavor than the Floridian types.

One day in June 2008, I visited Double Diamond Acres, an enormous hydroponic greenhouse operation about a mile from the shores of Lake Erie in Leamington, Ontario. The company was thirty years old and expanding rapidly—one of its state-of-the-art greenhouses was only three years old, and the entire operation was fully computerized. To anyone who has spent time in a dirt vegetable patch, it's a little spooky to walk through a greenhouse that's dedicated to food farming. Even a healthy tomato field has plenty of brown, curled-up leaves and a certain number of weeds, and bugs and birds, and some tomatoes that are either rotting or green mixed in with the ripe ones. These greenhouse tomato plants had perfect foliage, to the point that I found myself pinching the leaves to be satisfied that they weren't plastic.

The productivity of this greenhouse was a little mind-boggling, too. According to the boss, Nick Mastronardi, on each of the twenty-five acres devoted to tomatoes, there were ten thousand plants and each plant produced fifty to sixty pounds of tomatoes from the time it was transplanted, just before Christmas, until the vine was cut down the following November. The plants grew out of rockwall, an inert rooting medium in which water, fungicide, and water-soluble nitrogen, potassium, and phosphorus fertilizer circulated in quantities set and controlled by a computer. Ozone was bubbled through the runoff water to kill microorganisms and reoxygenate it before it was recycled. A factory down the road supplied bottled carbon dioxide, which was used to enrich the atmosphere. Extra CO_2 was like steroids for the tomatoes, increasing their yields by 50 percent. Giant awnings closed over the glass roof and windows at night, conserving energy. For heat the greenhouses used bunker fuel—low-grade refinery junk left over from gasoline production. No pesticides were used—local companies raised aphid- and worm-eating wasps for the greenhouses. When the wasps weren't eating bugs, they lived in pots of wheat that grew at the end of the rows of tomatoes and peppers.

The greenhouse used Dutch and Israeli technology—from the computerized environment to the tomato seeds. One popular greenhouse cultivar, the Campari—a spherical tomato whose size is midway between a cherry and a small beefsteak—was developed by Enza Zaden, a Dutch company based in Eikhuzkoven. Its creators used Japanese breeding lines—the Japanese like really sweet tomatoes—in the mix that went into Campari, which Safeway and other big supermarket chains sell in plastic clamshells.

I toured Mastronardi's plant with a group of processing tomato farmers and canners from places like California, Iran, Chile, Tunisia, and the Dominican Republic. The visitors had been attending the eighth World Processing Tomato Congress in Toronto the week before—southern Ontario is one of the world's leading areas for growing processing tomatoes and has the oldest Heinz ketchup plant in the world. Mastronardi, a blunt-spoken, stout little guy, was born in southern Italy to farmer parents. He did poorly in school and quarreled with his dad but took up farming just the same, and the tomato tourists warmed to his colorful way of putting things, especially after learning that he'd been a processing tomato grower himself. He'd switched to hydroponics in the mid-1970s, a time when many of the local farmers decided to go greenhouse.

"When I was growing processing tomatoes, I used to beg the canneries to give me more acreage. The last year I grew them, I said, 'I've been trying to kiss your ass all these years to get more acres. Well, you can kiss my ass now; I don't want them,'" he said with a hearty laugh. "The greenhouse industry has increased its yields just as much as you guys have. When I started out we'd get twenty pounds per plant."

Salmonella hadn't been a problem in Mastronardi's operation, which uses tap water in its operations and sterilizes the water it recycles. During the 2008 salmonella scare, sales went up 10 percent, he said. "We're very fortunate. I wouldn't mind advertising our safety record, but how do you do that without putting down the other guys?" Instead of being picked green and gassed with ethylene, the Double Diamond tomatoes were picked with at least a blush of color, sometimes later. They were packaged in fifteen-pound boxes and could be shipped to much of the East Coast of the United States (more than half of Mastronardi's market) in less than two days.

The high cost of heating is the biggest problem for greenhouses. Cogeneration plants, which provide heat as a by-product of electrical generation, are used for Canadian greenhouses, but it's still an expensive proposition in the middle of a northern winter. That's why outfits like Eurofresh Farms, a Dutch-founded company that grew tomatoes, cucumbers, and bell peppers on 318 acres of greenhouse in Arizona, were expanding. Purists may object to greenhouses, but the industry has shown it can produce tasty products in a controlled environment that reduces the need for petrochemical-based inputs.

Eurofresh's product is especially popular on the West Coast, as I learned one morning in April 2008, when Kanti gave me a chance to see how the tomato business looks from a wholesaler's perspective. That was one of the few enticements that would have gotten me to wake up at 4:00 A.M. (I overslept anyway) to make a visit with Bobby Pizza (his real name) at his "What a Tomato" shop in San Francisco's wholesale vegetable market, near Cesar Chavez Street in the southern part of the city. Pizza, whose father was a vegetable wholesaler, has had the business since 1986 and told me he sold more tomatoes every year. As prices rose and fell, he might be buying tomatoes that came anywhere from California to Mexico to Florida, but he tried to stay away from the Florida tomatoes because "they don't taste as good."

My visit came in the middle of a disastrous spring for the fresh-market tomato business. The FDA had incorrectly implicated tomatoes in an outbreak of *Salmonella saintpaul* illness that sickened more than twelve hundred people and killed two of them. The episode had been painful but not devastating for Pizza. He'd had to throw out five thousand boxes of tomatoes and lost maybe $50,000 (the price of each twenty-five-pound box is $5 to $14 wholesale—heirlooms go for about $20 for a ten-pound box). But he wasn't worried about the long term. "Tomatoes will recover. They're a staple item."

We looked around Pizza's lot, poking and prodding and taking a bite here or there. Then a load of tomatoes pulled up to the dock. It was a refrigerated truck carrying tomatoes along with lettuce and other vegetables, and inside it was 45 degrees, or colder. No amount of breeding, whether it's done in the lab or the greenhouse, can overcome the disastrous effects of prolonged refrigeration on tomato flavor.

"They tell you they don't refrigerate tomatoes," Kanti said. "But they do."

He shrugged. While he was in pursuit of excellence, he doesn't expect the world to follow. "People like me and Jay Scott and Gary Ibsen are puritan whole-ists who want to find that ultimate tomato under the umbrella of nature, right off the plant," he said. "We're the crazies pursuing the fleeting flavor of the ultimate tomato. As for the rest of the world? Come on!!"

CHAPTER SIX

Are Things Better in the Old Country?

We don't know who was the first to think of marrying pasta and tomato. He surely deserves a monument.

—Jeanne Carola Francesconi, *La cucina napoletana*, 2007

 In September 2001, customs agents seized 160 tons of rotting, worm-infested Chinese tomato paste at the Italian port of Bari. Much to their horror, Italian consumers soon learned that some of the tomato paste on their grocery shelves—worse than that, some of the paste they had cooked with, eaten, enjoyed—was Chinese. In China, it was pointed out, there were few guarantees in regard to cleanliness, pesticides, or heavy-metal contamination. "Italy—Invaded by Chinese tomatoes!" screamed a *Corriere della Sera* article. This "perfectly legal invasion," as one magazine writer called it, spooked the Italians in a profound way. The alarmist language used to describe these imports— words like "invasion" and "flood" appeared frequently—pointed to a

cultural pessimism that went beyond a few producers' complaints of dumping by the Chinese.

In 2005, Italy imported 157,000 tons of Chinese paste. That year, low prices led Italian farmers who grew paste tomatoes to leave half their crop in the field to rot; newspaper accounts suggested that Chinese imports were responsible for undercutting prices. "National cultivation is at risk," went the headline in *Corriere*. The Chinese paste imported by Italy was a drop in the bucket compared to the 5.23 million tons of processed tomatoes produced in Italy. But tomatoes were a fundamental of Italian food culture, perhaps the cornerstone of southern Italian cooking. If Italy could not maintain the quality and uniqueness of its food, what, exactly, did it have? "By universal consent," as a writer in the Italian gourmet magazine *Gambero Rosso* put it, "the Bel Paese's production represents the cutting edge of quality when it comes to this fruit that travels the world with pizza and spaghetti. The tomato is one of our undisputed culinary glories, a true red gold because of its flavor and economic value."

The Italian farm organization Coldiretti raised one million signatures demanding a ban on Chinese imports. In response, the government decreed in March 2006 that every container of *passata*—the ground-up tomatoes that go into Italian pizzas and pasta sauces—carry a label indicating the region and country it came from, the date the raw material was harvested, and a certification that it was made "directly from fresh tomatoes." China exports nearly all its tomatoes in the form of concentrated tomato paste, so this last requirement was aimed at squeezing the Chinese out of the Italian market. Industrial paste is used around the world—including Italy and, of course, the United States. The highly concentrated paste, made in vast quantities in modern factories, is then reconstituted to make spaghetti and pizza sauce, ketchup, salsa, tomato juice, and other products. Many food experts consider tomato sauces made from industrial paste inferior, though this is the subject of some debate. But in Italy, the fine print of the argument was ignored. Coldiretti declared June 12, the day the new law went into effect, National Italian Tomato Day.

Although China's entry in the market had hurt Turkish and Australian producers more than the Italians, the latter were especially worked up over what they viewed as a kind of Faustian bargain their industry had made with the Chinese. In the 1990s, searching for cheap product for their export markets, Italian companies began setting up tomato processing plants in China to provide paste, which Italian canners repackaged in Naples or Palermo, slapped with "Made in Italy" stickers, and shipped to Africa. Soon, the Chinese had figured out a way to market their paste directly to the Africans—and began selling it in Europe as well. The Chinese grew most of their tomatoes for export in the westernmost province of Xinjiang, near the borders with Russia and Kazakhstan. Xinjiang is China's largest province, an area of massive snowcapped mountains and arid highlands studded with yurts and oil derricks and camel herds that ramble among them. One of the two large producers there is Chalkis, an affiliate of the military's Xinjiang Production and Construction Corps, which is said to have about a million employees, more than any other company in the world.

You couldn't blame the Italians for being defensive and even horrified at the idea of eating Chinese tomato paste. Food traditions in many parts of the world are intimately connected to feelings of identity. The *Gambero Rosso* writer invoked the "fraud" committed against Italian citizens, who "without knowing it found themselves eating a product cultivated in a country with very different health rules than ours," tomatoes that were "brutally transformed and transported hundreds of kilometers with little interest in the nutritional properties and antioxidant substances in which the tomato is so rich." Well, yes and no. Sure, the Chinese tomatoes might have had a few traces of pesticides in them, but their nutritional level was probably the same as paste produced in Italy. The real difference was aesthetic, and existential. Is there anything wrong with rice grown in Louisiana? No, but the Japanese resist importing this rice, and they heavily subsidize their own rice farmers—to preserve a way of life, not to mention all those lovely rice terraces, fragments of continuity with ancient times that flicker past like scroll paintings on the windows of the bullet train.

But what, exactly, in the case of Italian tomatoes, was being protected? Was it the farmer? The canner? The consumer? Was it the traditions associated with small landholders, the warm memories— sometimes borrowed, perhaps—of the *cucina di mamma* celebrated in a thousand tomato can labels, magazine ads, and television commercials? Was it the aesthetics, real and contrived, that link a product with its *terroir*—that combination of climate, topography, and soil that the French insist is so important, and upon which they base all their finicky rules for which wine gets to be called *champagne*, which brandy *cognac*? Were the Italians scared they'd lose control of the tomato products that go into their exacting, very particular cuisine? Did they fear losing their brand? Or was there an element of culinary xenophobia? There might be real concerns with the safety of Chinese food products, but was it safety concerns that actually created the anxiety about the Chinese tomatoes? Or was the country with Europe's lowest birthrate extra touchy because its citizens felt overwhelmed, more generally, by non-Europeans, the *extracomunitari* who were an increasing percentage of the otherwise shrinking population?

With the exception of Mexico, there's no country on earth where the tomato is more indispensable to cuisine than Italy. And this is stranger than it seems, because as recently as a century ago, most Italians didn't even eat tomatoes. The story of how Italy fell in love with the tomato is intimately related to the story of how its diverse population—only 2.5 percent of whom spoke Italian as a first language in the mid-nineteenth century—was unified, emptied by emigration, traumatized by fascism and war, and turned prosperous after World War II.

In the sixteenth and seventeenth centuries, wandering Arabs and Jews, thrown out of Spain by the *reconquista* and pogroms, were the vectors of new foods in the rest of Europe. The Arabs brought the eggplant to Italy and may have brought the tomato as well. Or it may be that Spanish Jews brought the tomato to the Parma area. Scholars aren't sure, but these are two leading theories, though there may have been multiple fronts in the tomato invasion. Whatever the case, it's probably no accident that the "traditional" tomato-growing areas of Italy—Sicily, Sardinia, Campagna, and Emilia-Romagna— were the regions ruled by the Spanish Bourbons beginning in the late sixteenth century. No Spanish cookbooks remain from the immediate post-Columbian period, but the earliest tomato-containing recipe in Italian cookbooks is *"pommodoro alla spagnuola"* in Antonio Latini's *Lo scalco alla moderna* (The modern kitchen master), published in Naples in 1692. In this and other early recipes, the tomato remained essentially Mexican—roasted with hot chili peppers. By 1747, however, in Juan de la Mata's *Arte de repostería*, the tomato had been decoupled from the spicy chili pepper, though it was not yet an omnipresent component of southern cooking. Other New World foods penetrated faster. By the sixteenth century, the polenta eaten by northern Italian peasants was already made from corn rather than the barley, millet, and buckwheat of past generations. Tomatoes moved in more slowly. Vincenzo Corrado's 1778 classic *Il cuoco galante* (The gentleman's chef) had tomato sauce recipes, but these sauces were for meat, not pasta.

In the countryside, things may have been different. Tomatoes grew easily in the Mediterranean climate, and later folkways suggest that the peasantry made good use of them. They used a number of ways of preserving tomatoes and tomato sauce for year-round use. Larger tomatoes could be split in half, salted, dried in the sun, and hung on strings. Cherry tomatoes were dried whole by hanging stems up on twine, forming grapelike bunches. "Strings of dried tomatoes are familiar sights in southern Italy and Sicily at every house in the country and even at the houses of the lower classes in large cities like Naples," an American visitor wrote in 1915. Entrepreneurial souls made crude tomato pastes like *conserva nera,* prepared by cooking strained tomatoes down to a quarter of their original volume and stirring the mash to the consistency of a marmalade, which was then dried in an oven or in the sun. The resulting tomato cakes could then be worked over by hand with olive oil, shaped into cylindrical patties, and baked in the sun until they were quite solid and nearly black. At the larger enterprises, the cakes were wrapped in oiled paper and packed into boxes for sale.

If you went back far enough, the southern Italian diet was heavy on greens, fruit, and meat. But pasta arrived, possibly through the Arabic occupation of Sicily in the tenth century, and it became a convenient way to feed the peasantry. By the mid-nineteenth century, the Neapolitan workman's lunch was often bought on the street from itinerant or streetside pizza makers and pasta sellers. The latter would throw a pinch of cheese and a dollop of tomato sauce onto the pasta for an extra penny or two—it wasn't uncommon for customer and vendor to bicker over a few drops. Only the richest customers ate sauce and cheese; some of the poor could only afford the broth in which the macaroni was cooked.

Food, and tomatoes, are frequently mentioned in accounts of Italian unification. When Garibaldi's northern Italian army whipped the Bourbon troops at Caserta and arrived triumphantly in Naples in 1860, the troops caught their first whiffs of pizza and pasta with red sauce. The Neapolitan pizza maker Raffaele Esposito, whose Da Pietro parlor had been around since 1760, honored the new Italian queen, Margherita, with a red, green, and white pizza, its colors representing the flag of the new country she ruled. Whether this was really the first tomato, mozzarella, and basil pizza served in Naples was beside the point. The important thing was the symbolism, the "invention of a tradition," as food historian Franco de Cecla puts it. *Pizza margherita* embodied the myth of unification. The north extracted more taxes from the south. But it also ate southern food. The queen was bored with French cooking. Of course, the Bourbon monarchy had eaten pizza, too—Esposito served it at the Savoy court. But that was just bread with tomato sauce—this was the pizza of unification!

National food integration was consecrated in Pellegrino Artusi's 1891 cookbook *La scienza in cucina e l'arte di mangiare bene* (Science in the kitchen and the art of eating well). Artusi's book is to Italian cooking what *The Joy of Cooking* is to American cuisine, and Escoffier's *Guide Culinaire* to the French. But *l'Artusi*, as Italians still call it, was more than that. Written in witty prose by a Florentine banker who'd been raised in the countryside, the book consolidated dozens of regional Italian cuisines into a single whole that both respected the differences and articulated an insouciant but careful approach to the preparation of simple food with good ingredients.

Manzoni's novel *I promessi sposi (The Betrothed)* is often cited as the novel that unified Italy by disseminating a standard national language and an accepted national history. But *Scienza in cucina* may have done more for national unification. "Artusi's gustatory principles created a code of national identification where Manzoni's stylistic and linguistic principles failed," wrote the historian Piero Camporesi. "This is understandable, because not all of us read, but we all eat." And the single most important ingredient in *l'Artusi*, argues Camporesi, was tomato sauce. After Artusi, tomato sauce and spaghetti were warmly accepted, one might even say canonized, in the Italian national culinary system. The new Artusian national cookery owed much to the triumphal arrival of the tomato into what might be called Risorgimento cooking, or even Garibaldian cooking, because after Garibaldi's March of the One Thousand in 1860, tomatoes triumphantly overran the whole peninsula. They gave new flavor and body to the eclectic and depersonalized romantic cuisines, mainly brought in by the French, which survived in tired form without originality or flair even during the Restoration. The tomato, much more than the potato, is the new explosive and revolutionary element of the Italian cuisine of the nineteenth century.

Italy was very poor after unification, too poor to sustain a national food industry or to form a national cuisine. It was the Italian diaspora, more than *l'Artusi*, that accomplished that end. By 1920, nine million Italians—a quarter of the population—had emigrated. In the early twentieth century, demand for the foods that the world would come to identify as characteristically Italian—pasta, olive oil, tomatoes, and hard cheeses—came from outside Italy, not within. When they got to the United States (or Canada, Argentina, or Australia), the Sicilians and Neapolitans and Calabrians and Florentines of disunited Italy were now identified, whether they liked it or not, as Italians. Consumer demand within Italy was weak, but the humblest bricklayer ate well in the United States, where wages were ten times higher. Remittances, and the demand for these foods from Italians living abroad, strengthened a food industry that couldn't have survived on the internal market alone. And the turn of the century was also a period of technical innovation in the canning industry.

In 1897, Italy had exported 2 million kilograms of tomato products. By 1911, that figure had expanded a hundredfold, to 230 million kilograms. "The enormous number of our compatriots who have gone globetrotting in search of better fortunes has facilitated the export of this product," an industry analyst writes. "These men demand the motherland's product from all corners of the earth, and through their habits they spread word of them to the inhabitants of the places they have colonized."

The champion exporter was Francesco Cirio, a Sardinian who founded Italy's first modern canning factory in Turin 1856. In 1900, Cirio built an enormous cannery at San Giovanni a Teduccio, on the eastern edge of Naples. The tomatoes were grown on the volcanic soils of Vesuvius, usually on nonirrigated land. The packers liked that better—less water meant more intensely concentrated, better-tasting tomatoes. The classically scripted Cirio labels, with their tiny copies of medals won at international fairs, became a familiar sight in urban groceries around the world. When emigrants returned home, they brought back a national cuisine that hadn't previously existed. "Food and acts of consumption became ways to reproduce an identity not quite rooted in experience, but perhaps rooted in how previous experience should have been," writes Carol Helstosky in her 2006 book *Garlic and Oil*. "This is still the case today, at least in the United States, where nostalgia for authentic Italian cuisine goes hand in hand with memories of grandmother's kitchen and the family table."

The ultimate commodifier of Italo-American nostalgia was chef Ettore Boiardi of Piacenza, whom the opera singer Enrico Caruso brought to New York in 1913, where Boiardi became chef at the

Knickerbocker Hotel and, later, the Plaza. In 1926, Boiardi moved to
Cleveland, where his Giardino d'Italia restaurant was so popular that
he began canning its spaghetti and meatball sauce. Sold as Chef Boy-
Ar-Dee sauce, the stuff made Boiardi a rich man, especially after the
military made his dish part of its K-rations. He died in 1985 at age
eighty-seven in Parma—Parma, Ohio, that is, a suburb of Cleveland.
Spaghetti and meatballs didn't exist in Italy—it was invented by Italian peasants in America enthralled by the availability of cheap meat.
Veal parmigiana was another Italian-in-America invention.

Brightly colored Italian tomato labels played upon the cultural
themes of the day. In 1938, the label on a can of Progresso tomatoes,
grown and packed in San Marzano for a Brooklyn wholesaler, showed
a Roman soldier on a chariot with various symbols of fascist progress
behind him—a train going through a tunnel, imposing fascist architecture, airplanes, ships. A 1950 label for Sophia Brands offered a sensual
breath of the *dolce vita*, with Sophia Loren in a low-cut dress standing
in front of two-peaked Vesuvius and the sea. A tiny puff of smoke rises
from the volcano.

When Mussolini and the fascists seized power in 1922, they set out to
control every aspect of food consumption and to nationalize Italian cuisine, sometimes by making all Italians consume less food. The regime
touted the economic and nutritional benefits of the Mediterranean diet
because the practice fit with its political goals: food autonomy and soldiers who were well nourished enough to fight effectively in the national-
ist missions Mussolini planned for them. The fascist era saw the arrival
of Futurism, which provided an aesthetic cover for the political manipulation of diet. In his *Manifesto of Futurist Cooking*, Filippo Tommaso
Marinetti called for the abolition of pasta, which he called an "absurd

gastronomic religion" that drained Italians of their energy, creativity, and intelligence. To the mayor of Naples, who declared that "the angels in Paradise eat nothing but *vermicelli al pomodoro*," Marinetti replied that this only confirmed his suspicions that it was boring in Paradise. Eventually, food would be replaced by vitamin pills and supplements, the Futurists said, but in the meantime, they advocated symbolic dishes such as *carneplastico*, or meat sculpture, *pollo Fiat*, a stuffed chicken on whipped cream, or *porco eccitato*, aroused pig—a salami placed at a right angle to the plate, doused with coffee and eau de cologne.

The Futurists dispensed aesthetic judgment on the poor people's efforts to feed themselves. Meanwhile, *Il Duce's* nutritional diktat changed in rhythm with his erratic economic policy. One month bread was in, the next it was out. Farmers needed special licenses to grow tomatoes. During the 1920s, when Mussolini was pushing wheat to the exclusion of other crops, a tomato shortage caused southerners to tear out their hair. By 1936, the crop had recovered enough (despite other food shortages) for the fascists to organize a contest to pick the most innovative use for canned tomatoes. About three thousand people took part, according to the fascist media, contributing tomatoes stewed in Marsala sauce, slathered in cream, ground up in meatballs, and so on. "The new Fascist discipline of production has concerned itself with the problems of the tomato," a propagandist declared in 1940, "and has sought to give farmers and industry an economic base through fundamental directives of discipline and economic defense of culture."

Hunger intensified during the war, but within a couple of decades, Italians were eating better than they had ever eaten before. And then, suddenly, the diet of necessity became cool.

In 1959, Margaret and Ancel Keys put their official stamp of approval on the Mediterranean diet with their book *Eat Well and Stay*

Well. The Keyses, American physicians, had compared the rate of heart attacks in people around the world and found that those who lived on pasta, fresh vegetables, and olive oil were among the healthiest. Just as the fascists had maintained, it was a good thing to live on a diet imposed by shortages of meat and animal fats. So many Italians settled into a cuisine focused on pasta and sauces, a way that mocked the hunger of earlier eras. "Italian cuisine, built of scarcity and necessity, now constitutes a formalistic language where the attention to the smallest detail is mind boggling," writes Franco la Cecla. "Is it not incredible that the dried pasta industry produced not two or three shapes, but six hundred? The culture of poverty in Italy is often a culture of variety, thousands of types of bread, thousands of ways to cook the same food, and thousands of shapes of pasta and types of pizza."

The legacy of poverty remains in the basic elements of Italian cuisine and in the obsession with detail. You don't serve beans with spaghetti or pasta shells with pesto to an Italian. Light sauces only on *taglioline*, please, while *vongole* must go on linguine or spaghetti. How the pasta is cooked and which sauces go with which pastas are part of the national cultural framework.

Which brings us to Carmelo D'Agostino, the Tomato Man of Testaccio. Italian chefs are not nearly as particular about their tomato choices as they are about pasta. Yet it's certainly logical that Italy should have a D'Agostino. He's the only retail food seller in the world that I know of whose trade is entirely in fresh tomatoes.

"Why should I talk to you?" D'Agostino asked when I first approached him. He was a shortish, worried-looking guy in his fifties with a dirty gray ponytail and big, rather sweet brown eyes. He stood at the apex of a pyramid of tomatoes—maybe one hundred boxes of them, laid out in a dazzling display around his stand in the Testaccio market of Rome. Most of them were different varieties, and they were tomatoes you just didn't see in American markets: big, irregular Beefhearts; green round Camones; ribbed Casalinos; long, slug-shaped San Marzanos; tiny date-shaped Datterinos. Picadillys, Pantanos, Thomases, Salamones, Merengues. Tomatoes shaped like big strawberries and tomatoes shaped like bell peppers. They were at all stages of ripeness, too—some half-green, a few nearly rotten. There were boxes of wrinkled, little reddish brown oblongs that an American grocer would have tossed out weeks ago. There were even tomatoes hanging to dry on wires in a little glass cage, the kind in which cured Chinese ducks hang by their roasted necks.

"I've been on SkyTV, I've had articles in the newspapers, the magazines. I've been quoted in books. They buy the books and newspapers. They don't buy my tomatoes," he sighed by way of explanation for being rude. It was mid-August, dead time in Rome. Testaccio, a food market that occupies a city block a mile or so south of Rome's historic center, was very quiet. I couldn't blame D'Agostino for being in a bad mood when he was approached by a gawky American speaking Spanish with an occasional word of Italian thrown in. Nobody was buying tomatoes.

So I asked if I could look at his press clippings, which he had laminated, and I retreated to an empty crate several feet away to read. This was how I was introduced to D'Agostino's calling. In *Aroma* magazine, he is quoted as saying, "I've always had a particular gift. My mother when I was little would always take me shopping with her because I always picked the best stuff. Eventually I transferred this faculty exclusively to the tomato, which I have studied in depth." Hundreds of varieties had passed through his stall: "It all depends on what your taste is, you see. Some like it this way, some like it that. You think tomatoes are all the same?" he asks. "For background for example you might want

Casalino, which is creamy and aromatic, for fish maybe a more delicate tomato, maybe a Ciliegino."

D'Agostino was the son of rural people from Calabria. More than tomatoes, he was selling knowledge. "His real value to the gourmet is his advice," a chef told *Il Messaggero* in 2005. He was all about finding the right tomato for the right job.

Seeing me there, diligently reading and taking notes, D'Agostino had a change of heart, came over, and began his lesson in earnest. "In the U.S., you have enormous areas, all the same. Here we've got the sea, the mountains, and the twenty to thirty miles between them, and in all these lands there are so many different soils and climates. That's why we can have such diversity of the tomato." Just as they do with their six hundred kinds of pasta, Italians categorize their tomatoes by shape— the leading text lists twenty-seven types ranging from round to pear to oblong to elongated and everything in between. Finding the right tomato, from this Italian master's perspective, can be just as intuitive and complex as finding the right-shaped pasta for a sauce.

To get on D'Agostino's good side—and of course, to conduct my own taste test—I bought $20 worth of his tomatoes: Ciliegino, Casalino, Salamone, Datterini. They weren't cheap, at €6 per kilo, and I carefully noted down his instructions about how to use each one, and arranged to conduct a proper interview a few days later. When I returned to my rental apartment, after a cursory taste test of them raw—these are good, these are great, these are pretty good, ho hum—I threw them all into a skillet with onions and made a big pasta sauce out of the whole lot. I'm hopeless when it comes to the *comme il faut* of gourmet cooking.

When I returned to D'Agostino's stand, I came with my friend Marjorie, who speaks flawless Italian and had offered to translate. D'Agostino grimaced slightly when I described how my family had eaten his tomatoes, but he acknowledged that some of his directives might be hard to follow.

This fed into an interesting conversation, because Marjorie, though American, has lived in Rome for years and learned to appreciate the finer points of Italian life. She's also a fairly strong-willed organophile and an adherent of Slow Food, the movement to return to small-scale, traditional foodways. Like most Slow Fooders, she was skeptical of hybrid tomatoes—favoring original flavors and ancient ways of farming. But D'Agostino, it turned out, was not so interested in organic tomatoes or heirlooms. He was all about the flavor—and much to our surprise, he was not particularly nostalgic on that score.

"Ancient flavors," he sniffed. "There are a lot of great new flavors!"

D'Agostino had locally grown tomatoes from all around Rome and the province of Lazio, but he also had tomatoes from the Piedmont, from Puglia, Campagna, even Sicily, whose greenhouses supply the rest of Italy and northern Europe during the off-season months. As he saw it, this was an exciting time to be a tomato connoisseur.

"Once upon a time, if you wanted a winter tomato, the only kind you could get were the Vesuvian ones, strung up in the summer," he said. "I sold them from the end of October until January. Then in the 1980s, there began to be hybrids, which made it easier to sell a larger number of varieties during the course of the year." Starting in the 1990s, D'Agostino decided to sell only tomatoes. In the summer, he could hardly control his fanaticism. In the old days, he always had the *costoluti*, the ribbed tomatoes that are surprisingly similar to the tomatoes one sees in the old sixteenth-century woodcut illustrations. He had the little Neapolitan tomatoes, called Lampadina for their lamplike shape, and San Marzano, which grow in the triangle of land formed by Naples, Salerno, and Mount Vesuvius. The San Marzano disappeared for a while after it was attacked by a fungus, but in the 1990s, federal researchers recovered it with a breeding program. When he made his own tomato sauce, he used cherry tomatoes like the Pommadarella from Abruzzi. "You can't eat them in a salad—they're bitter, brutal. But make them into a sauce and they're divine." He didn't make his own sauces anymore, though. His mother had died three years earlier, and now he had no one to cook for.

He showed us a big ribbed Beefheart, grown around Turin. "I can make a fabulous sauce with this. I can eat it raw with mozzarella—fantastic. But if I make a fish, it's not right. It goes with greens, not with fish or meat. These earlier ribbed varieties"—he rummaged in his stall—"these go well with fish." When I pointed out that no American market of any kind would try to sell the wrinkled little Datterini, D'Agostino frowned. "They're wrinkled because they've been exhaling, getting more intense and concentrated as they go. Do they change in flavor? I'd say yes. But that's a discussion for biologists. You feel the intensity. If it was a sweet tomato to begin with, it gets sweeter. The acid ones get more acidic."

Marjorie asked if any varieties he liked had disappeared. "None," he said. "There are three hundred twenty varieties in Sicily alone." We started talking about the tomato they call the Pachino, a prized cherry I'd been hearing about that was grown around the town of Pachino in southeast Sicily, where the Eighth British Army began the Allied invasion of Europe. "The Pachino isn't really from Pachino," he confided. "It's an Israeli tomato. An Italian farmer was in Israel and tasted them. He said, 'These are so good I'll bring them back to Sicily.'"

As for organic farming, he wasn't particularly enthusiastic. "For one thing, you're in the countryside; there are trucks going by a few hundred yards from your farm. There's pollution in the air. It's everywhere, you know? How organic is that? I don't feel it makes any difference. The tomatoes all have the same ingredients. The flavor is probably inferior in organic. And they don't last as long, and they lack as many varieties as there are in hybrids. You want to taste a good tomato?"

He took us over to a crate full of little *pomodorini* and fed us some round ones that were creamy but not very sweet. Then he handed us little date-shaped tomatoes called *scarpariello*—"classified as a bananiform dwarf," D'Agostino said.

Whoa. These were delicious tomatoes—high sweet, high acid, pungent. Like something in a porno movie, they exploded in your mouth. They were like candy—or rather, they were the platonic ideal of tomatoness. "That's a new hybrid," D'Agostino said, "from Sicily."

Italy is such a tomatophilic culture that it would be impossible for a person with my resources to explore all of its nooks and crannies, so I decided to limit my investigations to southern Italy. A few days after visiting with D'Agostino, I set off south from Rome, family in tow. On its Web site, the village of Villalba, in Sicily's Caltanisetta province, promised an annual *sagra del pomodoro*, a tomato festival that fell on every third Sunday in August. So we ferried across the Straits of Messina and drove three hours into the parched heart of Sicily. I don't know what we were expecting as we cornered a mountain road and headed into the whitewashed, hillside town around 2:00 P.M. on Sunday, August 17. Gaily costumed dark-hued men and women, drinking wine out of goatskins and throwing their heads back in hearty peasant laughter, maybe. But there was nothing going on in Villalba at all, except for a few African clothing salesmen sleeping in the shade by dusty wooden stalls in the center of town. No crowds, no music, no hearty laughter, no *sagra*, no *pomodori. Niente.* Nix.

There was an annual festival, it turned out, but it mostly occurred between the hours of 11:00 P.M. and 4:00 A.M. No produce was involved, and no farmers, either, despite the name of the festival, advertised on bills posted around town that read "Tomato and Lentil Festival." Famished, we found the only café in town and convinced the owners, who were in the midst of a very long family luncheon, to bring out some spaghetti with *ragù* and a *tiramisù*. While we waited to eat, and in due time ate—and not badly, though the *bistecca* was as tough as the hide of the cow it was cut out of—the toddler grandson in a muscle shirt and shorts loudly marched around blowing on a toy horn, occasionally stopping to grasp a hank of cheek from my eight-year-old daughter, who promptly named him Pinchio.

Eventually, the head of the tomato farming cooperative was rustled up somewhere, and he sat for an interview while my family gamboled around the sun-washed town square being gawked at by passing motorcyclists and a man with a truckload of squealing pigs. This wasn't a town that attracted a lot of tourist action.

He was Giuseppe Tatano, a charming, blue-eyed, twenty-seven-year-old chain smoker. Things weren't what they seemed on the Internet, he explained. The *sagra*? They'd been holding it for three decades, but it had devolved into an occasion for emigrant Villalbans to visit from Belgium or Germany or wherever and party with their friends. Although most of the remaining townsfolk made their living growing tomatoes, they didn't bother to bring the harvest into town, because no one was interested in buying tomatoes. Tatano's father had started growing tomatoes in the 1970s, and the co-op was formed a few years later. But it had been gradually falling apart as the politicians who set it up to gain a name for themselves moved on to other interests. The co-op hadn't paid its fees to the chamber of commerce for a decade, to give you an idea.

The tomatoes were grown mostly on nonirrigated land and sold to individual families in surrounding towns and cities, or sometimes to truck drivers who bought them on spec with clients in mind. Almost all these tomatoes, Tatano told me, would end up being made directly into sauce in people's kitchens. Many Sicilians and southern Italians still spent a couple of days each summer making sauce and putting it up in beer or soft drink bottles. If they didn't grow enough tomatoes themselves, they'd buy them from a farmer. There was no such thing as a canning industry anywhere near Villalba. And times were tough. "The politicians here don't do anything for us once they're elected," Tatano noted. "They ask us for a few bushels and say they'll use them for promotion, but they just give them away to their relatives and friends." The farmers were desperately in need of irrigated water, especially since climate change, in his view, had created weird weather. It had hardly rained the whole season except for a few days in December. "It's been a bad year for tomato growers, but nobody cares. The mayor's a cardiologist. The politicians think farmers are idiots."

Tatano took me to his warehouse, gave me a bag of lentils, and wished me a happy voyage.

After the letdown in Villalba, I decided to check out Pachino, near Syracuse in southeastern Sicily, even though it was off-season. After some purposeful loitering in municipal offices in the town's nondescript central area, I located Sebastiano Fortunato, the head of a consortium of one hundred producers and packers. What I learned from Fortunato was that Pachino's treasured tomatoes had a tradition that went back all of thirty years.

Pachino is the sunniest town in Europe, and its water table has a salinity approaching 5 percent, which is high. That makes it a very good place to grow tomatoes. But until about 1970, the main crop was grapes, which were primarily made into grappa. Fortunato, who was fifty-two years old, grew up in Toronto, where his father had a fabric business. In 1975, after his grandfather had returned to Italy and begun investing in tomatoes, the whole family followed him home. The Fortunatos organized a network of farmers to grow tomatoes in plastic greenhouses. They produced several varieties, but the leader was a cherry called the Chern, produced by Hazera, a big Israeli seed company. The Chern had the *rin* gene, which gave it a shelf life of up to a month. As in Mexico, there seemed to be a great deal of fighting among big farmers for control of the best seed, and Fortunato told me that all of Syngenta's prized Camone tomatoes were being grown in Sardinia now.

By the 1990s, there was considerable demand for Sicilian tomatoes during the winter, and the Pachino-area growers decided they needed to develop a niche. "We wanted to be the Ferrari of tomatoes, so we could charge a little more," Fortunato said. Around 2000, the district won a prized IGP, a sort of geographic trademark that gives their tomatoes a special cachet. To put Pachino IGP on your tomatoes, you had to grow them within a certified area around the town. You needed the right amount of salt in the water, and you were forbidden from producing more than fifty thousand kilograms of tomatoes (110,000 pounds) per acre, in order to keep the prices up and to keep farmers from overwatering to increase yield. To make sure they reached the limit, the farmers tended to overplant. At the end of the season, they often had several tons of leftover fruit that couldn't get the Pachino IGP label.

After a while, Fortunato started to sound like Tony DiMare, a guy with a lot of gripes. Maybe all farmers sounded like this. They couldn't find good help. Italians didn't want to work. The Moroccans and Tunisians were undercutting them with crappy, cheap produce. Fortunato had visited North Africa five times, looking into putting operations there, like some of his French and Spanish competitors. But the poverty was dismal and there weren't any good managers. "It would probably be the right thing to do from a business standpoint," he said. "But it would be such a sacrifice to spend all my time there." So he was sitting pat. And business was getting worse, inputs more expensive all the time—everything was going to hell. "I've never seen anything like it," he told me. "I think we're heading back to the day of the family farm. One acre, and one family living there. That's the only way you can make it as a farmer."

I got similarly gloomy fare from Luigi Salvati when I interviewed him at his large cannery in Mercato San Severino, a town in the triangle of craggy volcanic land on the Italian mainland between Vesuvius, Naples, and Salerno. This was the true heart of Italian tomato country, and Salvati was a craggy, mordant southern Italian with dark eyes. He canned San Marzanos—the famous handpicked, delicate, elongated heirlooms—under the Fontanella brand (Dececco, in the United States), as well as San Marzano–shaped hybrids, which sold for a third the price. He told me that things were as bad as they had been since his uncle started the business fifty-one years earlier. "I'm very worried," he said. "It's not so much the lack of tomatoes, or the financing. It's that people don't want to work anymore. Nobody wants to get up at six A.M. and go to sleep at ten, which you have to do during the season. In the old days, the workers were uneducated, but they were precise and dedicated. Now they want to knock off after eight hours and go home. The truth is, without the *extracomunitari*, we'd be finished. They're better workers, more dedicated—the Ukrainians, the Romanians, the North Africans. It's our own fault and the fault of the parents. We're doing so well that we aren't willing to sacrifice. We don't want to work. We want the safe job."

It's the same sad story all over. Italy is still the world's second-largest canning tomato producer; its red-and-yellow-colored tins stock shelves around the world. But it isn't like the old days, when the Italian juggernaut was the terror of tomato farmers around the world. A half-century and more ago, American farmers couldn't compete with Italian coreless tomatoes like the Re Umberto and San Marzano. These tomatoes were cheaper to produce and of higher quality than American standbys like the Marglobe and Santa Clara. Blight and other microorganisms that plagued the eastern United States were unknown in Italy. Canning was the sixth-biggest export industry in Italy. The Naples area produced canned whole tomatoes, while around Parma, sophisticated factories cranked out double-concentrated paste using steam-heated vacuums. But even as business boomed, signs of trouble were starting to appear. A U.S. tariff commissioner who visited in 1929, five years before the United States slapped prohibitive tomato tariffs on Italy, noted that sixty thousand Italians worked in six hundred canneries in the Naples area. But land was getting scarce. Prices had gone from $234 per acre in 1900 to as much as $1,573 per acre in 1926.

Even today, Italy makes more cooked tomato products than any other country in Europe—about five million tons a year. The north-south division of labor continues. About 40 percent of tomatoes are grown in the Po Valley to be made into bulk paste. Another 50 percent are grown in the south and are canned whole, diced, or as sauce. But the increase in land costs cited in the 1929 report has meanwhile grown acute. Although tomatoes are still canned in the Naples area, most of them are grown up to two hundred miles away in Apulia, around the cities of Foggia, Bari, and Brindisi, where land and labor are cheaper than in Campania.

"This area is too industrialized," Salvati told me, as we watched a truckload of Apulia-grown tomatoes, packed in sixty-pound crates, roll into his factory, where they were unloaded by forklift. "In Apulia, they have flat lands and bigger farms, and the harvest is mechanical." Topography and land price don't explain the whole problem, Salvati said. The San Marzano geographic trademark includes forty-two towns in the three provinces of Naples, Salerno, and Caserta. But farmers in only a few towns actually grow them. There just aren't that many people who are willing to put the effort into growing San Marzanos. Instead, Salvati claims, people use the San Marzano DOP *(Denominazione d'Origine Protetta)* without using real San Marzano tomatoes. "Fraud is cheaper," he said. "But it penalizes those of us who are making the effort."

While the big Italian producers faced new challenges, a few artisanal producers in the south seemed to be getting by producing traditional varieties. Since 1996, the San Marzano had been reemerging in recipe books and on fancy food Web sites. It had caught on big time among American food snobs. "Ask any chef what the best tomatoes for sauce are and you'll hear a unified chorus: San Marzano," wrote a critic in the online food magazine *The Nibble*. "A tomato so distinctive and high-quality that it is the only cultivar that can be used for true Neapolitan pizza."

A lot of gilt-edged, phony mythology surrounds the San Marzano. According to one entirely unsubstantiated rumor carried on various Web sites, the San Marzano was a gift of the king of Peru (whoever that was) to the kingdom of Naples in 1770. Accounts more fact-based state that the variety arose near the town of San Marzano on the slopes of Mount Vesuvius around 1900, as a spontaneous hybrid of two old open-pollinated varieties, the Fiaschetta and the Fiascona. The San Marzano is an elongated tomato that's about the size and shape of a large banana slug. When cooked, the tomato tends to fall apart, leaving scraps of its stringy self behind. The adjective you hear most often to describe this tomato is "delicate"—it's relatively low on acids, unlike some of its lip-puckering Vesuvian cousins.

One man's "delicate" is another's "insipid," but in any case, disease virtually wiped out the San Marzano by the late 1960s. Everywhere it was grown, wilts attacked, and eventually growers had to introduce other plum-type tomatoes, especially the USDA-bred Roma, to take its place. Enter the Japanese. Somehow, Japanese food buyers got wind of the San Marzano and would accept no substitute. In response to the demand from those faraway islands, the Cirio Research Center in Naples, with money from the national research agency, set up a program to preserve the variety. They did this by selecting seeds from farmers' collections until they found some that were resistant to wilts. The most resistant selection was the Cirio 3, which is grown by Salvati and the other big producers under a DOP—like the IGP, a regional designation linking a food crop to a *terroir*.

On the Internet, I found a fan club called "I Devoti del San Marzano," whose activities included "tours of the San Marzano area for specialty journalists." I had the damnedest time getting any of the members to respond to my e-mails. Finally, the head of the group sent me a desultory message that he'd be out of town when I was there. So I showed up at the group's headquarters. La Fabbrica dei Sapori (The Flavor Factory), two miles outside a battered little Campagnan town called Battipaglia, was an old tomato cannery on a dusty industrial route. It had been refurbished in industrial grays and brown into a vast and very chic restaurant where pizza was being served when I arrived. The owner, a devotee named Cosimo Mugavero, studied cooking in Paris, began making pizzas in the 1970s, and is one of the most prolific dough spinners in the world; as of 2005, he'd served more than two million pizzas at restaurants throughout Italy. Mugavero wasn't around, so I ordered a mozzarella, olive, and escarole pizza on one of his "anti-aging" crusts, a whole-wheat dough with eight raw vegetables baked into it. For a healthy food, it was surprisingly fabulous, as even the pope had agreed, after a private tasting at the Vatican in 2007.

After many cell phone calls and hand gestures, I was instructed to return a few days later to talk to Mugavero. He was a balding, raven-haired middle-aged guy dressed in blue jeans and loafers, with spectacles around his neck on a cord. To explain the difference between San Marzano DOP and regular San Marzano–shaped tomatoes, he said, would require a taste test. We went back to his enormous kitchen and strode up to a spotless stainless-steel counter. As his pizza chefs studiously watched, Mugavero opened three cans of tomatoes—San Marzano DOP, San Marzano hybrids, and *pomodorini*, canned cherry tomatoes—and turned them onto plates in front of me. The first we tried was the San Marzano. *"È più tenero,"* he said—more fragile, stringy even. The ersatz San Marzano was darker and held together more. "Both are great tomatoes," he said. "The difference is in how you use them. When you use the San Marzano, the tomato flavor dominates. Not so much with the other one."

To me, they tasted about the same, maybe with a slight preference for the ersatz variety. "The difference is slight," he acknowledged with a disappointed air, "it's a shading." The *pomodorini*, on the other hand, were much stronger-flavored than either variety. Stronger sweets, stronger acids. "These have a more intense, aggressive flavor," Mugavero said. "You sense the swing between bitterness and sweetness."

On the one hand, all this obsession with a forgotten, reborn tomato seemed like so much charming marketing bullshit to my crude American palate. On the other hand, the pizza I ate with my family at the Flavor

Factory was certainly the best any of us had ever tasted. The flavors were well blended but strong and tomatoey, the crust was crunchy and tasted like well-seasoned olive oil. The pizza with tiny mozzarella balls made from the local buffalo mozzarella filled our mouths with a buttery vinaigrette. The four-cheese pizza with diced tomatoes sprinkled on it that my son ordered was perfectly spiced, the cheeses not too salty, as they are in the United States. Dare I doubt the judgment of a man who produces such an obviously superior product? I dare not.

It turns out there is a revolution in the San Marzano revolution, a group of tomato Mensheviks who decry the San Marzano DOP crowd as what one critic called the "evil San Marzano empire." A faction of this rebel group is led by Sabato Abagnale, an otherwise mellow-seeming food entrepreneur in the town of San Antonio Abad. Abagnale and eleven of his partners grow their own San Marzanos using a second subvariety, the Smec-20. The Cirio Research Center also developed the Smec-20, but purists claim that it's closer to the San Marzano strain that prevailed before it crashed and was scientifically resurrected. Abagnale calls his product the Miracle of San Gennaro, and he puts a "Made in Campagna" sticker on it to "show that our region makes good things, too, not just garbage for the Germans to haul away." (In the summer of 2008, the Naples area was in the news because its mobbed-up garbage workers had been on strike so long that streets were clogged with the stuff.)

The Slow Food movement prefers Abagnale's tomatoes, which he doesn't peel before canning. Several swanky restaurants on the Sorrentine Peninsula swear to its superiority. "The color should be an intense red, the red of fire, like the eruption of Vesuvius," a chef named Alfonso Jaccarino rather poetically put it.

San Antonio Abad, like many of the towns in the area, is old and industrial. There are sixteen different tomato canneries lining its narrow streets. As my family and I slowly made our way through pestilent traffic down its main road, we caught glimpses into the yards of the warehouses, where thousands and thousands of tin cans were stacked on wooden pallets, ready to be slapped with labels that would appeal to customers half a world away. With a few detours, we found Abagnale's house near the central square, and while my wife and kids played badminton in the backyard with his wife (an industrial chemist) and their teenage daughter, Abagnale gave me a tour of a field near his home, on a palm-tree-dotted plain surrounded by Vesuvius and its folds on one side, the imposing Lattari Mountains on the other.

Abagnale's father had been one of the biggest San Marzano canners in town until the late 1960s, when the fungi drove him out of the business. Abagnale started out with a little fresh-vegetable market but decided to go into farming after his tomatoes caught on with the local gourmets. He rotated the tomatoes with beans and little artichokes, which he covered with clay pots while they matured to keep them tender and purple. The tomato harvest took place from mid-August to mid-September. "It's a very delicate process, and it's all manual," he said. He produced only about fifty thousand jars of San Marzanos during the season, selling most of them to local restaurants. Everything had to follow traditional rules and superstitions. To make sure the fruits were red and juicy, you had to harvest them at night and have the cooked tomatoes packed in juice by six o'clock the next morning. You couldn't make love for two weeks before the harvest, he told me with apparent earnestness. And every family in town had its own seeds, which they gave little names.

"I don't do anything new. I do what the generations before me did," he said. The plants weren't "organic," but they didn't need many fertilizers, because of the volcanic soil. He used copper to attack *Alternaria*, a tomato fungus. Not too many farmers liked the Smec-20, because it fell apart when handled mechanically. Most of the canneries in town were processing hybrids. Abagnale and his partners had their niche. "It's the difference between a Fiat and a Ferrari," he told me. Italian tomato farmers apparently like car metaphors.

Abagnale seemed like a sweet guy with nothing to prove but a love for the game. If the tomatoes down here are all about the mixture of sea and volcanic soil, he's the gentle Tyrrhenian breeze more than the brute eruption. Our next stop in Vesuvian territory, however, was high up on the east side of the volcano, where the last eruption, shortly after the Allies captured Naples, destroyed eighty-eight B-25 bombers and buried the towns of Massa di Somma and San Sebastiano. At this site, Giovanni Marino, an aristocratic landowner, was preserving the *piennolo* —the thick-skinned cherry tomatoes that generations of southern Italians have hung up to slowly dry and preserve for making *passata* during the winter.

"What the heck? How can you save a tomato?" asked my daughter Lucy as we drove through the narrow, garbage-strewn roads between the A-3 superhighway exit at Herculaneum and the Casa Barone warehouse. We were met by Marino, who handed us off to his English-speaking agronomist, Sergio de Luca, a bearded forty-four-year-old in a yellow polo shirt. Brown-eyed and alert, de Luca warned us that he was *spigoloso*—which might be translated as "prickly." "I like people and things with strong opinions. I can't stand politically correct yes men," he said. We quickly got a sense of how de Luca fit into the local terrain and the difficult enterprise of preserving the *piennolo*.

De Luca had a degree in plant pathology from the University of Portici and had worked in academia for stretches between getting disgusted with the professors. He was not afraid to share his knowledge and opinions, both considerable. He had very particular tastes. The All-man Brothers blasted out of his Volkswagen at a high volume as he drove ahead of us toward the summit of Vesuvius. He played the guitar himself, though, of course, "no one has played electric guitar since Duane Allman and Jimi Hendrix died." He added, "I'm not a polite person. I say what I think. But I'm not used to thinking about what I say."

The first order of business was to set me straight about the cult of San Marzano. "In this area, to tell you the truth, nobody eats San Marzano, for some Campanialistic reason," he said, which I took to mean that people around here are ornery and like to do the opposite of what's expected of them. But anyway, they weren't missing anything: "There is no real San Marzano anymore. The best ecotypes were lost in the 1970s, killed by fusarium and viruses. They were also less productive and didn't ripen all at once. If people say they are growing San Marzano, it's not true." De Luca wasn't impressed by the "rescue" of Smec-20. "What's left is just the name. But no one will tell you this. San Marzano DOP? If you are making a good product, you don't have to call it something else. If you're growing something good, why did you have to call it 'San Marzano'? Because consumers stick to the labels more than the taste." In De Luca's view, the customer was almost always wrong.

De Luca, who had been working with Casa Barone for four years, said that he fought with Giovanni Marino, too. But Marino was one of the few producers he knew who wanted a high-quality product even if he lost money at it. "That's what's really visionary about organic and Slow Food," he said. "We've got tomatoes from China selling for seventy cents for a half kilogram, when you have to sell at least double that price just to break even." His dream was to turn back the hands of time, creating a farm like the ones that were here a century ago, with nothing more modern than a volcanic eruption to trouble their rustic authenticity.

In bright sunshine, we drove up the eastern slope of the volcano, then opened a gate blocking access to Vesuvius National Park, and left our cars. Casa Barone had been given permission to farm on a parcel of a few acres barely one hundred meters from the broad swatch of lava that belched out of Vesuvius in 1944. De Luca led me through a terraced hillside planted with tomatoes and grapevines. He'd been clearing roads through the lava, creating dry walls without using cement. "To save the identity of this place, we should return to the old state, using Vesuvian stones, basalt. We should save the old varieties that are strongly linked to the place." He didn't want to use herbicides, because "we prefer not to poison what's already damaged. We want to preserve the biodiversity of this place." His tomato rows alternated with vines that grew Falanghina and Catalanesca grapes, for making the appropriately named Lacrima Christi (Tears of Christ) wine. There was only about two feet of soil on the volcano. "Only a crazy agronomist would do this," he said. He opposed hybrids, too. It was a bad idea to breed in resistance, he said, because "soon another pathogen will move into the niche."

It was hard to find young workers who shared de Luca's enthusiasm. Like many farms in the area, Casa Barone was chronically understaffed, although unlike the others, Casa Barone did not employ Romanians and North Africans. "I can't understand why people don't like farming," de Luca said. "They work seven hours a day, have regular contracts, and get the same salary of someone in industry. And they get to work outside. But Italians associate farming with poverty and shame. It's all in people's heads." At the Casa Barone warehouse, three older guys were sorting through an enormous pile of tomatoes. I asked one of them if his sons farmed. One son worked in the supermarket, he said, and the other drove trucks. "Why?" de Luca asked. "Because there's no money in it," the old man answered. "All the money goes to the middlemen."

The men were picking out the tomatoes with black spots, which was caused by a cladosporium. These bacteria are hard to eradicate because they are transmitted through the seed, and the seedlings have no symptoms, de Luca explained. The bacteria spread easily because of the cultivation methods required by the sere, unirrigated soil in which the tomatoes grow. To protect the vine and maintain the intense flavor of the tomatoes, the workers pruned the plants three or four times a season. In doing so, they spread bacteria from plant to plant.

De Luca's team sorted the tomato racemes—the fruit-bearing branches—into piles that were affected or not affected by cladosporium. The spot-free racemes were prepared for hanging on a length of twine. Vincenzo, one of the men, showed me how it was done—one raceme at a time, placed on the one below it, until there was a mass of tomato vines hanging together like a bunch of grapes. About a thousand bunches hung in the warehouse, each containing about 120 cherry tomatoes.

Some of the tomatoes had nipples, and some didn't. The nippled ones were a sweeter cultivar called Riccia, or San Vito. The other was the Patanara; its leaves resembled those of the potato plant. Not that de Luca expected us to notice the difference. "Give your kids foods loaded with sugar and salt, and as adults, they won't be able to distinguish between sweet and sour tomatoes," he said. "Someone who has been eating processed foods for the last thirty years can't distinguish between Patanara and Riccia."

So we tasted them. "Sour," said Lucy, and she spat it out.

"Delicious," said my wife, who's very polite. "Meaty. A little tart."

My twelve-year-old son Ike noticed that the skin was very thick. To me these tomatoes carried a strong note of dimethyl sulfide—the acrid flavor of cooked tomatoes. But there was no denying that these were tomatoes with intense flavor.

Before we left, de Luca invited the kids to a pastry at the bakery in San Sebastiano. Despite the gruff exterior, he too understood that excessively sweet things would pave the way from one heart to another.

Overall, my tour of the tomato in Italy had been both exhilarating and sad. Almost nobody cared whether a tomato was "organic"—the Italians cared profoundly about how it tasted. Yet though people knew how to grow fabulous tomatoes and cook them in delicious dishes, the mood was deeply pessimistic. Instead of being self-righteous about their farming techniques, the way American organic farmers were, they were bitter about people who did things differently. In America, the world of tomato possibilities was expanding. Here, it seemed to be shrinking.

If the small farmers, except for a few obsessives like de Luca and Abagnale, stopped producing tomatoes, leaving the field to big farmers and processors, did it matter whether these were Italian or Chinese? They were all making paste roughly the same way. The Chinese used the latest Italian machinery and American, Israeli, and Dutch seeds, just like everybody else.

In 2007, I toured the Chinese tomato industry with the World Processing Tomato Council. It was the middle of August, the height of the harvest in most parts of the tomato world, and there were forty-five of us—farmers and canners and food processors from California, Tunisia, Australia, Chile, and everywhere in between. China had recently passed Italy as the second-largest grower of processing tomatoes, after California.

The precipitous rise of the Chinese tomato industry, which scarcely existed before 2000, surely ranked as one of the weirdest of the country's economic boom. To begin with, the Chinese themselves are not big tomato eaters. In Beijing, I was told, the Chinese eat tomatoes one of two ways: scrambled with eggs, or as a dessert, sliced with a liberal sprinkling of sugar. Sometimes you find them in soup. After the Spanish conquest, peppers and sweet potatoes became firmly entrenched in the Chinese diet, arriving by way of the Philippines and Japan. The tomato found few friends, except in the cuisines of the tropical south and a few other areas. We say *tomato*, but the Mandarin Chinese say "foreign eggplant" *(fan qie)*. Eggplants aren't native to China, either, but they got here from India long before the tomato.

The story of mass tomato production in China was a story of socioeconomic imperatives. The tomato paste business was started from scratch by generals who needed to find gainful employment for the hundreds of thousands of soldiers posted in the remote province of Xinjiang during the standoff with the Soviet Union.

After the Chinese built the first for-export tomato cannery in 1987 at Manas in Xinjiang, the military, using the company name Chalkis, soon started building factories with names like "3rd Battalion Tomato Paste Factory," according to Australian tomato industry consultant Barry Horn. The managers were former army generals who still used their military titles. By 2007 the majority of the canning tomatoes were still grown in Xinjiang, China's largest province, a landlocked territory along the old silk route whose native inhabitants include Muslim Kazakhs and Uighurs. In 1993, a big private company called Tunhe started growing tomatoes until it went flamboyantly bankrupt and was taken over by a Chinese state-run food conglomerate, COFCO.

Although COFCO Tunhe was making inroads on Chalkis's territory, the connection to the military is keenly felt to this day. Many of the farmers we encountered wore fatigues. One told me, through a translator, that "Chairman Mao told us to put down the sword and pick up the plough." In the historical museum of Shirezi, a sparkling town of five hundred thousand that the army built from scratch, one of the exhibits was, in fact, a rifle turned into a plough in the early 1950s.

The point of growing all these tomatoes in Xinjiang—as well as Inner Mongolia and Gansu provinces—was not so much to secure vital ketchup ingredients for China as it was to create jobs for all the Han Chinese sent to the region during the heroic age of Chinese communism. The companies have given small plots of land to tens of thousands of tomato farmers. At harvest, the tomatoes were collected in cloth gunnysacks, dumped into trailers, and driven by truck, motorcycle, and even donkey cart to ultramodern, Italian-designed tomato processing factories. There, using the standard method for creating industrial tomato paste, most of the tomatoes were heated to about 200 degrees, which caused them to blow up. The resulting paste was partly evaporated and flowed into sterile drums that went by rail across the country to the east coast and were shipped around the world—especially to the Middle East, Asia, Eastern Europe, and Africa.

A certain tension permeated the tour, because while some of the visiting tomato farmers and processors were looking for business opportunities, all were seeking intelligence as to how serious a threat China's tomatoes were to their operations back home, where tomato growing was sometimes not just a business, but also a way of life. The rise of the Chinese industry had wreaked some havoc, and not just in Italy. The Senegalese claimed that cheap Chinese tomato paste was driving tomato farmers off their land. The Turks, Aussies, and Russians had similar complaints. The Chinese sought to reassure their guests that they were really enthusiastic about tomatoes, too, and not just for the money. But it didn't seem to be a coincidence that none of the guests were Italians, except for an engineer from Rossi Catelli, a big food-processing machinery maker.

At a symposium in Beijing, Ning Gaoning, the president of COFCO, offered the following happy explanation of the tomato boom: "Tomato is such a beautiful fruit," he said. "It brings us taste and nutrition and health, and also it brings us business. It is a foreign thing. But it is more and more an important thing in the 'New Socialistic Country-side.'" Speeches like Ning's would be punctuated, during the tour, with the plinking of glasses of Chinese wine and of the sickeningly sweet COFCO brand tomato juice. Accompanied by lots of French fries, doused in ketchup. There were, in fact, ketchup packets at almost every meal, including the inevitable eleven-course banquet (among the courses, mysteriously, were chicken wings and French fries from KFC), and our stop at the Laoshe Teahouse, a glitzy tourist trap off Tiananmen Square, where we were entertained with a simultaneously translated floor show featuring a tubby dancer "balancing porcelaneous flower jug on head and throw it in the ambience of the evening," and the fabulous "face smearing of the Sichuan opera also called blow facing!"

Eager to assure their foreign guests that Chinese tomato production would not grow at the expense of foreign producers, the Chinese stressed that their young people consume more tomatoes all the time—in the form of pizza sauce or ketchup on fries and burgers, at the three thousand or so fast-food emporia opened in China over the past couple of decades. This junk-food explosion, and the recognition that China was starting to have an obesity problem, however, seemed slightly at odds with the World Processing Tomato Council's chief marketing pitch, which was that processed tomatoes were good for you—full of lycopene and other molecules that may help prevent cancer and heart disease.

"So the way to save the world's tomato industry is by getting the Chinese to eat more junk food?" I whispered to the representative of a major food-processing company.

"You weren't supposed to notice that," she responded.

What of the quality of the Chinese produce? The consensus seemed to be that while China was doing a plausible job making tomato paste, it had a ways to go. Juan José Amezaga, a handsome, chain-smoking, hyperkinetic Spanish tomato consultant, rushed around the factories, eyeing the weak spots. (Late blight! Rust in the trucks! Long lines waiting to enter the plant, with tomatoes rotting in the sun!)

"A sheety tomato is a sheety tomato," he was heard to say.

Amezaga wasn't the only one with doubts. Tomatoes are very difficult to keep pest-free, and in some of the Xinjiang fields, the visitors observed varieties of mold and viral infections they didn't even recognize. Jim Beecher, a sharp, outgoing Fresno farmer, stooped over a patch of black-spotted tomatoes and calculated its yield at about twenty tons per acre—about half the average of his fields in California. But that particular field was being farmed for Chalkis, and our tour guides were all from COFCO Tunhe, which led some of the guests to speculate that COFCO Tunhe was just trying to make its competitor look bad.

While free land and cheap labor gave China advantages, tomatoes are finicky fruit and tomato production a tricky business. A month after the visit, word arrived in Western tomato capitals that China had lost nearly a third of its crop—an uncontrollable mold had ruined the tomatoes of Inner Mongolia. This episode produced a certain schadenfreude among tomato people in the West.

"Serves them right," an Italian canner told me.

The next year, though, Chinese production had climbed back to about seven million tons. And in 2009, despite the ethnic riots in Urumqi, the harvest was similarly high. Xinjiang's tomatoes were here to stay. The tomato, born in Peru, nurtured in Mexico, and trained to perfection in Italy, was continuing its conquest of the world.

CHAPTER SEVEN

Messy Business

Our kitchens are built near tomato fields so we can pick, prepare and pack our tomato sauces the same day.

—From an old Five Brothers pasta sauce label

 WE CITY FOLK HAVE AN ENTIRELY CONFUSED PICTURE OF rural life. We like to think of the farmer rising early to a hearty breakfast before slogging through manure to milk the cows while twiddling straw in his mouth. It's a peaceful, low-stress idyll, and it couldn't be further from reality. The American farmer's day is more likely to involve traveling vast miles in a gas-guzzling pickup while on the cell phone to bankers, labor contractors, seed salesmen, and dozens of other people, even politicians. These farmers have more to worry about in the course of a week than many of us deal with in a year. Maybe the rains will come too late, or too early. Maybe one of a dozen or more threatening viruses, bacteria, molds, or insect problems will suddenly strike. Maybe, if you live in California, where the

biggest, wealthiest farms are, you won't get any water this year, forcing you to give up the profitable tomato harvest because you have to divert your entire water allotment to the almonds or walnuts or peaches. If the trees don't get water and they die, you lose seven or ten or twenty years' investment. And you've got hundreds of thousands or millions of dollars in loans that have to be serviced. "'Farm,'" said Jim Beecher, a Fresno tomato farmer and processor, "is a four-letter word."

Most of the tomatoes sold as cooked products are now grown in California, and the industry has grown increasingly concentrated since Jack Hanna's day. The largest tomato processing company in the world, the Woodland, California–based Morning Star Company, produces three million tons of concentrated tomato paste every year, most of it in a three-month period starting in late July. But with only about two hundred employees, even Morning Star is a small company that's subject to the same problems as any other tomato grower.

In early 2009, there was a new storm brewing in the tomato business, and it would prove to be even more challenging than the natural disasters that constantly plagued the industry. In April, federal agents raided the Lemoore, California, offices of SK Foods, the second-largest tomato processor after Morning Star. The raid hadn't gotten much press, because most of the locals figured it was an immigration raid, an increasing occurrence in the food industry. In fact, the agents seized paperwork and computers as part of a four-year investigation of bribery and price fixing in the tomato processing industry. The probe focused on Scott Salyer, SK Foods' owner, but also involved some of the biggest food companies in the United States and, at least peripherally, two other major tomato companies—Ingomar Packing Company and Los Gatos Foods.

Some people in the business saw the raid as inevitable. The structure of the industry, which involved fewer and fewer players with more and more power, invited corruption, they felt. While no one in the business thought that Chris Rufer, the founder and owner of Morning Star, was anything but an honest and upright businessman, some, including his competitor, Jim Beecher, believed that Rufer's relentless drive for efficiency might have contributed to conditions that gave rise to corruption. Rumors of price fixing and dirty field men who squeezed extra bucks out of the farmers in exchange for tomato-growing contracts had a long history in the processing tomato industry. According to one version of events, it had been one of Rufer's former employees who had attracted federal investigators to begin with.

That account went like this: At a January 2002 meeting of the California Tomato Growers' Association, a farmer named John Poundstone told an elaborate story about kickbacks in the tomato fields. The kickbacks revolved around one or more "field men," the cannery employees responsible for contracting farmers to deliver a certain tonnage of tomatoes at a certain time during the harvest and making sure the tomatoes get harvested on time. Poundstone, who said angrily that he was tired of playing ball, accused a particular Morning Star field man named Jerry Gilbert of taking advantage of the complexities of the business to personally enrich himself. There were a variety of ways of doing this. If a farmer was contracted to deliver, say, 20,000 tons of tomatoes but, due to the vagaries of weather and seed, had yielded a bumper crop of 25,000 tons, the field man would offer to buy the extra 5,000 at a reduced price. In the meantime, he'd have set up a dummy contract under another grower's name. He'd take the first farmer's 5,000 tons and sell them, at full price, under the second farmer's name to Morning Star—splitting the difference with the second, dummy-contract farmer. Since tomatoes in the early 2000s were selling for about $50 per ton, that simple transaction could net a crooked $125,000, to be split two ways.

A colleague brought the allegations to Rufer, and after obtaining evidence that supported them, the Morning Star chief asked Gilbert to come clean. But Gilbert said it was all a misunderstanding. A short time later, he left Morning Star and was hired by a friend working at a competing company. In January 2003, a Winters, California, grower named Andres Bermudez sued Gilbert and Morning Star, claiming they had reneged on an agreement to buy his tomatoes.

Bermudez himself was a tough entrepreneur who'd entered the U.S. as an illegal alien, worked his way up to owning land, invented a machine that transplanted tomato seedlings in the field, made millions of dollars, and returned to his hometown of Jerez, Zacatecas, where he was elected mayor. Bermudez died early in 2009 of a heart ailment. His lawsuit, which claimed that Gilbert had demanded kickbacks in exchange for Morning Star's business, was news to Rufer. A few weeks after he attended a deposition on the lawsuit with Bermudez, Rufer, and their lawyers, Gilbert committed suicide by shooting himself in the head. The allegations were never published, and the case was quietly settled. But it may have kicked off the wider investigation into industry corruption that followed.

Rufer was plainly disgusted and disappointed over the affair. A full-bore libertarian, he believes that if you take something from someone without their permission—whether you're a government collecting taxes or a mugger with a crowbar—you're equally guilty of theft. Rufer was born in Los Angeles in 1949 but grew up in the Central Valley, where his father was a truck driver. He studied economics at UCLA and got a master's in agriculture at California Polytechnic State University and an MBA at UCLA. During summers, he drove a tomato truck. He's a lanky guy with intense blue eyes, a prominent beak, and one of those clean California accents with just a hint of western twang. He speaks matter-of-factly, with annoyance when discussing the government and other wrongheaded people. He has a fax machine in his bedroom, and his traveling office is a white Bentley (which had four hundred thousand miles on it last time I asked). He works *all* the time.

Rufer is recognized as Mr. Processing Tomato within his industry, but it might be more accurate to think of his company as the FedEx or Toyota of tomatoes. Not to be confused with Morningstar Farms— which makes vegetarian products—Rufer's Morning Star Company in 2008 provided about 40 percent of the paste that goes into pizzas, soups, juices, spaghetti sauces, salsas, and all the other tomato products in America. Most of us probably consume, at least a few times a week, food whose ingredients were handled by Morning Star, yet who has ever heard of the company?

"You know, it could have been widgets," Rufer told me in an interview. "I mean, I love tomatoes but that's not it. Tomatoes happen to be what I evolved into. Why do you marry the person you married? Why did you meet Harry in fifth grade and he's your best buddy? It just happens. Even as an undergraduate, I wanted to be in business. I like L.A., but I wanted to be in the valley. I thought maybe I'd be a farmer, but I wanted to be something bigger in size than my father. Agribusiness. That was what I wanted. So I oriented my education to that."

What Rufer did was to introduce the latest methods of production, engineering, and inventory control into the tomato field and cannery, creating a tomato growing, harvesting, and processing giant in a very small company. The business grew out of Rufer's natural engineering ability. "My mind sees patterns and numbers flowing into patterns. I look at the economic picture, the technological picture, keep balancing things around until they make sense."

When Rufer was driving a truck in the early 1970s, most of the canneries were in the Bay Area, far from the tomato fields in the Central Valley. Not so long ago, there had been fields and orchards in San Jose and Oakland; even the Cannery at Del Monte Plaza, on San Francisco's Fisherman's Wharf, was an actual cannery until 1937. Interstate 5, the straight, fast, numbingly dull highway that connects the Central Valley and the rest of the state, wasn't finished until the mid-1970s, and the California Aqueduct was completed in 1969. The high cost of land and urban water pushed fruit and vegetable farms out of the Bay Area in the 1950s, but the canneries remained there a while longer. "Factories were buying tomatoes at longer and longer distances until they couldn't handle the cost structure," Rufer said. As he made his runs to Hayward, Oakland, and Sacramento, waiting in traffic, waiting at the grading station, waiting in the field, smoldering at mankind's stupidity, he began devising more efficient ways of doing business. Canneries were already moving closer to the tomatoes when Rufer started his company. He built new ones and designed them to work like efficient factories.

"In those days, we would stand four hours getting a load. Now it takes thirty minutes. I'd get eight or nine loads a week, harvested during the day. Now we go twenty-four hours a day, seven days a week, and the trucks get up to fifty loads a week. I spent two hours at a grading station. Now our drivers spend fifteen minutes. All the systems just improved. The bulk hauling of tomatoes [in 28.4-ton gondolas] was a big deal. The harvester was a big deal. The switch to electronic sorters in the 1970s. The yields changed quite a bit, allowing you to harvest more tons per hour. And the processing plants changed location. Sacramento doesn't have a tomato cannery anymore. The last Bay Area cannery closed ten years ago. Hunt-Wesson had canneries in Davis and Hayward. Those factories are gone." Most of the jobs were gone, too, but so were the noise and pollution and idling tomato trucks.

In 1983, after going into business with two large farmers as Ingomar Packing Company, Rufer built the world's first all-paste tomato factory in Los Banos, a key step in the transformation of the canned tomato business. In the past, food companies like Del Monte, Hunt-Wesson, and Heinz had taken tomatoes that farmers brought in and sorted them according to quality. The good ones became "peelers"—whole or chopped peeled tomatoes—that became finished canned products on the spot. The broken ones went into paste, or ketchup.

At Los Banos, everything coming into the plant was turned to paste, which was stored in sealed, antiseptic boxes that could be kept for months or years without spoilage. The food companies could purchase as much or as little paste as they wanted, depending on the market for their finished products. The pictures on the labels of products like spaghetti sauce and salsa were the only tomatoes the big food companies ever saw. To be sure, the "kitchens" were "close to the fields." But they weren't the kind of kitchens that old Italian grandmas cooked in. The tomatoes were processed by Chris Rufer and a half dozen other big raw-material handlers. No hands ever touched the fruit.

Rufer's design was to seamlessly integrate the planting, harvesting, and processing. The tomatoes would be planted in a staggered fashion within the harvesting area that fed the factory. As they matured, the factory would have the capacity to process them. The processors negotiated the tonnage and price with farmers in January, so that everything took place in a regular, more or less orderly fashion.

"I don't think there was anyone who had a more burning desire to start a plant than Chris. He was the sparkplug, and the other partners were the bucks and the horsepower," says Charles J. "Chuck" Rivara, an almond farmer and the director of the California Tomato Research Institute. "And there were prices to pay. If you were a farmer who threw in with Ingomar, you'd lose your contracts with the other canners. They'd say, 'Now you're our competitor.'"

Rufer left Ingomar after a few years to create his own company. Ingomar became one of his competitors, along with Tri-Valley Growers, which later went spectacularly bust. Two other big players later entered the business: J. G. Boswell, the secretive "King of California" who controlled a massive land empire in the southern part of the valley, and Boswell's onetime nemesis, Scott Salyer.

Americans were buying increasing amounts of finished tomato products, like ready-made spaghetti sauce and frozen or take-out pizzas. Developing better economies of scale for making paste, Rufer could produce paste more cheaply than a Kraft, Campbell, Del Monte, or Heinz. Instead of producing finished tomato products from scrap at their canneries, the leading tomato-product retailers increasingly let Morning Star and its competitors make their paste for them. Because it focused almost exclusively on paste, Morning Star contracted farmers to grow high-viscosity tomatoes that produced more consistent paste.

More than ever, the farms that grew processing tomatoes on thousands of acres in Maryland, Pennsylvania, Ohio, and Indiana moved to California, where the business was cheaper and less risky. By 2007, 95 percent of processing tomatoes were grown in California. "The way we used to make the finished product is, you made spaghetti sauces, juices, soups, and so on, the same day," says Rufer. "With the changes in the processing technology, you could make paste and then store it." The canneries, many of which were back East or in the Midwest, converted to remanufacturing paste from California. This allowed them to make final products yearlong to specifications. "You didn't have to guess eighteen months in advance which product to manufacture that day in the summer when the tomatoes were ripe," Rufer said. "You put them in bulk paste, and make ketchup and tomato sauce closer to where the consumer eats the product."

In 1972, 20 percent of California's processing tomato crop was packed as bulk tomato paste. By 1995, when Morning Star opened the largest tomato cannery in the world at Williams, in Colusa County, 60 percent of the tomatoes went into paste, and by 2005, more than two-thirds became paste. Since the early 1970s, the inflation-adjusted price of tomato paste has dropped from about $1.20 to $0.35 per pound.

The quantities involved were staggering. In a single hour, the Williams plant could take 600 tons of raw tomatoes—1.2 million pounds—and convert them into 200,000 pounds of tomato paste (6 to 1 is the standard ratio of raw tomatoes in highly evaporated industrial paste). It was a remarkably automated industry. Gone were the days when a small army of Mexican laborers scoured the fields, stacking boxes of tomatoes to be manually cored in the cannery. In 2006, only 2 percent of the average California paste operation's expenses were seasonal labor. Some 46 percent went to the tomatoes, 9 percent to containers, and 13 percent to heat the boilers and pay for electricity.

"Chris with his MBA ran the cannery with the lowest number of people imaginable," Kanti recalled. "I remember him coming to a breeding meeting at UC Davis and I asked him, 'How can you get away in the middle of the season?' He said, 'My job is to make an operation that can run without me.'"

Gradually, Morning Star became an integrated processing tomato business. In the 1990s, it began offering to harvest the farmers' crop and, several years later, insisted on it. Around 2005, as seed prices shot up, the industry shifted to growing out the seed in greenhouses and transplanting the seedlings, instead of directly seeding the fields. This method used about 85 percent less seed. Morning Star did the transplanting, and Rufer also bought into a nursery business.

His operations were efficient and therefore were "greener," too, but Rufer wasn't particularly thrilled by organic farming. "Chicken shit as fertilizer—that's cleaner?" he'd ask. He produced organic paste, of course, because there was a demand for it. The customer was always right. The idea of sustainability resonated with him and with the big farmers, and they were moving in that direction, if slowly, through better use of technology. GPS-guided machinery, drip-fed fertilizer and pesticide, and lower-intensity cultivation mean fewer inputs and soils with better tilth. The biggest obstacle to switching processing tomatoes to organic in California was the amount of nitrogen they required to obtain their high yields—about 250 pounds per acre. "These tomatoes are zombies," said Juan José Amezaga, the Spanish consultant. "If we don't give them their cocaine, they don't grow."

Though he was very much the boss, Rufer ran a dispersed, decentralized company that gave managers responsibility for running their own departments. No one had a title. The system wasn't for everyone, but while some employees left, they usually maintained a deep respect for Rufer. Not all of them, of course. In 2004 and 2005, three of Rufer's senior sales executives left and went to work for SK Foods, a major competitor. One of them pleaded guilty in 2009 to embezzling nearly $1 million from Morning Star; the two others were implicated in a bribery scandal that by mid-2009 had also led to guilty pleas by five other people.

During the production season, harvest and delivery were computerized and calculated down to the last mile and minute. The goal was to have trailers full of tomatoes sit no more than an hour at the factory before they were processed. Rufer would get the tons he contracted for, the farmers would earn the money for their tons, and the tomatoes would be processed as fresh as possible. But things didn't always work exactly as Rufer and his partners hoped.

There was always jostling, among the farmers, to get harvesting contracts for July or August, when the yield of a harvest was likely to be best. Rufer wanted to maximize the tonnage of high-quality tomato products he ran through his factories from July to October. Sometimes, this conflicted with the growers' interests. Some owned harvesters and preferred to amortize them rather than pay Rufer to do the harvest— but he insisted that his harvesters collect their crop, on his schedule. He wanted the irrigation water cut three weeks before the tomatoes were harvested. Cutting the water caused the foliage to shrivel up, which made it easier to harvest the tomatoes, and concentrated the fruit's soluble solids—the sugars, acids, and minerals that are dissolved in it. Morning Star's customers wanted tomato paste with good soluble solids, though they all had different specifications. From the farmer's perspective, the juicier the tomato, the more it weighed, and the more he or she got paid.

And if the foliage dried up too much, exposing the fruit to a lot of intense sun, the tomatoes developed sunburned areas that were attacked by black mold. During heavy harvest years, some farmers complained that by the time Rufer's harvesters got to their fields, mold was rampant and the crop was ruined.

Don Cameron, who managed a 5,500-acre farm near Fresno and negotiated with Rufer and the other processors as chair of the California Tomato Growers' Association for two years, found Rufer to be a tough negotiator. Every January, the growers sat down with all the processors and hammered out a price for the tomatoes that would be harvested beginning in July. Rufer never gave an inch. "We'll spend days arguing over an extra twenty-five cents per ton," Cameron told me over breakfast in Urumqi, China, during the Processing Tomato Council's visit there. "Chris wants people to think he knows what's right—but he's not always right. He goes from shouting to being a nice guy."

In a sense, Rufer's actions were to be expected, given the way his business had evolved. Tomato paste had become a commodity. Although there were quality differences, in general paste was paste no matter who produced it, as long as they were being honest about their product. The demand for paste was inelastic, because although you could tell people that lycopene was good for them until you were blue in the face, they still wouldn't eat it at every meal. "Rufer is all about squeezing the efficiency out of everyone—not expanding the market. It's typical of someone in a low-value-added business," said Kanti.

Politically, Rufer was similarly inflexible. "Taxing. That's not voluntary," he told me. "America used to be farms, and the government served the function of protecting individuals' property and agreements. Now you vote for a senator because he's going to steal more money from other states to bring to your state. They become arbiters of theft." But isn't it necessary, I asked, to compromise a bit to make a workable system? Aren't there degrees of compromise? "Nnnnooo there's not. If you can establish principles that work, you can't compromise. You can't believe that gravity works and try to make it work differently. If you think persuasion is better than coercion, it's better. I don't think there's a subscript to the biblical commandment that says 'Thou shall not steal.'"

Big food companies have profited from Rufer's single-mindedness. Take H. J. Heinz, for example. Traditionally, Heinz had bred the seed for its tomatoes, contracted farmers to grow and harvest the tomatoes, and turned them into ketchup and other products in its canneries. But Heinz got out of the business of contracting with U.S. tomato growers in the 1990s. And its factory in Tracy, California, which sent paste to the ketchup factories back East in big tanker trucks, closed in 1997 after fifty-one years in operation. It was cheaper and less of a headache to let Morning Star make the paste.

"It was gospel that no one could do it like Heinz," said Dale Smith, head of Heinz's global seed division. "But gosh—they could."

Now, Heinz mostly performs only the first and the last steps on the production chain. The company tells Morning Star what kind of Heinz seeds it wants farmers to grow (and sells its seed, independently, to farmers who want to grow it for other customers). And it takes the finished paste and turns it into ketchup. The rest of the job it leaves to Morning Star and companies like it. The new labels on Heinz ketchup in 2008, featuring a homegrown-looking tomato and the phrase "Grown not made," are true to a point—but it isn't Heinz that's growing the tomatoes.

Heinz traveled the world looking for places to sell its seed and for farmers to grow the seed out to make paste for its ketchup. In 2006, Heinz bought Petrosoyuz, a Russian company based in St. Petersburg, and was using Chinese paste to make Russian-brand ketchups. (McDonald's demanded Turkish paste, which was more reliable, for the Heinz ketchup used in its restaurants in Russia.) The quality of Heinz seed was beyond dispute. Before contracting with Chinese paste makers, Heinz had tried to set up a joint venture in Uzbekistan, a Russian Heinz official told me. "But there was a lot of corruption. When we got the tomatoes for the paste, they were lousy quality." It turned out that once they'd grown out the high-yield Heinz-seed tomatoes, farmers could make more money selling them to merchants, who peddled them fresh in the bazaar. They'd grown tomatoes with off-brand, cheaper seeds and tried to use them to fulfill their contracts with Heinz—and company officials weren't amused.

The streamlining of Heinz's business, the eternal search for the cheapest product that met quality standards, was very much in keeping with the philosophy of Heinz's CEO in the 1980s. Tony O'Reilly wanted to get rid of the company's factories while adding brands. As for the raw material it needed, O'Reilly squeezed suppliers to lower their prices. Rufer, on the other hand, had no interest in getting into the higher-profit end of the business.

In 2008, the World Processing Tomato Council elected as its president a charmingly gawky Italian named Marco Serafini, president of a company called Desco. I met him at the council's meeting in June, and he graciously invited me to visit his new cannery south of Rome, though he barely had it up and running. The Desco factory is located in the former Pontine Marshes near Terracina, midway between Rome and Naples. The draining of the marshes was one of the few real achievements of the fascist era. Mussolini succeeded where generations of earlier politicians and engineers failed. Then he brought two thousand politically reliable peasants from the north down to live there, giving them houses and land. I saw flat farms studded with ditches that lead into a canal fed by several pumps that run constantly, draining the below-sea-level area. The labor force was increasingly made up of men from northeastern India—they came to manage the water buffalo, whose milk creates buffalo mozzarella. Sweet corn to feed these hefty creatures accounts for much of the acreage planted in the area, I was told.

Serafini produced specialized pastes for pizza, juice, and saucemakers. He relied on the same Heinz and Syngenta seeds that Rufer used, and like Rufer's tomatoes, his were harvested by machine. But the harvester he used looked like something out of the 1970s—the tomatoes were funneled into boxes that guys wrestled into place on the trailer, rather than the giant twenty-six-ton gondolas they fill automatically in California.

Serafini told me that his customers, mostly northern Europeans, would pay extra for a good product. "Our tomatoes are grown close to the sea. The sea and the winds give the perfect ripening to the tomato and a wonderful taste and color to our products. Our product is more tailor-made than a big company like Morning Star."

Was there a significant flavor difference between Serafini's "tailor-made" and Rufer's mass production? It depended on whom you asked. In the days since Jack Hanna first took his hand to the tomato, the fruit used by paste makers had continued its transformation. With the current varieties, 80 percent of the fruit flowers at the same time. The tomatoes are tough, so they can sit on the vine for an extra week or two, allowing the laggers to turn red in the meanwhile. And the tomato looks entirely different. Today's processing tomatoes are almost entirely pericarp, with very small locules. This makes it hard to get decent brix. Most canneries want processing tomatoes with a brix rating of at least five—which means that 5 percent of the tomato is soluble sugars. That translated to 30 percent sugars in the concentrated paste.

Did any of this make a whit of difference in the manufacturing of, say, ketchup? No. "With ketchup, you're looking for the tomato to contribute color and viscosity," said Rufer. "Vinegar, spices, sugar—things like that provide the flavor." Heinz orders Morning Star to produce paste that's the right viscosity, so that it can make its ketchup without adding starch, as ketchup makers did in the old days. The enemy of ketchup is runniness ("high syneresis," to the expert), as we all know from those old ketchup commercials featuring the Carly Simon song "Anticipation." Serafini doesn't make paste for ketchup anymore. A decade or so back, a Kraft official pulled him aside and showed him ketchup made from Desco tomatoes and others. Even Serafini couldn't tell the difference. "You don't need flavor and color for ketchup," he told me.

Whether the same principle holds true for spaghetti and pizza sauces is the subject of considerable debate. Stanislaus, a Modesto company that supplies restaurants and food service companies, turns its tomatoes directly into diced products and sauces and uses higher-sugar tomatoes to make them. Because the tomatoes become sauce directly, without being turned into industrial paste that is then watered down and cooked into a sauce, the company estimates that its sauces have been exposed to only a quarter of the heat used to make your average Prego-type sauce. Its sauces taste better and have some additional nutrients as a result, Stanislaus maintains, and many pizza makers and restaurateurs agree. So do some other tomato processors.

Jim Beecher, a partner in Los Gatos Tomato Products, tells a story of how his staff once helped out a Stanislaus driver whose truck had broken down. "My wife said to me, 'Maybe they'll send us a case of tomato sauce as a thank-you.'" When I asked the Serbian-Americans who run Italian Pizza Kitchen, a higher-end Washington, D.C., pizzeria that my family favors, I wasn't surprised to learn that they use Stanislaus sauce on their 'zas.

Stanislaus, a private Italian-American-owned company since 1942, has appealed to the courts and the federal regulators to make sure its distinct method of sauce making is noted on labels. In the 1980s, Stanislaus tried to get the FDA to require labeling on tomato products similar to the kind used in the juice business, where "made from concentrate" is distinguished from "fresh-squeezed." Tropicana, which is not made from concentrate and advertises heavily on that theme, has "kicked the crap out of the market for the last twenty years because they pack fresh," a Stanislaus official told me. "Minute Maid is made through the cheaper remanufactured route, and they had their lunch handed to them."

Nearly all of the spaghetti and pizza sauces you buy in a supermarket are made from reconstituted paste that was originally produced by Morning Star or another big processor. The restaurants that buy Stanislaus and other smaller-scale, direct tomato-to-sauce products emphasize the flavor. "If you're a small restaurant, you can't compete on price," the official said. "The only way to get business is with flavor and service. And these restaurants prefer the taste of tomato products packed fresh in season."

In 1992, Stanislaus sued Campbell's Soup over the latter's Prego spaghetti sauce and, in 2001, sued Heinz. In both cases, Stanislaus wanted companies that used industrial paste to include the wording "reconstituted tomato paste" on their labels. Papa John's, which used Stanislaus pizza sauce, sued Pizza Hut for the same reason. But the largest food companies in the world used bulk paste in their tomato products, and they fought Stanislaus tooth and nail. The compromise is visible on the labels of most tomato products. The FDA required companies using bulk paste to list the ingredients as "tomato paste, water." It would take a pretty savvy consumer to get the implications of this wording. When I asked Rufer about the taste difference, he equivocated. While he agreed that a lot of people felt the Stanislaus-type product was better-tasting, industrial paste gave food companies the flexibility to make their final product closer to the time of sale, he said. "Some people will tell you that a fresh-made sauce that's been sitting in a can for twelve months tastes worse than one that was reconstituted from our paste a month ago."

If at times he came across as rigid, Rufer's cohorts agreed that he was straightforward and very open about his business. He allowed me to see any aspect of it that I wished. My first visit to one of his fields was on a windswept day in April 2007, in the company of Cameron Tattam, the director of production for Morning Star's northern district.

Morning Star's production area stretches from Bakersfield to Williams, with three-quarters grown south of the Sacramento River. Seeds go into trays in January, and the company starts planting the seedlings in March; the harvest may go as late as November, depending on the weather. As we headed out to a transplanting operation in Tattam's pickup, he filled me in on the year's problems. Tomato yellow leaf curl, a virus known throughout the Mediterranean, the Caribbean, and Florida, had popped up in Southern California the year before, and people were on the lookout for it. Another virus, curly top, was being spread by leafhoppers, and the state had restricted spraying Malathion to stop them, because the chemical killed beneficial insects as well. A new race of fusarium wilt was on the rampage. The spores, carried in soil and water, entered through the roots and wrecked the leaves, dramatically cutting into yields.

Costs were going up—with oil prices soaring, so were prices for petroleum-based products like fertilizer, pesticide, and drip tape. The minimum wage had jumped from $6.75 to $8.50 an hour in two years. "It's all migrants," said Tattam, who hails from Australia. "You can't get a white kid to come out and do this stuff." The company had had to break a "Mexican mafia" of "people who want to get their nephew a job even though he's as dumb as a rock. We've weeded out people who think that way. We don't care where they're from. We don't care about any of that crap. We try to get people we need to do the job."

And seed prices kept increasing. Heinz was the market leader, competing mostly with a small group of multinational seed companies—Monsanto, Nunhems. These three giants had multimillion-dollar laboratories that used molecular marker technology to speed the development of new varieties. Starting with Charley Rick's work, geneticists had identified molecular markers on pieces of DNA that were linked to hundreds of particular attributes—shape, color, lycopene content, soluble solids, ripening attributes. Using genetic techniques, breeders could examine new hybrid sprouts to see if they had the desired markers, rather than waiting until the plant fruited.

But marker technology wasn't entirely dominant. The single leading processing tomato, for example, the AB2, was sold by the Dutch company De Ruiters (later bought by Monsanto). Breeders at the Hebrew University in Jerusalem had developed it by crossing a high-sugar wild species, *L. chimielewski*, into the mix. Another important cultivar, the Haley 3155, had been going strong since the 1980s when Haley Vick developed it, using traditional techniques, for a small Hollister, California, company.

Heinz's geneticists worked in Stockton and tested their seed in plots that spanned six continents. Making hybrid seed continued to be a labor-intensive business, which Heinz contracted to small businesses and sometimes entire villages in low-wage countries like Thailand, India, and China. And as Chinese rural labor grew more expensive, the company had started an operation in northern Vietnam. Heinz sold several billion hybrid seeds each year—the result of perhaps one hundred million individual acts of hand pollination (each time you successfully cross-pollinate a flower, it produces a fruit with an average of seventy-five hybrid seeds).

As late as the early 1980s, the processing industry mainly used open-pollinated varieties that cost about $8 for one hundred thousand seeds. The first hybrid processing tomato varieties came on line in 1976, and between 1984 and 1994, the percentage of hybrids used went from 8 to 80 percent. Yields over this period jumped from twenty-five to thirty-five tons per acre. "Before hybrids, yields in tomatoes were unpredictable," Kanti told me. "A slight change in the weather could screw you." If there were too many underripe tomatoes in the mix, the sauce turned dark and would have to be thrown out.

You could look at the improved yields of hybrids as both a cause and an effect of the changes in the processing tomato business. "In the old days, people didn't eat as much tomato sauce, and it was a loser industry," says Kanti. "But production in California is now about twelve million tons a year." Demand was huge, but it was difficult to open a new cannery in California because of increased regulation and tight water supplies. Processors like Morning Star had to be sure the fields would reliably produce the tomato yields they required to run their factories at full capacity.

There were disadvantages to hybrids, too, the biggest being price, which had risen steadily as farmers got hooked on them. Hybrid seed prices started at $50 per 100,000 in 1976. From 2004 to 2005 alone, the price jumped from $350 to $1,000 per 100,000 seeds. The predominance of hybrid seed also drove the universities out of the breeding business and put intellectual property of the leading varieties into fewer hands. The universities had shared their varieties with anyone who wanted them, and you could reproduce the open-pollinated types simply by planting them and harvesting the seed. In the era of hybrid seed, the hybrid's parents were a secret closely guarded in the vaults of companies like Heinz.

Rufer and growers alike had responded to the seed price hike by increasing the use of transplants. They needed about eight thousand seeds to produce enough seedlings to cover an acre with tomatoes, as opposed to the fifty thousand seeds required for direct seeding. Transplanting also reduced the use and cost of chemical pest and weed controls, because the fields could be sterilized before the transplants went in. According to Tattam, the seed companies responded to the increased use of transplants by selling two classes of seed—one for "transplant" and one for "direct seeding." As far as Tattam could tell, it was the same seed, except that the seed companies had killed about a quarter of the "direct" seed, by baking or microwaving it. "I guess that's to keep you from transplanting it," he said. "I asked one of the guys, 'I legally can't use [the direct seed] for transplanting, or you don't want me to?'"

A few miles outside Woodland, where Morning Star has its modest, four-suite offices above a restaurant, we visited a 133-acre field owned by family farmer Dan Best. The varieties growing there were ps849 from Seminis, which was owned by Monsanto; 6368 from Nunhems, owned by Bayer; and Heinz 9663 and 2401—two of Heinz's proprietary ketchup varieties.

Morning Star was transplanting seedlings grown at a Tracy greenhouse that was co-owned by Morning Star and an Italian company. The joint venture charged the farmer $19.50 per 1,000 plants. The seedlings had arrived in a box on a pallet, 450 cells per tray, and 36 trays per box—each big cube contained 16,250 plants, roughly enough to cover two acres. The trays were loaded onto a carousel planter that was mounted on the front of a big tractor. As the tractor moved slowly down the row, three women sitting on what looked a bit like bicycle seats that jutted out in front of it separated the seedlings and placed them in one of ten cups. Each second, a metallic finger would clasp a seedling from a cup and drop it into a six-inch trench with a squirt of water. A perforated metal wheel under each woman's seat tamped dirt around the seedling. With the wind whipping along fiercely, the machine was only moving about a mile an hour. If it went any faster, the seedlings would blow over as they were dropped through the space between the loader and the hole. Three other workers walked behind the transplanter, straightening blown-over seedlings.

Tattam carried around a thick binder full of computerized metrics, all aimed at producing a smooth harvest that kept the big Morning Star processing plant in Williams moving at full capacity in the high summer. In Best's field, each row was 2,414 feet long. The space between furrows was precisely 60 inches, so the GPS-guided harvester's movements would be tracked by computer and the driver could harvest at night. Some of the seedling leaves had a slight yellowish color, which was normal. To ready the plants for the harsh outdoors environment, they'd been starved the last several days in the greenhouse. "You have to toughen the plant," Tattam told me. He held up a couple of the seedlings, grasping them from the top. If the seedling had a healthy, firm stem, he said, the stem and bulb stuck straight out. "I explain it to farmers as 'Viagra for plants.'"

Morning Star planted as many as 50 varieties in any given year. Heinz, Morning Star's largest customer, was using only 4 of its 120 varieties for its ketchup in 2007. They were planted for Heinz and Heinz only—other companies were free to order paste made with any of the other 116 Heinz types.

If you used another tomato in its paste, would Heinz notice? I asked. Tattam laughed. "They know their varieties so well that they would notice if we slipped other stuff in," he said. Plus, each truckload of tomatoes, with information about the seed type, time of planting and harvest, and all other relevant information, is computerized, so that any batch linked to salmonella, mold, or some other contaminant—God forbid—could be traced back to the field where it grew.

The drive for efficiency and mechanization was relentless and global. In June 2008, I toured some farms around Leamington, Ontario,

with a group of farmers and processors. Although Ontario gets brutal winters, once spring comes, the breezes off Lake Erie in the Leamington area provide a good climate for growing processing tomatoes.
About thirty of us spilled off the bus at Walt Brown's third-generation
farm in Leamington just in time to watch the transplanting operation.
In California, the planting starts as early as March, but here the growing season was just starting. As we looked out over a fine, gently slop-
ing field, a mechanized transplanter moved down the row toward us.
Four Mennonite women, clad in bonnets, were operating the planter
as it dropped seedlings into their holes. The machine could plant an
entire forty-acre field with 350,000 plants in one day. Two months later,
the egg-sized tomatoes would be harvested and turned into juice and
ketchup at Heinz's Leamington cannery, built in 1909.

In the middle of the field, Brown was tinkering with an even more
automated transplanter. This machine had a driver but no human plant-
ers; a set of computer-driven arms brought the seedling trays into position and tumbled the seedlings into the ground. Yet as we followed the
planter, we could see it was botching the job. Many of the plants weren't
properly inserted into the soil and lay on their sides, roots exposed.

"Interesting juxtaposition," said Ross Siragusa, a Heinz production
expert. "The Mennonite girls win—for now."

"It's only a matter of time before they're replaced, though," said Chuck
Rivara. "The goal of agriculture now is to get rid of labor. The truth is, no
one wants to be working out here in the wind and sand and dirt."

Four months after watching the planting of the Best field near Woodland, I returned to it with Cameron Tattam. Best was scheduled to
deliver to Morning Star 42,454 tons of processing tomatoes, for which
he'd be paid approximately $3 million. Since April, the fields had been

irrigated, sprayed with pesticides once, and fertilized twice. Pest control advisers had come out and inspected for wilts, nematodes, beetles, wire worm, viruses, and bacterial speck and spot. Because it doesn't matter what processing tomatoes look like, they need a lot fewer pesticides than what commercial fresh-market growers typically used on their crop. Ironically, Chris Rufer's ultraefficient, factory-farm, ketchup-destined tomatoes were probably sprayed less than some of the fresh ones that organic-loving foodies put in their arugula salads.

"It's really been a perfect year," Tattam said. Tomato plants shut down above 100 degrees, but this year, temperatures had been in the solid 90s. Diseases weren't bad—a little spotted wilt but nothing serious. Some fields were yielding sixty-five tons per acre—ten times what they'd produced thirty years before.

Morning Star was in the midst of its "Heinz pack"—several weeks of the season when everything entering its cannery was destined for Heinz ketchup. We stood in a field of ketchup, as far as the eye could see—thirty-four truckloads of Heinz 2401, which would become 1.3 million pounds of tomato paste and, eventually, hundreds of millions of ketchup packets. I cut open one of the oval-shaped, egg-sized tomatoes. The walls were thick, the locules small, with few seeds. It tasted OK: basic tomato flavor, with no highs or lows. A ketchup tomato.

To my untrained eye, this field looked a bit ill—"crispy," Tattam called it. Leaves were curled and yellow, and many of the tomatoes had sunburn or black specks where dew had set on the flattened burn spots, allowing mold spores to germinate. There were stink beetle bites, too—an entryway for bacteria. Because the season had been so good, with few crop losses, Morning Star was racing to harvest all the ripe tomatoes. Though it wasn't bad to have some of the foliage die back, this field probably should have been harvested a week or so earlier. "We're a little late here," Tattam said. But it would still pass inspection. He picked up a couple of shriveled, blackened tomatoes. "These don't matter in a whole field. And by not kicking out the green and moldy ones, we increase the farmer's yield. The bad tomatoes could be safely mixed in with the rest. "If a field is 10 to 15 percent old, we'll take it. If too many fields are like that, it can be a problem," Tattam said.

We got in the pickup and drove over back roads to I-5, and up the freeway to Williams. We passed enormous pistachio, almond, and walnut orchards in neat rows, and many white tractor-trailers brimming with red tomatoes as they bounced down the highway. Outside Williams, we headed down a flat dirt road into a field being harvested by a double-row harvester. It was an awesome sight. As the machine moved along at 5 mph, a rotating metal cage ran along the ground, ripping out two rows of plants and placing them on a chain that moved up over the cab. Above and behind the cab, a counterweighted shaker jiggled the plants, separating fruit from vine, and a groaning suction fan blew out a froth of tomato waste behind. A sorting machine made by Woodside Electronics Corporation "eyed" the fruit as it came down a conveyer. The machine had ten electronic sensors, one for each of its flexible black plastic fingers. Programmed to object to green tomatoes, its finger popped out and poked them as they tumbled from one conveyer onto another, and the green ones bounced into the space between the conveyers and onto the ground. I asked whether the machine could sort out moldy tomatoes, but Tattam said that because it used a laser beam that identified color, this wouldn't be practical. The mold spots were black, but on any given tomato, the beam wouldn't be likely to hit the mold spot as the tomato bounced past.

Four human sorters, two on either side of the cab, plucked out the remaining dirt clods, green tomatoes, and the odd watermelon or squash that had sprung up in the field—probably "volunteers" from the previous year's harvest. Smashed tomatoes and fruit piled up on the steps. In the time we stood talking in the field, half an hour or so, the machine harvested 114 tons of tomatoes, filling four trailers. The driver of the tractor got a salary; the sorters were earning $7.50 an hour. It was easy to see why labor was such a small part of this business.

Before the harvest ended three months later, this single machine, running twenty-four hours a day, would gather up about three hundred million tomatoes, and the Williams plant would convert some ten billion tomatoes into crushed and concentrated paste stored in aseptic three-hundred-pound boxes. The paste would be shipped to companies like Heinz, Campbell, Pizza Hut, and Domino's and made into spaghetti sauce, ketchup, tomato juice, soup, salsa, and pizzas.

We drove into the Williams plant following a tomato truck that pulled up to the grading station, where a long cylinder was dropped into a section of each of the two trailers. Following a randomized computer map, it scooped up fifty pounds of tomatoes and dropped them into a bucket, which emptied in a room where a group of women examined and sorted the fruit. Moldy tomatoes were put into a gray bucket, green ones into a green bucket, and everything else into a black bucket labeled MOT (material other than tomatoes). "I've gotten frogs, crickets. Once, I picked up a mouse," a sorter told me.

A state agency employed the inspectors on behalf of both farmers and processors, to make sure each side got a fair shake. They checked pH, solids, and color and separately weighed the defective and healthy tomatoes to get a proportion. Not a single load had been rejected this season, Tattam told me. But if the mold count in a load was high, technicians mixed it with a low-mold batch. "All that matters is the final product," he said.

The truck drivers earned between $12,000 and $25,000 in a

three-month season, depending on their hours. The ones who worked twelve-hour days, six days a week, earned about $20,000. Inside the control room, where the truckers hung out griping and waiting for a new load, a big screen showed where each harvester was in relation to Williams. Another screen located the drivers, most of them Mexican immigrants scrambling to make a buck for their families back home. Business was conducted in Spanish. Morning Star tried to keep the wait down to one hour maximum. "Lower inventory means lower number of drivers and fewer tractors and trailers, and higher-quality product," Tattam told me. "The trucking companies don't like it."

When we arrived at the plant, twenty-two graded trailers were waiting for processing—half an hour's worth of tomatoes. Tractors barreled around the yard, hooking up to the trailers and pulling them up a one-hundred-foot ramp to the dumping station, where a boom lifted the trailer, filled it with water, and tilted it slightly. Then the driver opened a four-by-four hole on the side of the trailer, and the tomatoes washed out into a stainless-steel flume. From here, they moved to their destiny by gravity. Rufer had designed the system, Tattam said proudly. "Everyone else hoses out their loads" (until the others started copying Morning Star).

As the tomatoes moved down the flume at the rate of 582 tons per hour, a rotating rake fished out pieces of vine. We saw some blackened corncobs in the mix, and a couple of dwarfish watermelons, from the field we had just visited. And a plastic water bottle. The watermelons weren't really a problem (sweeter paste?), but the bottle was.

"That's not good," Tattam said. "But they'll catch it."

If you stared at the flumes long enough, it was mesmerizing: a long, jumbled parade of red and some green and a few yellow circles bobbing in a mosaic of white foam, an acre of tomatoes moving by every five seconds. The flume divided into twelve lines before sorters had the last chance to pick out impurities like water bottles. The flume was too wide for the sorters to reach across, but if they saw something bad, they could stop the line by pulling a wire. We didn't see whether they caught the water bottle.

The tomatoes plunged into a series of machines that burst them apart, heat them to stop the ripening process, and evaporate the liquid. In the first phase, the chopping pump, a series of paddles rip the tomatoes into small pieces. The tomato bits pass at high speed through sieves of different sizes, depending on the customer's interest (spaghetti sauces can have thicker pieces than pizza sauce), then flow at high speed through a machine that "breaks" the ripening process by heating and deactivating the tomato enzymes that break down pectin and other solids contained in the tomato cell walls. As described in Chapter 2, a "hot break" was used for ketchup and most American sauces, with the tomatoes heated to 100 degrees Celsius. For making tomato juices and most European sauces, the tomatoes are heated only to about 65 degrees Celsius, for a "cold break." Cold-break processing deactivates fewer enzymes, so the resulting tomato sauce is soupier, since more of the pectin has been broken down. The lower heat also results in less cooked-tomato flavor and brighter red color, and possibly a more nutritious paste. In both types, the heating happens as the tomatoes flow rapidly through tubes, to prevent burning. After the "break," the paste goes into a refiner and from there to a vacuum evaporator that concentrates the material. Finally, the paste passes through tubes into sterile metallic bags that are stabilized in plastic-framed 300-pound boxes.

About one hundred people work full-time at the plant, divided among three shifts. "When we started in 1995, with twelve trucks an hour, it seemed like we were balls to the wall. Now that seems slow," said Brian Hagle, the guy in charge of the evaporator. He took pride in the natural-gas-powered generator, which allowed the plant to make power as a by-product of the steam it used to cook and evaporate the tomato paste. If it had to, Hagle said, "we can completely isolate from Pacific Gas and Electric. We can be off the grid." A copy of *God, Guns, & Rock 'n' Roll,* by the former Amboy Dukes guitarist Ted Nugent, lay open on the console, rounding out the libertarian atmosphere.

Over lunch with Tattam at Granzella's, a local dining institution, I remarked that this way of producing tomatoes didn't really resemble the image portrayed in TV commercials and advertising. Tattam's attitude toward farming was in keeping with the company's politics. "It's a business," Tattam said. "Do you want to be out there with a hoe? Yeah, right. Want to be like a Third World African nation? Everyone would starve to death. How are you going to feed three hundred and fifty million people?" His reaction to organics was much the same. "They don't have anything to do with health," he said. "They're trying to sell a product, is all. Try comparing organic and nonorganic paste. They taste the same. You can't tell the difference. Of course," he added, "getting rid of a few pesticides wasn't a bad thing."

On our way back to I-5 and Woodland, we passed an SK Foods plant producing organic tomato products for the Muir Glen label of Small Planet Foods. SK's main plant, the second-largest in California, is down south in Lemoore, near Fresno. The northern plant was shrimpy compared with the Morning Star behemoth down the road. "They don't even do a tenth of what we do an hour," Tattam scoffed. Two years later, in legal hot water, Scott Salyer would sell both plants to Olam International, a Singaporean food conglomerate.

As people in the business described them, Chris Rufer and Scott Salyer couldn't have been more dissimilar in their personalities and management styles. There were frictions between them and, eventually, blood in the water. In February 2008, during the annual meeting of the California League of Food Processors, Rufer was chatting with associates at the bar of the Sheraton Hotel in Sacramento when a process server stepped up to him. SK Foods was suing Rufer, charging that Morning Star had conspired with a New York–based food company to fix prices for processing tomatoes in order to drive SK Foods out of business. The suit arose when SK Foods lost a contract with Heinz to Morning Star and the New York company.

Three months later, without having filed any specifics to back its claim, SK Foods dropped the suit. Salyer had other problems on his hands. In May, IRS and FBI agents raided SK Foods offices, as well as those of Los Gatos and Ingomar, two other processors. In September, the Feds filed racketeering charges against Randall Rahal, a New Jersey trader who sold SK Foods paste to food companies. Rahal, in collusion with Salyer and other SK officials, had bribed at least six purchasing agents to get them to buy inferior SK products or buy its paste at inflated prices, the indictment charged. In one case, a purchasing agent at Kraft Foods admitted buying from SK Foods paste that was contaminated with illegal mold levels, and altering bills of lading to hide the problem.

The suit named major food companies like Safeway, Kraft, Frito-Lay, and ConAgra, and it stunned the processing tomato business. One of the alleged bribe recipients was a ConAgra executive identified in the suit as P. C., "director of agricultural operations." That was Pat Coe—an executive who had been elected chairman of the California League of Food Processors, the leading industry trade group, in 2008. Everyone had been wondering why Coe hadn't shown up at the league's meeting. In one taped conversation, Rahal told a colleague that P. C. was worried that the paste SK Foods was sending him was so bad it might make his bosses wonder what he was up to. "We pack garbage for them anyway and they always take it," Rahal said, "but we've hit new lows."

The problems for SK Foods had been brewing for some time. Salyer's grandfather, a freewheeling farming entrepreneur named Clarence "Cockeye" Salyer, arrived in Central Valley from Virginia in 1918 and at one time controlled eighty-eight thousand acres of land. But in the 1980s, the Salyers lost most of their empire to the rival Boswell family. In 1990, Salyer started SK Foods and later bought the Colusa County Canning Company plant near Williams—the one Tattam sniffed at—as well as Cedenco Foods, a big processor in Australia and New Zealand. But SK seemed to be fraying by 2007. Boswell's company, which had been processing three to four hundred thousand tons of tomatoes annually at SK's Lemoore plant, decided to build its own factory, cutting off SK's tomato supply.

Salyer had rubbed some people the wrong way. A take-no-prisoners negotiator, he traveled the world in a company jet and turned up at food industry conferences in a chauffeur-driven limousine, always nattily dressed. Rahal—who pleaded guilty and agreed to cooperate with the investigation—was "very New Jersey. He's quite bold," said a Morning Star executive. "And he dresses like one of the Sopranos."

What made Rufer wince was that three of the SK employees who are listed in the affidavit as participating in the fraud had quit Morning Star to work for SK Foods in 2004 and 2005. One of them, Tony Manuel, pleaded guilty to embezzling $975,000 from Morning Star. According to a lawsuit that Morning Star filed in May 2009 against Manuel, Salyer, and Jeff Beasley (who left the company in 2004 and pleaded guilty to corruption charges in August 2009), Manuel and Beasley plotted with SK while working at Morning Star to steal the company's clients. Kraft, which had been buying fifty million pounds a year of Morning Star paste for twenty years, suddenly canceled its contract. And Rufer found he couldn't get in the door with other big clients of SK's. In the two years after Beasley's departure from Morning Star, SK's market share skyrocketed.

In a wiretapped July 2007 conversation, according to an FBI affidavit, Rahal suggested that a company might start buying more SK paste and rejecting its competitors' products if a bribe were paid. "You never know what can happen, a little bit of money in the right place can do," Rahal said. Salyer, according to the suit, agreed: "I've heard about that type of shit happening, sample bags thrown away, there's all kinds of shit can happen." Food companies get samples of the paste, which they test for mold, brix, and other properties. In a business where a few cents per pound, either way, can make a huge difference in profits, manipulation of these figures could change everything. In one incident mentioned in the complaint, Rahal told Salyer that a buyer at a major food company should be approachable because he "needs a retirement program." Salyer asks, "How fast are you going to reel in that fish? I want that sucker on speed reel." In August 2009, a judge sentenced a Kraft executive to twenty-seven months in prison and a $1.6 billion fine.

This could be an isolated case of corruption. But two class action suits filed in December 2008 and January 2009 raised questions about the structure of the whole business. The lawsuits, filed on behalf of food processors, claimed that SK Foods, Ingomar, Los Gatos Foods, Rahal, and "unnamed co-conspirators" had fixed prices for tomato paste. The allegation seemed to lack evidence against Ingomar or Los Gatos; the only specific accusation was that they had formed an export association with SK Foods to jointly market their products abroad— a perfectly legal enterprise. But the lawsuits gave a pretty accurate account of an industry in which most of the country's tomatoes were grown for a handful of companies that strived for sameness. In 2007, for example, more than half of the processing tomatoes produced in California were five specific varieties of tomato: the AB2, Heinz 9780 and 9557, Haley 3155, and Hypeel 303. The standardization of paste into a commodity that was almost as interchangeable as corn or wheat or pig bellies "makes collusion easier."

With a small number of suppliers, it was hard for a company like Kraft to get what it needed, and that gave the tomato processing salesmen like Rahal a lot of clout. Meanwhile, the high value of a tomato-growing contract put a lot of power in the hands of the field men—who negotiated directly with the farmers and arranged their planting and harvesting schedules. "It's a perishable crop, a limited delivery window, with high capital investment required for growing and processing," one farmer told me. "You have to have a lot of trust in some of these positions in the supply chain."

In the end, Morning Star seemed to benefit from the outcome of the scandal. The company was gaining strength internationally, exporting sixty thousand tons of paste to Italy in 2008. Cheap Chinese paste was undercutting paste from Turkey, Chile, Russia, and Australia in many Third World markets, but Western Europeans insisted on quality they weren't sure China could deliver, and some were turning to California. Some Chinese tomatoes were contaminated with pesticides from the cotton fields next to them. And Chinese companies, I was told, sometimes reneged on contracts without explanation. "My customers can't risk losing twenty years of business credibility just for that cheaper price," said Juan José Amezaga. "California is the most consistent producer. They have fantastic weather, the best technology, low-cost farmers, and megafactories with huge economies of scale. I don't think anyone can beat them at the field level or at the production level."

To be sure, some European companies were using Chinese paste, but cautiously. Unilever made some of its Knorr brand of ketchup with Chinese paste, said Sikke Meerman, a Dutch Unilever executive. "I follow the weather reports to know what we can expect," he said. When temperatures rose, Chinese farmers laid on the fungicide to deal with rots that thrived in the heat—resulting in high levels of unacceptable chemical residues. A big company like Unilever didn't want that kind of trouble. "If a recall is in the papers, all of a sudden people connect it to all of our brands. We can't afford anything like that, especially in Western Europe or the United States."

As we toured the Changji processing factory together in 2007, Amezaga said it was similar to plants he'd managed fifteen years earlier: "The boilers burning coal, the tomatoes pouring out of rusty trucks, the wood crates in contact with fruit"; these were illegal methods in Europe because of the threat of contamination. For the time being, Amezaga said, he saw China's tomato production as mainly a social project for the thousands of soldiers on its western border. The government subsidized the land, oil, and other inputs, making it hard to calculate what the industry's bottom line really was. Nevertheless, China was improving its techniques, and he saw no reason they couldn't continue to grow. "They don't have to be banned from the world just because they haven't done the hazard analysis that some bloody bastard at Walmart wants."

But if the industry was going to have enough business to go around with Chinese producers claiming their piece of the pie, it would need to expand. Tomato growers and processors in recent years have tried to convince consumers to eat more of their product by promoting its health benefits. This wasn't as easy as it sounded, because the nutritional science around tomatoes, like much nutritional science, was pretty murky. In 1998, researchers from the Harvard School of

Public Health presented a paper at a meeting of the processing tomato industry stating that levels of the cooked form of lycopene in blood plasma corresponded with protection against cancers and cardiovascular disorders.

The industry jumped on the study, issuing a news release and pushing for FDA permission to put news of lycopene's benefits on their cans and labels. But in 2005, the FDA responded to a petition from Heinz by ruling that while food makers could claim that tomato products had the potential to reduce cancer risk, they had to hedge the claim by noting there was little scientific evidence in back of it. While lycopene had been shown to reduce the rate of cardiovascular disease in both epidemiological studies and clinical trials in which people were given supplements, there weren't enough well-controlled clinical trials to definitively establish these benefits.

After the FDA ruling, the industry created the Tomato Products Wellness Council to fund and publicize research into the health effects of cooked tomato. As of this writing, the council hasn't turned up anything that would cause FDA to change its mind. This isn't to say that tomatoes aren't good for you. Several studies that compared people who consumed different amounts of tomato in their diet suggest that a diet high in cooked tomatoes was protective against prostate, colon, breast, lung, and pancreatic cancers. How this occurs isn't clear, though. In test tubes, lycopene (which is present to a lesser degree in red grapefruit and watermelon) prevents the oxidation of LDL cholesterol, a cause of plaque buildup in the arteries. These in-vitro studies have indicated that lycopene is more potent as an antioxidant than other carotenoids, such as vitamin E. But in another study, rats fed yellow tomatoes—which lack lycopene—had healthier blood than animals fed lycopene supplements. It may be that lycopene isn't really the magic element.

There were other healthy compounds in tomato—vitamin C, essential fatty acids, a little protein, plant fiber—all good for you.

Although it seems to counter common sense, there are some indications that cooked tomatoes provide better nutrition than the raw fruit. In raw tomatoes, lycopene is present in a structural form called *trans*-lycopene, which appears to be less biologically available than *cis*-lycopene, the form that the chemical takes when it is cooked and served in an oil emulsion. Pizza and tomato sauce cooked in olive oil have nutritional, as well as culinary, value, it turns out. And a tablespoon of tomato sauce contains five times more lycopene than a tablespoon of crushed raw tomato; in the sauce form, the solid part of the tomato has been condensed. "The bottom line," says Gwen Young, a flavor chemist at Kagome, a major Japanese food company, "is that it's much healthier to eat processed tomatoes than fresh. When you eat fresh tomatoes, the lycopene is stuck in the pectin and fiber, so tightly wrapped in the cell walls that a lot of it passes through your gut with the fiber."

But there are some caveats. One study showed that canned pasta sauces contain far less vitamin C than claimed, possibly because the longer the products sit on the shelf, the more this vitamin is degraded. Also, it seems that the area just under the tomato's skin, which is removed in whole peeled and most diced tomatoes—though not in tomato paste—is the most lycopene-rich.

Amezaga felt the industry had moved too fast with the lycopene news. "When the lycopene study was presented in Pamplona, we acted like we had discovered a vaccine against AIDS," he said. "That was only one study. I said we needed someone with scientific authority to tell us that we could make these claims. An industry can't give the image of selling smoke. The Mediterranean diet isn't just lycopene. I said, 'Let's focus on all the other things as well.' The Americans screwed it up. They asked FDA for the right to make health claims and it backfired, because the evidence was insufficient. So now it's a tough situation, because you will need much more evidence to win the right to make a claim. Greedy is greedy," he said.

Greed is the American way, too—whether you're working for Enron or Goldman Sachs or you're a lowly tomato broker for a company like SK Foods. For the rest of us, moderation is the wisest course. It's a good idea to be leery of anyone who's pushing you to consume more and more of any product.

"Processed tomatoes do seem to be healthier," Amezaga added. "But people who eat a lot of this stuff also seem to have unhealthy diets. Isn't that a contradiction? A complete one. And nobody can fucking deny it."

CHAPTER EIGHT

The Secrets of Flavor

They were large and delicious, these nineteen Brandywines.
Still, it doesn't seem like much. It isn't much.

—William Alexander, *The $64 Tomato*

 THERE ARE ABOUT SEVEN THOUSAND KNOWN FRAGRANCES
in foods, four hundred in the tomato alone. The fragrances
are called volatiles, and they are low-molecular-weight compounds that generally have little nutritional value. From an
evolutionary perspective, however, the aesthetics of smell and taste
carry important information for survival. Many of the fragrances and
tastes we enjoy in food help us and other members of the animal kingdom distinguish nutritious foods from dangerous or lackluster ones.
The human genome encodes a few dozen functional taste receptors,
but several hundred olfactory receptors. And it is the interaction of
the nose and the volatiles that underlies the diversity of the human
diet. For the purpose of discerning the nutritional meaning of plants,

the tongue is a blunt instrument, while the nose performs exquisitely. (Which makes you wonder who's the real aesthete in a household—you or your dog?)

The most abundant volatiles in tomato fruits, it turns out, are linked to valuable nutrients in the plant. Those associated with flavors that people in tasting experiments describe as "tomatoey," "green," or "grassy," for example, are derived from essential fatty acids such as hexenal. A second class of tomato volatiles is produced by the cleaving of essential amino acids—these volatiles include methylbutanal, which imparts a potatoey flavor, phenylacetaldehyde and 2-phenylethanol (which is rose oil), and methyl salicylate—oil of wintergreen. A third class of volatiles, the apo-carotenoids, increases during ripening, resulting in color changes that signal to seed-dispensing organisms such as human beings, "Hey, the fruit are ripe and ready to eat!" Among these volatiles are 6-methyl-5-hepten-2-one, derived from lycopene, and beta-damascenone, a powerful scent also found in berries, apples, grapes, and wine. Glutamate and aspartate, nonessential amino acids, produce flavors that our taste buds recognize as savory umami.

In an intriguing 2006 article in *Science*, geneticist Harry Klee and flavor scientist Stephen A. Goff used the tomato's volatile "noseprint" to make a point about an unanticipated downside of modern farming and food processing. The authors compared the intensity of seventeen of the most important tomato volatiles in Flora-Dade, a popular fresh-market cultivar released by the University of Florida in 1976, and LA1673, a collection of cherry tomatoes that Charley Rick found growing in some weeds in the Rimac River valley of Peru in 1985. Only one of these volatiles, 6-methyl-5-hepten-2-one, was present in greater concentrations in the Flora-Dade. The exception is not surprising, because this compound derives from lycopene, which breeding programs have pursued because it gives tomatoes deeper red color. The superior volatile profile of the wild cherries didn't necessarily mean they were healthier than the Florida hybrid. But they were sending a message of healthy promise. Tomato flavor, Goff and Klee write, "can be viewed as a set of cues that together reflect the ripeness and nutritional quality/nutritional availability of the fruit." We're probably programmed to associate insipid flavor and smell with poor nutritional value. In this example, the paltry flavor of the Florida hybrid was clearly sending consumers the wrong signal about its nutritional value. It was hiding its light under a bushel—even if it wasn't as nutritious as its wild Peruvian relatives, it had more value than its insipid flavor implied.

In short, domestication has had a negative effect on tomato flavor and smell. And this is a far-from-trivial concern. Jack Hanna aimed for bland when he was trying to help farmers by breeding his square tomato. "The more bland a food is, the more people eat it," he'd boast to reporters. That isn't a marketing approach that works, anymore—or if it is, it shouldn't be. Tomatoes, a wholesome food with clear nutritional benefits, have been bred to taste plain, while food chemists and the companies they work for have gussied up their corn-syrup-based snacks with savory essences culled from nature. As nutritionists recommend that we eat more fresh fruits and veggies, the food industry, until recently, has been making fresh fruits and veggies less interesting, while adding new taste thrills to processed foods. This is not, as Goff and Klee conclude gently, a healthy policy. "Dissociation of flavors from their natural nutritional context may create undesirable health consequences such as the overconsumption of highly processed starch or saturated fats," they write. "Flavor preferences together with health benefits should be considered in future food production and in crop-enhancement strategies."

"The tomato probably evolved volatiles to attract animals so they would eat the fruit and spread it," Klee told me in an interview at his office in Gainesville. In person, he's tall and youthful, with narrow-set eyes and bushy brown hair. "The fact that humans happen to be animals that find it appealing is no accident. But there has not been a strong correlation between what breeders have done and making the tomato more attractive to critters. What we've done as breeders is to add water to tomatoes, which makes them less nutritious and less flavorful." He was surprisingly cynical about the Florida tomato business for someone whose laboratory work was partly funded by that industry. "The more fruit on the plant, the more you max out its ability to put nutrients in the fruit, and you get bigger, prettier fruit with more water in them and fewer sugars, vitamins, and acids."

A second rule of flavor is that tomatoes picked ripe have more flavor than those picked green, even if the latter are "ripe" when eaten. By the "breaker" stage—the point at which the fruit is just starting to turn red—the tomato has all the sucrose it can get. But picking a tomato at this stage slows the reduction of sucrose to the sweeter fructose and glucose. A study led by Allen Stevens found that vine-ripened tomatoes had about 20 percent more reduced sugars than those picked at the breaker stage. Moreover, the industry has bred tomatoes for firmness. The full flavor of a tomato doesn't come out until the fruit has gotten pretty ripe, which means soft. But fast-food restaurants want a firm tomato. They rely on machines that cut a slice for, say, a McDonald's hamburger that is precisely four millimeters thick. The distributor in Boston or Minneapolis or wherever wants the tomatoes he or she brings to the grocers to last on the shelf. And firmness negates flavor. "I don't buy the big tomatoes myself," adds Klee. "I stick with the cherries and grapes."

So here's the situation for people like Klee and his colleague Jay Scott, the Florida state tomato breeder: They're working on behalf of an industry that has been totally committed to big, firm, green-picked tomatoes that are the enemy of flavor. As the researchers try to puzzle out a way to produce more flavorful tomatoes for this industry, the industry has tied their hands behind their backs. Volatiles are a key component of tomatoes, but from the perspective of flavor-minded tomato scientists, they are tricky to manipulate. In part, this is because some volatiles can be smelled at very low thresholds and others only at quite high ones. A nose can pick up the violet smell of beta-ionone even at the low, low concentration of 0.007 nanoliter per liter—7 parts per trillion. It can't detect the apricot smell of pentanol, on the other hand, until concentrations reach the micromolar, or parts-per-million, range. "Some of these chemicals we're not sensitive to, but they are abundant. Conversely, some we're very sensitive to, but they aren't abundant," said Klee. The other problem is that some of the chemicals that contribute to good tomato flavor are unappealing or even vile when sensed in isolation. The classic example is 2-isobutylthiazole—a grassy smell that consumers don't care for on its own (although, if you'll remember, Allen Stevens found that 2-isobutylthiazole was key to the flavor of Campbell's Soup's favorite tomato). There are probably one thousand genes involved in different aspects of the tomato ripening process, many of them interrelated through complex feedback systems we haven't begun to understand. To complicate matters, taste is subject to cultural and personal differences. Flavor scientists who run taste panels with different groups make the following generalizations: People in Asian countries like their tomatoes sweet; WASPs from the

Northeast put a premium on mouth-feel and like their tomatoes firm; Latinos tend to appreciate acidity.

Despite the complexity, Klee was trying to back-engineer flavor into a tomato production system that had done its best to kill it. "I think we can do a lot better at reengineering the ancient tomato flavors," he said optimistically. "What we have to do is pump up the good things in the plant before the tomatoes are put through the processing system." To create tomatoes with different flavor profiles, Klee and his lab mates at the University of Florida were searching for genes that had an impact on the elaboration of volatiles. For the time being, the food industry has no desire to try to sell a tomato with genes inserted into it in a laboratory. No matter how innocuous this process might actually turn out to be, parts of the public don't like it, and there could be FDA headaches as well; it's not worth the investment. In the near term, growers will shun genetically manipulated tomatoes, but if Klee and his team can create interesting tomatoes using lab techniques experimentally, it might be possible to use traditional breeding methods to bring these genes into play.

Some research has shown that you can improve tomatoes by dropping in a single gene here or there. A team of Israeli scientists, working partly with funding from the state of New Jersey (which wants to put its tomato industry back on the map), inserted a geraniol synthase gene, derived from lemon basil, into an M-82, the standard table tomato used by geneticists as a backdrop. University students who tried it in taste tests were enthusiastic about this transgenic. Eighty percent of them found it more flavorful, and 68 percent preferred its flavor to that of the control. The transgenic was higher in "perfume," "rose," "geranium," "tomato-like," and "lemongrass" notes. Pumping up the geraniol synthase gene catalyzed a reaction in the tomato leading to a bump in these scented volatiles.

Klee's lab has focused on inserting genes that crank up production of particular amino acids, three of which—phenylalanine, leucine, and isoleucine—are important in making volatiles. More volatiles sounds like better tomatoes, but not necessarily. "The volatiles derived from leucine and isoleucine are not very good," he said. "They produce flavor notes, such as 3-methylbutanal and 3-methylbutyric acid, that we'd call 'vegetative.'" Taste panels have described 3-methylbutanal as "malty"; 3-methylbutyric acid as "sweaty" or "dirty socks." The same notes may be called "earthy" in some wines, but above certain levels in tomato, they are a definite bummer. The Klee lab has had better luck with phenylalanine, whose breakdown results in the fresh scents of rose and wintergreen oils.

In November 2007, I spent a morning at Klee's lab with his colleague, Denise Tieman, a Purdue-trained horticulturalist. I'd wondered what the key tomato volatiles smelled like on their own, so Tieman got the little two-ounce bottles out of the fridge and put them on a tray for me. We opened each one in sequence. Geranylacetone is "floral," and methylsalicylate is, as advertised, oil of wintergreen. Some of the others don't really register. 6-methyl-5-hepten-2-one is "piney," according to the *SAFC Flavors and Fragrances Catalog*. To me, it smelled like a chemical. Same with 2-isobutylthiazole, hexenyl alcohol, and ethyl vinyl ketone. According to *Flavors and Fragrances*, the latter is "pungent mustard." It knocked the top of my head off—the fine print on the jar warned "lachrymator!" "irritant!" "possible carcinogen!" The smell of 1-nitro-2-phenylethane was subtly nauseating, while isovaleronitrile was downright nasty. So was 2-methylbutyric acid. When I had smelled a dilute solution of *cis*-3-hexenal in Buttery's laboratory, it had smelled like tomatoes. But in its pure essence, it was just another chemical smell.

"I usually open these outside," Tieman said belatedly. "When I do it in here, I get yelled at."

A graduate student, Michelle Zeigler, had built a tomato high in methylsalicylate for her Ph.D. dissertation. The idea was that by raising the volume of this volatile, it might be possible to create a tomato that tasted OK and was also more resistant to insect damage—wintergreen being a natural insect repellent. It was a neat, gee-whiz experiment. To make the transgenic, Zeigler used a method similar to the one Calgene had employed in the late 1980s. She grew pieces of replicating bacteria called plasmids containing three special elements: a petunia flower gene that produced methylsalicylate, a promoter sequence from the cauliflower mosaic virus, and a gene that rendered the plant resistant to the antibiotic kanamycin. New M-82 tomato buds were grown in a kanamycin-containing solution with the plasmids; the ones that survived and grew had presumably incorporated the bacterial plasmid DNA into their genomes and "transformed" into transgenic individuals.

The day of my visit, field extension agents had just brought in a bag of the wintergreen-juiced tomatoes. A taste panel run somewhere on campus was preparing to feed them to a bunch of student volunteers. Since I happened to be in the lab, I got to be a guinea pig as well. Tieman sliced up a tomato, removed the seeds (she doesn't want me inadvertently "dispersing" this transgenic organism), and fed it to me. I wasn't impressed. It had a slight wintergreen taste, which wasn't something I really wanted in a tomato. Then again, maybe the tastiest part of this transgenic tomato was in the locule, which had been cut out with the seeds. Despite my reaction, Tieman wasn't deterred. She and other members of the Klee lab weren't in the business of creating a commercial tomato. They were doing science. And they had shown you could heighten wintergreen flavor by boosting a gene in tomato.

Like so much in the tomato world, the road to this experiment had led through the laboratory of Charley Rick. To determine the potential for boosting volatiles using tomato germplasm, Klee and Tieman were relying on the research of Dani Zamir, a Rick student who headed a laboratory at the Hebrew University of Jerusalem. Using techniques he'd developed partly as Rick's student, Zamir and his colleagues had created seventy-five introgression lines, that is, hybrids—in this case, M-82s— that each contained a defined piece of the genome of a wild relative, in this case, the Peruvian tomato *Lycopersicon pennellii,* inserted into its genome. Now, *L. pennellii* alone produced tiny, green, hard-as-a-rock fruit. As a tomato for human consumption, it was worthless; as a source of tomato germplasm, priceless. The next step for Tieman was to take the introgression lines and characterize the volatiles they contained. What she discovered was that the wild *L. pennellii* contained a treasure trove of hidden smells that popped out when bits of its genome were inserted into a commercial tomato. The fruit of one introgression line, designated 8-2-1, for example, smelled like cheap perfume, or roses. When she analyzed the fruit of these lines using gas chromatography, she found fifty-fold higher levels of 2-phenylethanol, or rose oil, the well-known scent of detergents, bathroom freshener, dollar-brand perfume, and the like. The taste of this tomato was not good—Tieman described it as "like toilet water." Although *L. pennellii* contained this genetic material, its fruit didn't smell like that. "They have other weird things in them that mask the smell," Tieman said. "But when you take that piece of the *pennellii* genome and put it into the tomato background, it smells very rosy."

"It's very complicated," she added. "This should keep us busy for a long time."

"By the way," I asked, "do you eat tomatoes?"

"Not really. I used to like them. Now it's too much like work. Sometimes I buy them and they sit there and I ask myself, 'Do I really want to chop another tomato?'"

The science was fun, but where was it leading? Klee wasn't sure. "I have lots of colleagues and friends who are tomato breeders. They didn't deliberately set out to make tomatoes that taste worse. They ignored flavor, and the reason they ignored it is because it's so difficult. With transgenes we can take a tomato that has all the things a grower wants—yield, resistance, size, shape, and color—then go back into the background to restore tomato flavor. It's easier for us to do that than it is for traditional breeders to make a good one from scratch with the materials they're using. But the companies have to step up and do it."

Marker-assisted breeding is the new big thing in breeding programs. It's a way of using advanced molecular technology to create a shortcut for developing new plants. It works like this: Breeders now know the chromosomal location of many genes, which are linked to well-marked pieces of DNA that can be easily identified using molecular techniques. So a breeder who wants to find out whether a plant contains the relevant gene can test it soon after germination. Let's say a breeder wanted to use *L. pennellii* to make a rosier-smelling tomato. This could easily be done by doing repeated crosses with Dani Zamir's 8-2-1 introgression line. Along the way, you'd want to get rid of 99 percent of the remainder of the *L. pennellii* genome containing undesirable traits. If you grew out one hundred plants, you'd have to figure out which one had the rosy genes. This is a lot easier if you can test the plant soon after it germinates. You could do this for heirlooms, too, Klee noted, and thereby introduce some of the more vivid flavors of an heirloom into a more modern variety. This might be easier to do once an alliance of government and academic plant geneticists called the Tomato Genetics Cooperative finishes sequencing the genome of the tomato, which Klee expects in a few years. "Then we could go in and say, 'This locus on chromosome 1 increases the level of this volatile, and this is the gene,'" he said.

Steven D. Tanksley, a Rick student who has published a number of breakthrough papers at Cornell University, recently created a genomics company to bolster the use of gene marking technology in crop breeding. "We use computer science to look at breeding as an engineering process and optimize it, for tomatoes and a lot of other species. The idea is that plant breeding and genetic improvement is a process that isn't that different conceptually from manufacturing a device or scheduling airline flights or optimizing Wall Street strategies. It hasn't been treated like that. It's been treated more as a mixture of art and science. We're looking to make it quicker and easier—doing what humans have done for thousands of years, just more efficiently." But just as the past two decades are littered with failed financial experiments, genetic technology turned out to be a bit overhyped. And in the view of Jay Scott, who has been breeding tomatoes and thinking about them for many years, there's little hope of a quick breakthrough in tomato flavor, despite recent scientific advances.

"Companies making big investments in biotech naturally want a big hit, like the Flavr Savr was supposed to be," he wrote recently, "yet historically, it's exceedingly rare for a single cultivar to be so good that it's grown for a long time." The major biotech-led improvements have occurred in crops where companies can easily get a return on their investment, specifically Bt corn and cotton (in which a natural pesticide-producing gene from a bacterium called Bacillus thuringiensis is cloned into the plants), and Roundup Ready soybeans. All three crops are planted on enormous acreage. Only a few horticultural crops have gone the genetically modified route, and that was out of desperation—viruses threatened the viability of papaya and certain squash crops, so specific resistances were genetically engineered into them. With Flavr Savr off the shelf, there isn't a single fruit or vegetable in the supermarket whose flavor, appearance, or nutritional value stems from genetic engineering, nor is there likely to be one anytime soon.

Public distaste for genetically modified foodstuffs aside, it just isn't that easy to create a valuable new food plant in the laboratory. A lot of genes are involved in tomato flavor. A few simple ones that improve sugar content have been identified, but it's hard to breed them into commercial varieties because they decrease the yields. And there are nasty "off flavors" associated with some high-sugar tomatoes, so selecting for high sugars alone doesn't guarantee good flavor. As for volatiles, even after years of work, no one knows what combinations make a better-tasting tomato. "The only way to determine the range of flavors of a tomato genotype," writes Scott, "is to taste the fruit a number of times under various growing conditions and seasons." In one experiment, Scott grew out a bunch of tomatoes, taste-tested them, then planted seeds from the ones with the highest scores. But the next generation of this same variety scored lower on taste tests. Sometimes, fruit from the same plant had widely varying taste scores. Current science is clearly inadequate to develop an infallibly tasty tomato.

Evolution is a series of random events; the "fearful symmetry" of plants and animals is the accumulation of an endless series of blind trial and error. A system built this way isn't engineered the way a building is. There is no true blueprint, despite the fact that some scientists have described our DNA that way. There's too much random duplication, erasure, and insertion in our DNA to accurately call it a blueprint. DNA contains not just genes but also stretches of code that promote genetic transcription, or stop it, or make it go haywire. When it comes to breeding a tomato—trying to make an approximation of a blueprint for one—changing the soil or climate introduces new variables, and so does postharvest handling. And even the deftest tongue experiences "taste fatigue," which makes it difficult to know whether you have a good tomato or not.

Scott is among the most sophisticated tomato flavor breeders. In addition to sweet and sour, he has categorized tomato fruit with flavor descriptors such as musty, bitter, astringent, ethanolic, sour, and metallic, as well as fruity-floral, mild sweet, and even "good" and "excellent" for the flavor panelists who lack other adjectives but still have strong feelings. Food panelists tend to be average university students looking to earn some beer money, not foodies. Yet after doing selections twice a year since 1998 to fix lines for the various flavor notes, Scott still lacked answers when I spoke to him in 2008 (though he had developed a pretty winning "premium market" cultivar, the Tasti-Lee). "Due to environmental influences, it has been difficult to obtain fixed lines. Some of the notes seem particularly ephemeral."

Will breeding ever be purely a science, and not a mixture of art and science? Kanti Rawal didn't think so. "Gene-marker-assisted breeding is a lot of crap," he told me. "Chemistry-wise, it's very difficult, because the components of the fruit are always changing under different conditions of temperature and so on. Look, when you put something in your mouth, it's the first impression that dominates. There are so many different pathways involved. Changing one isn't going to make a difference. For me, marker-assisted breeding is just a fancy way of being a pith helmet, stick-in-the-armpit agronomist who never gets his white uniform dirty. There's a lot of talk about it, publication of papers, but not much has come out of it. The growers aren't going to be impressed by the fancy biochemistry. They want a tomato they can market. If these biotech people don't go out into the field, nothing's going to come of it."

Over time, I found that Kanti had a more nuanced view. He was less definitive about what molecular biology *could* do for tomato flavor than what it *should* do. His resistance to it was based partly on scientific skepticism and partly on self-interest, but mostly on his philosophical notion of how breeders fit into the whole food chain, especially as he, Larry Jacobs, Sandra Belin, and their Mexican friends practiced it in Baja California. Jacobs and Belin were firm adherents to organic agriculture. Kanti tended to see organics as part of a bigger picture.

When you try to analyze the elements of farming and food production in their individual parts, the value of one way over another can seem arbitrary. Studies of the nutritional value of tomatoes, for example, are subject to the same frustrating limits as other efforts to ascertain the particular value of a food: The benefits of any given item are marginal in terms of overall health, and individual studies often contradict each other. That isn't to say there's no such thing as sound nutritional advice—just that, for the most part, it's quite simple. So far, nobody has come up with a better dictum than what your mama told you when you were a kid: "Eat your fruits and vegetables—they're good for you!"

Much the same may be true of organic farming. Following demand, some of the big processing tomato growers have been getting into organics. In the 2007 season, a big California grower, Don Cameron of Terranova Ranch, was earning $91 per ton for organic processing tomatoes, compared with $63 for conventional. "We even grow organic cotton," he said, smiling as if to say, "We'll grow whatever these idiots ask us to grow if the price is right." Even Pizza Hut had shown interest in making organic sauces.

But the evidence for the nutritional value of organic is mixed. Organic and conventional tomatoes have roughly the same level of sugars, acids, and micronutrients like lycopene. Heavy metals tend to be slightly higher in organic tomatoes, perhaps from the animal manure used to fertilize them. Generally, pesticides in conventional tomatoes

can be measured in parts per billion. To the extent that organic tomatoes taste better or have concentration of nutrients, this is probably due
to their getting less water and lower amounts of fertilizer. The stressed
organic tomato responds by producing more vitamin C and anti-
inflammatory flavonoids—the same chemicals that protect the plant are
also healthy for humans. The biggest benefit of organic farming was probably the reduced use of petrochemical-based inputs and the diminished
exposure of farmworkers to these chemicals—though the types used in
the twenty-first century were generally less toxic than in earlier years.

Chris Rufer produces organic paste when asked to—"the customer
is never wrong"—but he's openly skeptical. Growing with less fertilizer means using more land to produce the same amount of food, Rufer
argues, because less fertilizer means lower yields. "Where do we get
the acreage? Wetlands, forest?" On a society-wide basis, that's no plus.
And since organics cost substantially more, an all-organic supermarket
would mean lower consumption of fruits and vegetables. "Having an
increased rate of consumption of fruits and vegetables far outweighs
any minuscule imperceptible issue there may be with pesticides," he
says. Are petrochemical-based fertilizers and pesticides necessarily worse than spraying "organic" copper and sulfur and bacteria on
your plants? Is it more ethical to eat organic heirloom tomatoes driven
across the country than conventional ones grown fifty miles away? Is
it more ethical to ship five hundred tomatoes one hundred miles than
ten thousand tomatoes one thousand miles? At a Mollie Stone's supermarket in San Francisco recently, I found "locally grown" heirlooms
from the Capay Valley, a two-hour drive away, that were either unripe
or rotten, at $4 per pound, along with $3 Del Cabo cherries imported
from Mexico that had real flavor. Which was more "ethical" or, for that
matter, sensible? Sometimes it seems that going organic or pursuing

"traditional" crops is more about posturing than doing something real for health and the environment.

On its face, the answer to this conundrum is simple. As the writer and Slow Food activist Michael Pollan has written, "Eat food. Not too much. Mostly plants." Experts in nutritional science generally recognize the marginal significance of any individual study and give the same advice as Pollan. But as Pollan has argued in *The Omnivore's Dilemma* and *In Defense of Food*, the shifting narrative of nutritional advice directed at the shopper by advertising and half-baked news reports is mainly of value to the food companies that grab on to the latest study or headline to promote a new "value-added" food product—a product that, whether it is "heart-healthy" cereal, "low-fat" potato chips, or "antioxidant-rich" pomegranate juice, is only of slight nutritional benefit at best.

It is a bit strange how long it has taken us to recognize that whole foods, produced at home from actual grains, nuts, beans, fruits and vegetables, and the like, present a better nutritional package than products that have been stripped down to function well in a business environment. And yet, science and technology still have their roles to play. We can't all live on organic farms, and even if we could, we don't and won't. In the rush to condemn our way of life, the cultural critics among us sometimes miss the fact that technology, while enabling monopoly and greed and ridiculous products like frozen peanut-butter-and-jelly "lunchables," can also lift boats that have been stuck in an ebb tide for too long. Smaller is not necessarily more beautiful. Most of the farms in the developing world are small, and they generally produce barely enough to feed the people who live on them, let alone their compatriots. The majority of African farmers would be happy to be able to afford hybrid seeds or to feed their soils with even a smidgeon of the petroleum-based fertilizers so insufferable to organic farming purists. California farms do use plenty of fertilizer, but they also manage to grow enough food, in an area of several thousand square miles, to feed most of the country.

Kanti, who has moved from the mainstream of agriculture to the organic edge, agrees. "This is a natural greenhouse, the best in the world," he told me one September afternoon as we stood in a field next to a crowded shopping outlet in Gilroy, California. Every summer, Kanti rents a patch of land where he grows out his newer varieties and invites seed companies and farmers to inspect them. My son was with us, and my wife and daughter were next door buying high-tops at the Converse store. After a long career in the tomato business, Kanti was now focused on training Mexican agronomists and helping a cooperative of Mexican farmers maintain a whole way of life and avoid the desperation of low-wage migrant work. But the task of finding flavorful tomatoes that can survive bad weather, crop diseases, and two weeks' travel to the consumer is a never-ending one that requires him to constantly plant his seeds in a variety of climates and soil types stretching from Northern California to the tip of the Baja Peninsula. I have found the mixture of idealism and science that informs Kanti's worldview to be irresistible and quite relevant to the questions that food critics ask.

The cherry and pear tomatoes that Del Cabo grows in Baja are closer to the wild originals than the full-sized beefsteak tomatoes are. Unless we're Peruvian, we can't eat those wild tomatoes in the habitat where they arose, but thanks to Charley Rick and his students, it has been possible to reintroduce at least some of these plants' flavors into commercial tomatoes. One positive thing about living in a global economy is that we in the wealthy West can support people in poor countries, which have their own products to offer us in a division of labor that may be mutually beneficial. There's a certain logic to doing this in the deserts of Mexico, the birthplace of the cultivated tomato. This is what brought Kanti to Baja.

In his poignant account of the 1981 death of a farmworker named Ramon González, who apparently succumbed to pesticide poisoning, anthropologist Angus Wright asked, "Why is it that people like Ramon can no longer make a living from their own land and must work instead where they own nothing and control nothing and where their only apparent future is to move on to work in yet some other alien and unfriendly land?" Kanti and the Del Cabo folks had no answer to this—perhaps no one did. But in their own small way, they were struggling to maintain a zone of compassion at the southern tip of the Baja Peninsula. Larry Jacobs hoped that by continuing to add value to the farms and the people who worked on them, he could offer at least one group of vulnerable people a stable and comfortable life.

Developing flavorful tomatoes to grow in a particular environment and then ship a long distance is painstaking. But for Kanti, who began breeding tomatoes for Del Cabo in 2001, it was a great opportunity. "I was tired of breeding for the farmer. I want to breed for the consumer. I want people to buy my tomatoes. I breed for a tomato that tastes the same ten days after you pick it. We're not trying to sell seeds. We're trying to create tomatoes that the consumer will come back to." After Belin and Jacobs got to know Kanti, they wanted to sign a contract. "Larry doesn't want anyone to be disappointed," said Kanti. "But I told him, 'I'll only stop working with you if you commit murder, rape, or some other violent crime.'"

When they're working in southern Baja, Belin and Jacobs live in an old two-story adobe house not far from downtown San José del Cabo and just off Highway 1, the continuation of California's coastal highway and the road that takes you up the peninsula to most of the farms worked by the cooperative. They have a spare bedroom for Kanti when he's in town. The house is surrounded by a dirt yard with subtropical plants and trees. A concrete pathway and stone walls were designed and built by John Graham, an Oklahoma-born organic farmer who, along with his teenage daughter Ruby, also shares the compound. Most of their work seems to be done at a wooden dinner table on the porch outside the kitchen. Graham, who started organic cooperatives in Oregon and Washington after serving in the Peace Corps for many years, came to Baja as an organic inspector, but stayed after he got to know Belin and Jacobs. A car accident in northern Baja several years back left him crippled and in a wheelchair.

One night, Belin was cooking dinner—rice and tofu and veggies—and Jacobs was sitting at the dinner table watching some nerdy futurist TV program on his computer. Kanti and Graham exchanged looks and invited me up to Graham's place, on a terrace above the main house. We drank warm beer around a mosquito coil outside and talked about farms and music and the hippies, wealthy expats, and other Americans who peopled the southern tip of Baja. Kanti enjoyed the scene, and Graham was very much at the center of it. Belin and Jacobs kept their distance. They were workaholic idealists. For them, the inactivity of hanging out was painful. "Larry and Sandy have no life. They work all the time," Kanti told me as we drank. "We want to enjoy our lives. The precondition to work in our breeding program is, you have to be able to drink beer whenever I say so."

The last night of my stay in San José, however, I did manage to talk with Belin and Jacobs at a Thai restaurant to which I had invited them. It had taken more of my persuasive powers than I'm used to investing on a dinner invitation, since they couldn't see the point of spending money on something as lavish as a pretty good restaurant meal. I found that Jacobs was remarkably optimistic about the motivations of other people. Belin was thoughtful and introspective. They didn't have the slightest discomfort about being the gringos who were saving a way of life not their own. Jacobs said he'd experienced an epiphany while riding his bike through a slum outside Mexico City on his way to Guatemala, where the couple spent several years working as volunteers. "Holy Toledo! This is how the rest of the world lives! We were born with enormous privileges to do things few other people in the world could do," Larry said. "That kind of experience in your twenties really marks you for life." While on a brief vacation in Cabo San Lucas in 1982, they hit on the idea of growing tomatoes in Baja. By then, they were convinced that helping people form a business made more sense than doing charity. They borrowed $50,000 from relatives and friends to get the project off the ground and sold the idea to the local rural development honcho, Narciso Agundes. "They were happy to have us. They didn't have anything else going on." (It seems to have helped Agundes's career—in 2008, he was elected governor of Baja California del Sur.)

Twenty-six harvests later, the company was doing about $50 million a year in business. The tomatoes didn't look like much, oddly colored things in clamshell cases on the display shelves of the supermarket. But they meant the difference between a decent life and the fate of Ramon Aguirre to thousands of working people who depended on Del Cabo. Farmers who grew for the company made an average of $12,000 a year. Belin and Jacobs didn't pay themselves a salary at all until 1994. They've averaged about $80,000—combined—since then. "We think that's pretty good," Jacobs said. He declined to mention that the couple were still suckers for charity cases. When a woman in the packing plant needed $30,000 to get a kidney transplant in the United States, Jacobs and his family picked up the bill.

The Saturday before I left San José del Cabo, Kanti, John Graham, and I visited a farmer's market held every week on the grounds of a country club by the estuary on the city's outskirts. Graham and some of his friends had organized a conference to discuss issues like water conservation, recycling, and tourism, which had the Cabo region growing at a pace of 17 percent a year. The other panelists included an environmental scientist from a federal agency, a left-wing lawyer, a left-wing doctor, and a wealthy young American in flowing white robes who introduced himself by saying, "I come representing the earth."

Graham had organized the forum to get people thinking. "We have to decide how important golf courses are in relation to farming," he said. "If things keep going the way they are, farming in the immediate San José area will soon be a thing of the past." The panelists concurred. Several years of good rains were masking a lurking water crisis. A couple of years of drought would dry up all the water for agriculture.

On the other side of the green, vendors sold local fruits and vegetables, crafts, crystals, and books. About thirty people in tie-dye and faded muscle T-shirts stood in a circle, chanting and pushing incense at each other and banging on Indian drums and bells. I asked Ruby, Graham's wise-before-her-time twelve-year-old, what she thought of it all. "It's silly," she said. "But, whatever."

The hippie scene is just one part of the heterogeneity of southern Baja, which has a very globalized feeling with its desperate migrant workers seeking jobs in the burgeoning tourism industry, its middle-rich American sunbirds, and its tomato farmers. Natives of Cabo are a minority here. Even the farmers are often immigrants. I met a co-op member named Juan José Silva who'd come to San José in 1980 from Aguascalientes as a farm laborer. Seven years later, he bought land to join the co-op. His nine brothers and sisters were working construction or in the hotels. He was sure that he was the luckiest. "Life is tranquil and healthy on the farm," he told me. "The cooperative creates social cohesion.

The *cooperativistas* come from different places, and now we've all got a place where we can feel at home. You can't get that if you're a waiter."

Besides worrying about the biological pests that trouble the sleep of all farmers, the men were troubled by the encroachment of tourism on their land and their water. There were already eleven thousand hotel rooms in Cabo and San José, four thousand more approved, and plans for another twenty thousand rooms. There were 2 million tourists visiting each year, 180,000 inhabitants, and 40,000 temporary workers. Already, there wasn't enough housing for the construction workers, let alone the people who would move here to work the hotels. It was a boomtown that was probably living on borrowed time.

And though they have a lot of good friends and happy memories, Jacobs and Belin didn't feel entirely at home in southern Baja. They didn't indulge in the prelapsarian goo of the farmer's market, but "we don't feel part of the meetings at the packing shed, either," she said.

For Kanti, on the other hand, all of life is a stage. As the conference at the farmer's market was winding down, he couldn't resist getting in his two cents. Rising from his chair, he turned to face the audience of thirty or so people. "Capitalism works!" he shouted. "Let's use consumerism for environmental purposes. Create a company that sells pure, clean tap water. Take away the need for bottled water. We'll create a new service industry—drivers, water technicians, people who travel door to door collecting recyclables." The crowd cheered appreciatively. "Power to the people!" he added as a grace note. Then he sat down, to applause and laughter.

Like their compatriots everywhere, the Del Cabo farmers complained about labor and pests and money. Although everyone agreed that Kanti's little grape tomatoes were delicious, the farmers would rather grow cherries, because cherry tomatoes are slightly larger and thus cost less to harvest. Just as in any other part of the tomato industry, the salespeople wanted flavor, whereas the farmer wanted yield. There was some tension between Kanti and Jacobs and Belin as well. Jacobs was a sort of business visionary—in his purity and devotion to the cause, he actually reminded me a bit of Chris Rufer—and he found the idea of marker-assisted breeding appealing as a way to improve the crop. On the road one day, they had a heated discussion about it, and Kanti told Jacobs and Belin that the high-tech approach wouldn't work. There was no one in the tomato industry, he said, who could afford the basic research needed to make a truly superior product. "You need proven technologies to put out a new product. Only DuPont and Monsanto and a few others have the cash and the monopoly power. Even if you could come up with a new technology for grape tomatoes, how much money could you make from it?"

Kanti later added, "I can't do all the breeding with these markers. I'd have to go to Larry and say, 'Hire a guy for $100,000 a year and spend $350,000.' Your cost of entrepreneurship will go up. I object to that. It takes away from the contribution of people who could play an interesting role in bringing food to the table."

Jacobs told me that he couldn't figure out whether Kanti opposed biomarker technology because he thought it wasn't useful, or because it threatened him personally. "I'm trying to figure out, are they good tools or not?" he said.

The question went considerably deeper for Kanti. Marker-assisted breeding, with its technical requirements, intruded on his agrarian idyll. "Nobody teaches conventional breeding anymore at U.S. universities, nobody is there if you want to learn it. You can't take a course without getting brainwashed about the miracles of genetic modification," he said.

"The youngsters in the U.S. are lost boys—if they go into agriculture today, they are in white lab coats. They are so mesmerized by biotech that this art will die." His late friend Ed Tigchelaar—who discovered the *rin* and *nor* genes, used to lament that conventional geneticists like him were a vanishing breed, fighting a losing battle for funding. "If the world goes GMO [toward genetically modified organisms], then independent breeders like me have no future," Kanti said.

Nevertheless, Kanti was of two minds about biotech. He felt that more safety studies needed to be conducted, but he had also concluded that some of his organic-farming friends were being unreasonable in their blanket opposition to GMO. "Do they want to go back to the sixteenth century? How far back do we go?" he asked. He liked that genetically modified Bt corn controlled earworm and thereby eliminated the use of poisonous insecticides. "Roundup Ready corn and soybeans also eliminate the use of some dangerous chemicals.

"The bottom line," he said, "is that I'm pissed off at biotech for personal reasons. I worry that my kind of mom-and-pop operation probably wouldn't be feasible. You'll need millions to license someone else's technology, or develop your own."

I got my own tomatoes in the ground by May 15, and within a month, they had taken over the garden. Maybe I overfertilized, because the growth and flowering were really stupendous. The tomato vines in my twelve-by-six-foot patch had fused with the ones growing out of a dozen plastic pots next to them, forming a single, huge, green thicket that I could barely wade into. It was like a jungle setting out of a Tarzan movie. And then, just as the tomatoes were reaching their crescendo in late July, something seemed to go wrong. Leaves started to wilt, and a few turned brown. Even more distressing were the pale brown dots that began to appear on some of the stems. When I sliced into a few of the stems, I saw vascular damage that looked like wilt, if my interpretation of the photographs in the University of California Ag Division's *Integrated Pest Management for Tomatoes* was correct.

At first, the attack seemed to be confined to the San Marzano II and the Principe Borgheses planted in the back of the garden by the wall. Maybe I should have known better than to plant Italian heirlooms in damp, semitropical Washington, D.C. Then it spread. It didn't kill everything, but for some reason—and I'm sure there are a thousand home gardeners who could give me conflicting answers, all reasonable—the plants, after leafing and flowering like crazy, weren't producing many fruit. One or two Green Zebras popped out on the vine—after that, nothing. The Biisky Zhelty produced one elegant yellow tomato. Rutgers, Marmande, Burgess Mammoth, VF145—all duds. Clint Eastwood, Julia Child, Black Plum—next to *nada*. Even Jay Scott's hardy Tasti-Lee, after putting out a couple of beautiful and really delicious hybrids, went on strike.

That left mostly cherry tomatoes—lots and lots of cherry tomatoes. The wild Mexican ones, which I call Huachinango Reds, and the *L. pimpinellifolium,* too, produced scads of strong-tasting fruit, although the sticky gene they seem to possess posed some problems. You could pull them off the stem and eat them right then and there, still warm from the sun, but if you put them in a bowl, within a few hours, the tomatoes were deflated and leaking through the big hole that you ripped in the stem pore when you tore them off the plant.

Of the larger tomatoes, for some reason, the Speckled Peach alone was thriving. Its vine had proven superior to the others, reaching far above the madding crowd of tomato foliage, snagging the sun, converting it into scores of its peculiarly velvety, matte-dull, golf-ball-sized fruit. I probably got at least fifty Speckled Peaches over a six-week period.

I could pat myself on the back here for having chosen the Speckled Peach, which I had enjoyed so much when I tested them at Gary Ibsen's Tomatofest in Carmel the September before. But the sad truth was that these Speckled Peaches weren't anything like the ones I ate at Tomatofest, even though I bought them and grew them out of Tomatofest seed. They looked like Speckled Peach, but they didn't taste like Speckled Peach. They were pretty bland. Or maybe they had more acid, which overcame the sweet. They weren't like the sweet mango-tomatoes of that Elysian field at Carmel. It must have been the soil, or the sunlight. Or maybe they missed California. Maybe I didn't talk to them nicely enough.

From my friends, to whom I had hopefully distributed several dozen tomato seedlings, I didn't get a lot of feedback. Steve up the street is a very good gardener, and I could see that his cherries and Marmandes were prospering. But he got a lot of Speckled Peaches, too, and didn't care for them. No one else reported back except Martha, but that's because she's a smart entomologist who studies outdoor things for a living. Martha e-mailed me a photograph of one of the tomatoes in front of a ruler so I could see how big it had grown. However, she wasn't sure which variety it was. Clint Eastwood, maybe? Julia Child? Like me, Martha suffered from backyard gardener's amnesia. You set out thinking that you'll carefully measure the progress of your garden, but within a month, you can't even remember which varieties you planted. We all have busy lives. Who's got time to watch the grass grow?

I came out of this experience with a great fondness for growing tomatoes and extremely low expectations that I would be able to nourish my family with them. More than that, I realized there's a reason that agriculture, as opposed to gardening, is a profession and not a hobby. The food we eat is really cheap, and for the most part, that's a good thing. Cultivate your own garden, sure, but don't expect to feed the world with it.

As for the great tomato quest, Kanti and I agreed that there was no reason to end it.

"Every nation bitches about something gone wrong with at least one ingredient in its cuisines," he told me. "The French complain about how the baguette and croissants are limp nowadays, the Italians complain about how lousy the olive oil has become. We Americans—we always complain about the lack of flavor in tomatoes. But do we really want to find what we are looking for? If we reach our destination, we'll have nothing to do and nowhere to go. We really never want to get there! We do not want the journey to end. We are thirsty but want only a sip; we do not want to quench that thirst.

"If I found that ultimate, great-tasting tomato, would I be content?"

Acknowledgments

THIS BOOK WOULDN'T HAVE BEEN POSSIBLE WITHOUT THE ENTHUSIastic participation of Kanti Rawal, who guided me through many chapters of the tomato story. Gwen Young helped get me started and provided encouraging and intelligent advice along the way. David Plotz and Julie Zavon gave careful readings and important suggestions; Sarah Chalfant, Jack Shoemaker, Roxanna Aliaga, and Patricia Boyd have all been good shepherds. Tom Monmaney of Smithsonian Magazine was an early enthusiast and gave generous room to my story in the magazine.

Sandra Belin and Larry Jacobs fed and housed me, shared their thoughts, and showed me every part of their business in Baja del Sur. Chris Rufer and Kebede Gashaw threw open the doors of the Morning Star Co. to my inspection; Jim Beecher was another extremely generous and friendly guide to the processing tomato industry, as were Chuck Rivara, Cameron Tattam, Gene Miyao, and Juan José Amezaga. I'm also especially grateful to Amy Goldman, Cinzia Roveta, Sophie Colvine, Marco Serafini, Ann Hall, Sikke Meerman, Liang Zhongkang, Ross Siragusa, Duncan Blake, Huang Mu, Peter Tjia, Louis Chirnside, Barry Horn, Siva Subramanian, Carlos Colomietz, John Poundstone, Chris Woolf, Dave Epp, Walt Brown, Don Cameron, Dale Smith, Diane Barrett, Roger Scriven, and Don May. All hail the breeders and genetic untanglers of the tomato: Jim Dick, Ben George, Roger Chetelat, M. Allen Stevens, Ghurdev Khush, Jay Scott, Majid Foolad, Harry Klee, Yosef Mizrahi, Steven Tanksley, and Teresa Beck-Bunn. All props to Doug Gosling and his dazzling, delicious tomatoes. In Italy I was under the intrepid and open-hearted guidance of Marjorie Shaw, along with Giuseppe Tatano, Carmelo D'Agostino, Sebastiano Fortunato, Luigi Salvati, Cosimo Mugavero, Sabato Abagnale, and Sergio de Luca. Shara Wasserman generously loaned us her apartment and its cats. Florida grower Tony DiMare was generous with his time and open with his opinions, while Gerardo Reyes and Lucas Benitez were friendly guides to the fieldworking life. In Mexico I also enjoyed the thoughtful and sincere company of John Graham, Fabiola Rodríguez, Hugo Burgoin, and Juan José Silva. Thanks also to Mel Green, Andrew Brait, Gary Ibsen, Ron Buttery, Bob Pizza, Yiftach Giladi, Ding Shenglin, Andries Cronje, Mawuli Agbleze, John Rick, Frank Furman, Daniel Wakin, and Marie-Christine Daunay.

Last I thank my family, especially my parents Richard and Barbara Allen, who understand good food and shopped at farmer's markets long before they were hip, as well as my sisters Susie and Emily, brother Nick, and nephew Ben Coates for their help and encouragement. My son Ike and daughter Lucy were inspired company, excellent travelers, and sources of highly relevant suggestions for a book about a lowly vegetable. Finally I thank Margaret, who is always kind, helpful, and deeply insightful.

Selected Sources
and Notes

Introduction

The section on the early history of the tomato in the United States relies heavily upon Andrew Smith's tomato-related oeuvre, including *The Saintly Scoundrel: The Life and Times of Dr. John Cook Bennett* (Champaign-Urbana: University of Illinois, 1997); *Souper Tomatoes: The Story of America's Favorite Food* (New Brunswick, NJ: Rutgers University, 2000); *The Tomato in America: Early History, Culture, and Cookery* (Champaign: University of Illinois, 2001); his introduction to A. W. Livingston, *Livingston and the Tomato* (Columbus: Ohio State University, 1998); and *Pure Ketchup* (Washington, DC: Smithsonian, 2001). For general information on the tomato industry, I turned to Bill Pritchard and David Burch, *Agri-Food Globalization in Perspective: International*

Restructuring in the Processing Tomato Industry (Burlington, VT: Ashgate, 2003). I was inspired by, and borrowed, the concept of the human tomato from Mark Harvey, Stephen Quilley, and Huw Beynon, *Exploring the Tomato: Transformations of Nature, Society and Economy* (Cheltenham, England: Edward Elgar, 2004). I frequently dipped into the following specialized texts: Wilbur A. Gould, *Tomato Production, Processing and Quality Evaluation* (Westport, CT: AVI Publishing, 1992); J. Atherton and J. Rudick, eds., *The Tomato Crop: A Scientific Basis for Improvement* (New York: Springer, 1986); and M. K. Razdan and A. K. Matoo, eds., *Genetic Improvement of Solanaceous Crops*, vol. 2 (Enfield, NH: Science Publishers, 2007). An excellent review article on tomato genetics and its relevance to the tomato fruit is Majid R. Foolad, "Genome mapping and molecular breeding of tomato," *International Journal of Plant Genomics* (2007): 1–33. The Ellen Goodman quote comes from her column, "Summertime and tomatoes are ready," *Boston Globe*, August 28, 1987, B7. James E. McWilliams, *Just Food: Where Locavores Get It Wrong and How We Can Truly Eat Responsibly* (New York: Little, Brown, 2009), provided interesting food for thought. I was tipped off to the existence of Kanti Rawal by Terry McDermott, "Trying to strike gold in a yellow tomato," *Los Angeles Times*, November 13, 1999.

Chapter 1: The Architect of the Tomato

Interviews with author: John Rick, Roger Chetelat, Don May, Ghurdev Khush, Steven Tanksley, Kanti Rawal, Mel Green, M. Allen Stevens, John Scott, and Majid Foolad.

Sources for discussion of Hans Stubbe are Susanne Heim, *Plant Breeding and Agrarian Research in the Kaiserwilhelm-Institutes, 1933–1945* (Boston: Springer Science and Business, 2008); Ulrich Wobus and Ingo Schubert, "Science and politics: Hans Stubbe and the

Institute of Plant Genetics and Crop Plant Research at Gatersleben,"
Trends in Plant Science 7, no. 9 (2002): 418–420; Alison Abbot, "German science begins to cure its historical amnesia," *Nature* 403 (2000): 474–475; Hans Stubbe, "Über die vegetative Hybridisierung von Plfanzen," *Kulturpflanze* 2 (1954): 185–236; Hans Stubbe, "Considerations on the genetical and evolutionary aspects of some mutants of *Antirrhinum, Hordeum,* and *Lycopersicon*," *Cold Spring Harbor Symposium on Quantitative Biology* 24 (1959): 31–40; and Hans Stubbe, "Considerations on the genetical and evolutionary aspects of some mutants of Hordeum, Glycine, Lycopersicon and Antirrhinum," *Proceedings of the X International Congress on Genetics* 1 (1959): 247–260; Gary P. Nabhan, *Where Our Food Comes From: Retracing Nikolai Vavilov's Quest to End Famine* (Wellfleet, MA: Shearwater, 2008).

Tomato genetics papers by Charles M. Rick consulted include the following: "A new male-sterile mutant in the tomato," *Science* 99, no. 2583 (1944): 543; "Rates of natural cross-pollination of tomatoes in various localities in California as measured by the fruits and seeds set on male sterile plants," *Proceedings of the American Society of Horticultural Science* 54 (1949): 237–252; "Pollination of *L. esculentum* in native and foreign regions," *Evolution* 4, no. 2 (June 1950); Charles M. Rick and Donald C. McGuire, "Self-incompatibility in species of *Lycopersicon sect. eropersicon* and hybrids with *L. esculentum*," *Hilgardia* 23, no. 4 (1954): 101–124; "The tomato," *Scientific American,* August 1978, 77–87; Charles M. Rick and Paul G. Smith, "Novel variation in tomato species hybrids," *American Naturalist* 87, no. 837 (1953): 359–373; D. W. Barton, L. Butler, J. A. Jenkins, Charles M. Rick, and P. A. Young, "Rules for nomenclature in tomato genetics, " *Journal of Heredity* 44 (1955): 22–26; Charles M. Rick and A. C. Sawant, "Factor interactions affecting the phenotypic expression of the jointless character in tomatoes," *Journal of the*

American Society of Horticultural Science (1955): 354–360; *Tomato Genetics Cooperative Newsletter* issues, http://tgc.ifas.ufl.edu/vol9/v9p39.html and http://tgc.ifas.ufl.edu/vol6/v6p24.html; "Controlled introgression of *S. pennellii* into *L. esculentum*, segregation and recombination," *Genetica* 26 (1969): 753–768; "Potential genetic resources in tomato species: clues from observations in native habitats," in *Genes, Enzymes and Populations*, ed. A Hollaender and A. M. Srb (New York: Plenum Press, 1973); Charles M. Rick and J. F. Forbes, "Allozyme variation in the cultivated tomato and closely related species," *Bulletin of the Torrey Botany Club* 102 (1975): 376–386; Charles M. Rick, S. D. Tanksley, and H. Medina-Filho, "The effect of isozyme selection on metric characters in an interspecific backcross of tomato: basis of an early screening procedure," *Theoretical and Applied Genetics* 60 (1981): 291–296; same authors, "Use of naturally occurring enzyme variation to detect and map genes controlling quantitative traits in an interspecific backcross of tomato," *Heredity* 49 (1982): 11–25; Charles M. Rick and S. D. Tanksley, "Isozyme monitoring of genetic variation in *Lycopersicon*," *Isozymes* 11 (1983): 270–284; Charles M. Rick, S. D. Tanksley, and John I. Yoder, "Classical and molecular genetics of tomato: highlights and perspectives," *Annual Reviews in Genetics* 22 (1988): 281–300; "Tomato," in *Evolution of Crop Plants*, ed. J. Smartt and N. W. Simmonds (London: Longman, 1995); "Tomato resources of South America reveal many genetic treasures," *Diversity* 7, no. 1+2 (1991): 54–56; Charles M. Rick and Roger Chetelat, "Utilization of related wild species for tomato improvement," *Acta Horticulturae* 312 (1995): 21–38; Charles M. Rick and M. A. Stevens, "Genetics and breeding," in Atherton and Rudick, *The Tomato Crop*; Charles M. Rick and Roger Chetelat, "Past, present and future prospects for using wild germplasm resources for tomato improvement," *Proceedings of the 1st International Conference on the Processing Tomato* (1996); S. D. Tanksley and Ghurdev Khush, "Biographical memoir: Charles Madera Rick, April 30, 1915–May 5, 2002," at http://newton.nap.edu/html/biomems/crick.html.

Other scientific papers: T. C. Nesbitt and S. D. Tanksley, "Comparative sequencing in the genus *Lycopersicon:* implication for the evolution of fruit size in the domestication of cultivated tomatoes," *Genetics* 162 (2002): 365–379; S. D. Tanksley et al., "A new class of regulatory genes underlying the cause of pear-shaped tomato fruit," *Proceedings of the National Academy of Sciences* 99, no. 20 (2002): 13,301–13,303; José T. Esquinas-Alcazar, "Genetic resources of tomatoes and wild relatives," IBPGR Secretariat, September 1981; T. O. Graham, "Impact of recorded Mendelian factors on the tomato, 1929–59," *Report of the Tomato Genetics Cooperative* 9 (1959): 37; A. Frary et al., "fw2-2: a quantitative trait locus key to evolution of tomato fruit size," *Science* 289 (2000): 85–88; Y. Eshed and D. Zamir, "An introgression line population of *Lycopersicon pennellii* in the cultivated tomato enables the identification and fine mapping of yield-associated QTL," *Genetics* 141 (1995): 1137–1162.

Most of the accounts of early Mexico and the identity of early tomato uses in Europe come from Bernardino de Sahagún and Charles E. Dibble, *The Florentine Codex: General History of the Things of New Spain,* Book 9, *The Merchants,* and Book 10, *The People* (Salt Lake City: University of Utah, 1959 and 1961); I. Peralta et al., "Nomenclature for wild and domesticated species," *Tomato Genetics Cooperative Newsletter* 56 (2006): 6–13, at http://tgc.ifas.ufl.edu/vol56/vol56.pdf; Marie Christine Daunay and Henri Laterrot, "Iconography and history of Solanaceae: antiquity to the 17th century," *Horticultural Reviews* 34 (2008); George A. McCue, "The History of the Use of the Tomato," *Annals of the Missouri Botanical Garden* 9, no. 4 (1952); U.S. Department of Agriculture, "Descriptions of types of principal American varieties of tomatoes," USDA

Miscellaneous Publications no. 160 (Washington, DC: GPO, October 1933), 1–23; Rudolf Grewe, "The arrival of the tomato in Spain and Italy: early recipes," *Journal of Gastronomy* 3, no. 2 (1983): 67–79; Abbe François Rozier, *Nouveau cours complet d'agriculture theorique et pratique* (Paris: Deterville, 1823) 15: 417–418; L. C. Luckwill, "The evolution of the cultivated tomato," *Journal of the Royal Horticultural Society* 68 (1943); L. C. Luckwill, "The genus *Lycopersicon:* an historical, biological and taxonomic survey of the wild and cultivated tomatoes," *Aberdeen University Studies,* no. 120 (1943); Nikolai Vavilov, "Mexico and Central America as the principal center of origin of cultivated plants of New World," *Bulletin of Applied Botany, Genetics and Plant Breeding* 26 (1935): 135–199; Alfred Crosby, *The Colombian Exchange* (New York: Praeger, 2003); C. M. Jones et al., "Genealogy and fine mapping of obscurvaenosa," *American Journal of Botany* 94, no. 6 (2007): 940; Peter Dreyer, *A Gardener Touched with Genius: The Life of Luther Burbank* (New York: Coward, McCann & Geoghegan, 1975); Edgar Anderson, *Plants, Man and Life* (Mineola, NY: Dover, 2005); J. A. Jenkins, "The origin of the cultivated tomato," *Economic Botany* 2, no. 4 (1948): 379–392. I drew on the following materials from the James August Jenkins papers, located at the Bancroft Library, University of California, Berkeley: Carton 1: Charles Rick, E. B. Babcock, Carl Sauer, Edgar Anderson correspondence folders; Carton 13: Bound notebook dated September 1952–July 1953 on travels through Latin America; correspondence with Donald Brand, Junius Bird, Juan Rosales, Harold Key, Mrs. George Cowan; unbound notes listing tomato types.

Chapter 2: The Flavor Cravers

Interviews with author: Andrew Brait, Larry Jacobs, Sandra Belin, Kanti Rawal, Fabiola Rodríguez, Doug Gosling, Gary Ibsen, John Scott, William Foerster, Teresa Beck-Bunn, Ron Buttery, and M. Allen Stevens.

Literature consulted on tomato flavor chemicals includes M. A. Stevens, "Tomato quality: potential for developing cultivars with improved flavor," *ISHS Acta Horticulturae 93*, 1979; Ronald G. Buttery et al., *Journal of Agricultural and Food Chemistry* 51, no. 3 (2003): 722–726; Ronald G. Buttery, Roy Teranishi, and Louisa C. Ling, "Fresh tomato aroma volatiles: a quantitative study," *Journal of Agricultural and Food Chemistry* 35 (1987): 540–544; Ronald G. Buttery, Roy Teranishi, Louisa C. Ling, and Jean G. Turnbaugh, "Quantitative and sensory studies on tomato paste volatiles," *Journal of Agricultural and Food Chemistry* 38 (1990): 336–340; Ronald G. Buttery and Louisa C. Ling, "Volatile components of tomato fruit and plant parts: relationship and biogenesis," in *Bioactive Volatile Compounds from Plants* (Washington, DC: American Chemical Society, 1993); Ronald G. Buttery et al., "Analysis of furaneol in tomato using dynamic headspace sampling with sodium sulfate," *Journal of Agricultural and Food Chemistry* 49 (2001): 4349–4351; Ronald G. Buttery, "Quantitative and sensory aspects of flavor of tomato and other vegetables and fruits," in *Flavor Science: Sensible Principles and Techniques*, ed. Terry E. Acree and Roy Teranishi (Washington, DC: American Chemical Society, 1993); Florian Mayer et al., "Aroma of fresh field tomatoes," in *Freshness and Shelf Life of Foods*, ed. Keith Cadwallader and Hugo Weenen (Washington, DC: American Chemical Society, 2003); Florian Mayer, Gary Takeoka, Ronald G. Buttery, and Linda Whitehand, "Differences in the aroma of selected fresh tomato cultivars," in *Handbook of Flavor Characterization*, ed. Kathryn Deibler and Jeannine Delwiche (New York: Marcel Dekker, 2004); Mayer et al., "Studies on the aroma of five fresh tomato cultivars and the precursors of *cis*- and *trans*-4,5-epoxy-(E)-2-decenals and methional," *Journal of Agricultural and Food Chemistry J Agricultural* 56 (2008): 3749–3757;

R. A. Jones and S. J. Scott, "Improvement of tomato flavor by genetically increasing sugar and acid contents," *Euphytica* 32 (1983): 845–855.

Chapter 3: No Hands Touch the Land

Many of the papers relating to the mechanical harvester are unpublished but are available at the Shields Library, UC Davis. Firsthand accounts are given in A. I. Dickman, "Interviews with persons involved in the development of the tomato harvester, the compatible processing tomato and the new agricultural systems that evolved," Oral History Office, UC Davis, 1975, in *The Engineering of Abundance: An Oral History Memoir of Roy Bainer* (Davis: UC Davis Special Collections, 1975), and to a lesser extent in letters and loose papers contained in the G. C. Hanna Papers, UC Davis Special Collections. Other literature on the harvester consulted here includes William H. Friedland and Amy Barton, "Destalking the wild tomato," UC Davis, Department of Applied Behavioral Sciences, June 1975; O. E. Thompson and Ann F. Scheuring, "From lug boxes to electronics: a study of California tomato growers and sorting crews," Monograph no. 3 of the California Agricultural Policy Seminar, 1980; California Agrarian Action Project, "No hands touch the land: automatic California farms," pamphlet, July 1977; "Presentations before regents' committee on educational policy in regard to farm mechanization research in the University of California," Los Angeles, February 16, 1978; Charles E. Hess, "Agricultural research: its impact on farm size," *California Farmer*, June 20, 1981; Peter Schrag, "Rubber tomatoes," *Harper's*, June 1978, 24–28; Andrew Schmitz and David Secler, "Mechanized agriculture and social welfare: the case of the tomato harvester," *American Journal of Agricultural Economics* 52 (1970): 569; John H. Vandermeer, "Mechanized agriculture and social welfare: the tomato harvester in Ohio," *Agriculture and Human Values* (summer 1986): 22–31; John H. Vandermeer and Peter M. Rosset, "The confrontation between processors and farm workers in the Midwest tomato industry and the role of the agricultural research and extension establishment," *Agriculture and Human Values* (summer 1986); Michael Seiler, "Tomato man squares the circle," *Los Angeles Times*, March 25, 1975, D1; "New canning tomato developed by growers," *Los Angeles Times*, November 2, 1952, A20; "VFL-13 seed increase in Mexico," *California Tomato Grower* 7, no. 5 (May 1964): 4; James E. Bylin, "Lack of workers may limit tomato crops in California: higher retail prices seen," *Wall Street Journal*, August 12, 1965, 6; "Braceros stream into California," *New York Times*, September 5, 1965, 56; "Wirtz OKs use of 6,000 Mexicans in tomato harvest," *LA Times*, August 2, 1966, 3; Judith Miller, "Agriculture: FDA seeks to regulate genetic manipulation of food crops," *Science* 185 (1974): 240.

Material on Tillie Lewis is from Tamar Andreeva, "Tilly's profitable romance," *American Mercury*, February 1953, 84–89; Dorothy Walworth, "Tillie of the Valley," *Reader's Digest*, August 1952, 101–104; Amy Goldman, *The Heirloom Tomato: From Garden to Table: Recipes, Portraits, and History of the World's Most Beautiful Fruit* (New York: Bloomsbury USA, 2009), introduction; "Italian tomato growers here to study how to turn out paste more efficiently," *New York Times*, September 9, 1958, 55; and "Register of the Tillie Lewis Foods Collection, 1935–1978," San Joaquin County Historical Museum, Lodi, CA, available at http://content.cdlib.org/view?docId=tf6t1nb1s8&doc.view=entire_text&brand=oac.

Descriptions of some of the relevant genetics are in A. F. Yeager, "Determinate growth in the tomato," *Journal of Heredity* 18 (1927): 262; and Charles M. Rick and A. C. Sawant, "Factor interactions affecting the phenotypic expression of the jointless character in tomatoes," *Journal of the American Society of Horticultural Science* (1955): 354–360.

American food histories consulted include Harvey Levenstein, *Paradox of Plenty* (Berkeley: University of California Press, 2003); and B. L. Gardner, *American Agriculture in the 20th Century: How It Flourished and What It Cost* (Cambridge, MA: Harvard University Press, 2002).

Early tomato cultivar history is described in J. W. Day, D. Cummins, and A. I. Root, *Tomato Culture in Three Parts* (Medina, OH: AI Root Company, 1906); E. A. Miller, "Lessons on tomatoes for rural schools," Bulletin 392, USDA, 1916; and U.S. Department of Agriculture, "Descriptions of types of principal American varieties of tomatoes," USDA Miscellaneous Publications no. 160 (Washington, DC: GPO, 1933), 1–23.

For information on the UC Davis sustainable agriculture program, see "A Descriptive Survey of the University of California, Sustainable Agriculture Research and Education Program," at http://www.sarep.ucdavis.edu/about/SAREP_Report_2008.pdf.

Chapter 4: *Destino Cruel*

Interviews with author: Tony DiMare, Fritz Roka, Harry Klee, John Scott, Gerardo Reyes, Lucas Benitez, Cruz Salucio, Greg Abed, Wayne Robinson, Frank Furman, Robert A. Hanson, and several tomato pickers who wished to remain anonymous.

Readings on the growth of the fresh-market tomato market include Arthur D. Knox, *Tomatoes: Instructions to Growers and Shippers* (Nashville: Nashville, Chattanooga and St. Louis Railway, 1907); W. W. Deen, "Recent advances in mechanization of fresh market tomato harvesting in Florida," *Proceedings of the Florida State Horticultural Society* 83 (1970); and several articles in *Proceedings of the Florida State Horticultural Society* 85 (1972): P. H. Everett et al., "Growing fresh market tomatoes for machine harvest," 152–155; W. W. Deen Jr. et al., "Conditioning tomatoes for fresh market machine harvest," 156–159; Richard Fluck and Dwait Gull, "Mechanical properties of tomatoes affecting harvesting and handling," 160–165; P. H. Everett and W. W. Deen Jr., "Machine harvest of 'Florida MH-1' tomato: effect of harvest method on size and maturity," 166–168; Pat Crill and D. S. Burgis, "Occurrence of spontaneous mutations in the tomato variety 'Walter,'" 169–170; D. S. Burgis and Pat Crill, "Pruning test comparison of tomato varieties 'Florida MH-1' and 'Walter,'" 171–174; R. K. Showalter, "Sizing tomatoes into fruit diameter classifications," 178–181; R. F. Matthews et al., "Processing Florida tomatoes—the impact of mechanical harvest," 181–184; J. R. Hicks et al., "Consumer acceptance of machine harvested 'Florida MH-1' tomatoes and taste panel comparisons of 'Florida MH-1' and 'Walter' tomatoes," 184–186. Other sources include E. T. Sims et al., "Evaluation of a totally mechanized tomato harvesting system," *Proceedings of the Florida State Horticultural Society* (1976): 139–140; H. E. Studer et al., "Damage evaluation of machine harvested fresh market tomatoes," *Transactions of the American Society of Agricultural Engineers* (1981): 284–287; P. Crill et al., "Florida MH-1: a machine harvest tomato for the fresh market," mimeo report, Gulf Coast Station 717, Bradenton, FL, 1971; Roberta Cook, "Overview of the greenhouse vegetable industry: focus on tomatoes," IR-4 Project Greenhouse Grown Food Crops Workshop on Pest Control, September 11, 2006. See John Bowe, *Nobodies: Modern American Slave Labor and the Dark Side of the Global Economy* (New York: Random House, 2007), for an excellent account of the Coalition of Immokalee Workers and its achievements. Newspaper accounts include Steven Lewis, "US-Mexico tomato dispute comes to a head," *Food Chemical News*, September 9, 2002; Associated Press, "Price of Mexican tomatoes may increase," Associated Press, June 22, 2002; Jennifer Sergent, "Florida tomato growers don't like foreign trade bill," *Vero Beach (Fl.) Press Journal*, June 9, 2002, A17; U.S. House of Representatives, Select Committee on Small Business, "Hearing, distribution problems in the tomato industry," June 12, 1961 (Washington, DC: GPO, 1961); U.S. House of Representatives, Committee on Agriculture, "Hearing, imported tomato restrictions," October 4, 1977 (Washington, DC: GPO, 1977); Charlene M. Shupp Espenshade, "No more tomatoes for mid-Atlantic's largest producer," *Lancaster Farming*, March 28, 2008; Jane Zhang, "Florida vegetable growers urge regulation," *Wall Street Journal*, September 17, 2007; Cindy Skrzycki, "UgliRipe tomato proves alluring to regulators," Bloomberg.com, February 6, 2007; Elaine Walker, "Costs are squashing the tomato industry," *Miami Herald*, February 8, 2008.

Chapter 5: Fried Gene Tomatoes

Interviews with author: Dwain D. Gull, Kanti Rawal, Yosef Mizrahi, M. Allen Stevens, Majid Foolad, Nick Mastronardi, Dwight Ferguson, Frits Herlaar, Bryant Umblang, Adel Kader, Bobby Pizza, and Steven Tanksley.

Sources include Frederick B. Abeles, Page W. Morgan, and Mikal E. Saltveit, *Ethylene in Plant Biology* (San Diego: Academic Press, 1992), 267–270; F. Maul et al., "Predicting flavor potential for green-harvested tomato fruit," *Proceedings of the Florida State Horticultural Society* 111 (1998): 285–290; E. M. Chase, "Health problems connected with the ethylene treatment of fruits," *American Journal of Public Health* 24 (1934): 1152–1156; A. Whidden et al., "A history of commercial vegetable production in central and southern Florida," *Proceedings of the Florida State Horticultural Society* 117 (2004): 1–3; R. Robinson and M. L. Tomes, "Ripening inhibitor: a gene with multiple effects on ripening," *Tomato Genetics Cooperative Reports* 18 (1968) 36–37; W. B. McGlasson, H. C. Dostal, and E. C. Tigchelaar, "Comparison of propylene-induced responses of immature fruit of normal and *rin* mutant tomatoes," *Plant Physiology* 55 (1975): 218–222; *Plant Physiology* 55 (1975): 218–222; W. B. McGlasson et al., "Influence of the non-ripening mutants *rin* and *nor* on the aroma of tomato fruit," *HortScience* 22, no. 4 (1987): 632–634; Jeffrey Tomich, "Seeds grow Monsanto's business," *St. Louis Post-Dispatch,* September 20, 2009; "Workshop: Considerations in harvesting vine-ripe tomatoes in Florida," *Proceedings of the Florida State Horticultural Society* 111 (1998): 101–103; M. A. Stevens and Charles M. Rick, "Genetics and breeding," in *The Tomato Crop: A Scientific Basis for Improvement,* ed. J. Atherton and J. Rudick (New York: Springer, 1986); Belinda Martineau, *First Fruit: The Creation of the Flavr Savr Tomato and the Birth of Biotech Foods* (New York: McGraw-Hill, 2001); Philip Elmer-Dewitt, "Fried gene tomatoes," *Time,* June 24, 2001; Yuling Bai and Pim Lindhout, "Domestication and breeding of tomatoes: what have we gained and what can we gain in the future?" *Annals of Botany* 100 (2007): 1085–1094; Linda Calvin and Roberta Cook, "North American greenhouse tomatoes emerge as a major market force," *Amber Waves* 3, no. 2 (April 1, 2005): 20.

Chapter 6: Are Things Better in the Old Country?

Interviews with author: Chris Rufer, Kebede Gashaw, Giuseppe Tatano, Carmelo D'Agostino, Sebastiano Fortunato, Luigi Salvati, Cosimo Mugavero, Sabato Abagnale, Sergio De Luca, Marco Serafini, Juan José Amezaga, Jim Beecher, Sikke Meerman, Ann Hall, Liang Zhongkang, Ross Siragusa, Duncan Blake, Huang Mu, Ding Shenglin, Shixin Ming, Sophie Colvine, Peter Tjia, Louis Chirnside, Barry Horn, Maximilian Stirn, Francois Branthome, Gino Gugliotti, Ray Sellwood, Mohamed Laid Benamor, Siva Subramanian, and Carlos Colomietz.

Books and articles include S. Frederick Starr, ed., *Xinjiang: China's Muslim Borderland* (New York: M. E. Sharpe, 2004); Hasia R. Diner,

288   SELECTED SOURCES AND NOTES

Hungering for America (Cambridge, MA: Harvard University Press, 2001), 41–54; Pier Luigi Longarini, *Il passato del pomodoro* (Parma: Silva Editore, 1998); Carole Helstosky, *Garlic and Oil: Food and Politics in Italy* (Oxford: Berg, 2006); Margaret and Ancel Keys, *Eat Well and Stay Well* (New York: Doubleday, 1959); Franco De Cecla, *Pasta and Pizza* (Cambridge: Prickly Paradigm, 2007); *L'industria delle conserve di pomodoro* (Casale: Fratelli Ottavi, 1913); Renato Rovetta, *Il pomodoro: coltivazione-industria* (Milano: Ulrico Hoepli, 1914); U.S. Tariff Commission, *Canned Tomatoes and Tomato Paste* (Washington, DC: GPO, 1929); Claudio Benporat, *Storia della gastronomia italiana* (Milano: Mursia, 1990); Remigio Baldoni, *Il pomodoro industriale e da tavola* (Rome: Ramo Editoriale degli Agricolotori, 1940); Gianfranco Schiavo, *Il pomodoro nell'orto* (Verona: Edizioni L'Informatore Agrario, 1992); Alexis Shriver, *Canned-Tomato Industry in Italy* (Washington, DC: U.S. Dept. of Commerce, 1918); B. Casarini and M. Di Candilo, *La coltura del pomodoro* (Bologna: Edagricole–Eizioni Agricole della Calderini, 1996); P. Siviero and M. S. Motton, *La coltivazione del pomodoro da mensa* (Verona: L'Informatore Agrario, 1995); G. Silvestr and P. Siviero, *La coltivazione del pomodoro da industria* (Verona: L'Informatore Agrario, 1991); Reay Tannahill, *Food in History* (New York: Crown Trade, 1973), 202–328; John Dickie, *Delizia: The Epic History of the Italians and Their Food* (New York: Free Press, 2008); William Black, *Al Dente: The Adventures of a Gastronome in Italy* (New York: Bantam, 2003), 203–211; Filippo Tommaso Marinetti, *The Futurist Cookbook* (San Francisco: Bedford Arts, n.d.); Guido Rovesti and F. Piccoli, "Industrial tomato: the problem is not only China," *Informatore Agrario* 61, no. 11 (2005): 41–42; "L'invasione dei pomodori cinesi," *Corriere della Sera*, August 25, 2005; "E' tornado re pomodoro" (Castel San Marzano: Consorzio San Marzano, undated pamphlet); Gigi

Padovani, "The anti-oxidant pizza was born here," *La Stampa*, November 23, 2007; Pellegrino Artusi, *Science in the Kitchen and the Art of Eating Well*, introduction by Luigi Ballerini (Toronto: University of Toronto, 2003). I also drew heavily on the Piero Camporesi introduction to the 1970 Italian edition of Artusi, *La scienza in cucina e l'arte di mangiar bene* (Torino: G. Einaudi, 1970); Mara Nocilla, "Profondo rosso," *Gambero Rosso*, August 2008, 33–61.

Chapter 7: Messy Business

Interviews with author: Kebede Gashaw, Cameron Tattam, Chris Rufer, John Poundstone, Jim Beecher, Sikke Meerman, Stewart Woolf, Jim Dick, Walt Brown, Dave Epp, Don Cameron, Gwen Young, Juan José Amezaga, Marco Serafini, Dale Smith, Ben George, Michael Loktionov, Chuck Rivara, Diane Barrett, Roger Scriven, Scott Sullivan, Gene Miyao, Don May, Ann Hall, Liang Zhongkang, and Ross Siragusa.

Books and articles include Mark Arax and Rick Wartzman, *The King of California: J. G. Boswell and the Making of a Secret American Empire* (New York: PublicAffairs, 2005); A. Venket Rao, ed., *Tomatoes, Lycopene and Human Health: Preventing Chronic Diseases* (Caledonian Science Press, 2006); Ivan Fallon, *The Luck of Reilly: A Biography of Tony O'Reilly* (New York: Warner Books, 1994); Robert C. Alberts, *The Good Provider: H. J. Heinz and His 57 Varieties* (New York: Houghton Mifflin, 1973); Eleanor Foa Dienstag, *In Good Company: 125 Years at the Heinz Table* (New York: Warner Books, 1994); S. J. Kazeniac and R. M. Hall, "*Cis* to *trans*-3-hex transformation in tomatoes," *Journal of Food Science* 35 (1970): 519; Ben George, "Development of the California processing tomato, 1859–2004," *The Tomato Magazine*, July 2008. I also consulted records filed in U.S. District Court, Sacramento, in *U.S. v. Approximately $415,000.00 in U.S. Currency seized from Sun National Bank, et al.* (no.

2:08-CV-01899-GEB-GGH, E.D. Cal.), and related class-action lawsuits; and in Yolo County Superior Court, *Bermudez Brothers v. Morning Star Foods, Inc., Jerry Gilbert, Terry Hatanaka etc.* (CV02-1827).

Chapter 8: The Secrets of Flavor

Interviews with author: Harry Klee, Denise Tieman, Majid Foolad, Kanti Rawal, Steven Tanksley, Roger Chetelat, John Graham, Jay Scott, Juan José Silva, and Hugo Burgoin.

Harry Klee and Denise Tieman are the authors of many detailed papers. For relevance's sake, I mention only Stephen A. Groff and Harry Klee, "Plant volatile compounds: sensory cues for health and nutritional value?" *Science* 311, no. 5762 (2006): 815–819; the chapter epigraph comes from William Alexander, *The $64 Tomato: How One Man Nearly Lost His Sanity, Spent a Fortune, and Endured an Existential Crisis in the Quest for the Perfect Garden* (New York: Algonquin, 2007). Some good material on Mexican farmworkers and the Mexican tomato industry can be found in Angus Wright, *The Death of Ramon González: The Modern Agricultural Dilemma* (Austin: University of Texas, 1992); Laura Velasco Ortiz, *Mixtec Transnational Identity* (Tucson: University of Arizona, 2005); Javier Maisterrena Zubiran and Isabel Mora Ledesma, *Oasis y espejismo: proceso e impacto de la agriindustria del jitomate en el valle de Arista, SLP* (San Luis Potosí: Colegio de San Luis, 2000); Deborah Barndt, *Tangled Routes: Women, Work and Globalization on the Tomato Trail* (Lanham, MD: Rowman and Littlefield, 2002); David Mares, *Penetrating the International Market: Theoretical Considerations and a Mexican Case Study* (New York: Columbia University, 1987); Mark Arax, "The summer of the death of Hilario Guman," *West Magazine*, September 3, 2006; Tom Thompson, "Why they come here: U.S. agriculture policies spell disaster for Mexico's rural poor," *Seattle*

Post Intelligencer, May 21, 2006, D6; Gabriela Rico, "Displacement is a familiar story for indigenous people," *Statesman Journal*, November 12, 2005, 20; John Hubner, "Hispanic Indians, new workforce: almost half of state's 300,000 Indians have Mexican roots," *San Jose Mercury News*, August 4, 2001, 1A.